THE MUSIC HISTORY CLASSROOM

To the memory of

John Daverio
(1954-2003)

Teacher, Scholar, Mentor, Friend

The Music History Classroom

Edited by

JAMES A. DAVIS
State University of New York at Fredonia, USA

ASHGATE

Published by
Ashgate Publishing Limited
Wey Court East
Union Road
Farnham
Surrey, GU9 7PT
England

Ashgate Publishing Company
Suite 420
101 Cherry Street
Burlington
VT 05401-4405
USA

www.ashgate.com

British Library Cataloguing in Publication Data
The music history classroom.
   1. Music in universities and colleges. 2. Music appreciation – Study and teaching (Higher)
   I. Davis, James A. (James Andrew), 1962–
   780.7'11–dc23

Library of Congress Cataloging-in-Publication Data
The music history classroom / [edited by] James A. Davis.
   p. cm.
 Includes bibliographical references and index.
   ISBN 978-1-4094-3658-4 (hardcover : alk. paper)—ISBN 978-1-4094-3659-1
(pbk. : alk. paper)—ISBN 978-1-4094-3660-7 (ebook) 1. Music—History and criticism
—Instruction and study. 2. Music—History and criticism—Study and teaching (Higher)
I. Davis, James A. (James Andrew), 1962-

 MT18.M757 2012
 780.71—dc23

ISBN 9781409436584 (hbk)
ISBN 9781409436591 (pbk)
ISBN 9781409436607 (ebk)

Bach musicological font developed by © Yo Tomita.

MIX
Paper from
responsible sources
FSC
www.fsc.org
FSC® C018575

Printed and bound in Great Britain by the
MPG Books Group, UK.

Contents

List of Figures and Tables

Figures

Tables

Notes on Contributors

Eleonora (Nora) M. Beck is James W. Rogers Professor of Music at Lewis & Clark College, where she has taught since 1993. She has published widely on the subject of Italian medieval and Renaissance music and art, including her books *Singing in the Garden: Music and Culture in the Tuscan Trecento* (1998) and *Giotto's Harmony: Music and Art in Padua at the Crossroad of the Renaissance* (2005). Also a writer of fiction, in 2006 Beck published *Fiammetta*, which won Honorary Mention in the Writers' Digest International self-published book competition. The American Musicological Society named Beck Master Teacher in 2007. In 2000, she received the Graves Award from Pomona College for outstanding teaching in the humanities and in 1998 was named Lewis & Clark Professor of the Year.

José Antonio Bowen is Algur H. Meadows Chair and Dean of the Meadows School of the Arts at Southern Methodist University. Bowen has taught at Stanford, at the University of Southampton, England, at Georgetown and at Miami University. He has written over 100 scholarly articles, edited the Cambridge Companion to Conducting (2003), received a National Endowment for the Humanities (NEH) Fellowship, and contributed to *Discover Jazz* (Pearson, 2011). He is an editor of the six-CD set, *Jazz: The Smithsonian Anthology*. He has appeared in Europe, Africa, the Middle East, and the United States with Stan Getz, Dizzy Gillespie, Bobby McFerrin, Dave Brubeck, Liberace, and many others. He has written a symphony (which was nominated for the Pulitzer Prize in Music in 1985), a film score, and music for Hubert Laws, Jerry Garcia, and many others. He is currently on the Editorial Board for *Jazz Research Journal, Journal of the Society for American Music, Journal of Music History Pedagogy*, and *Per Musi: Revista Acadêmica de Música*. He is a Founding Board Member of the National Recording Preservation Board for the Library of Congress, and a Fellow of the Royal Society of Arts (FRSA) in England. Bowen has been featured in the *Wall Street Journal, Newsweek, USA Today, US News and World Report*, and on NPR for his Teaching Naked concept (http://www.npr.org/templates/story/story.php?storyId=111872191) (forthcoming as a book from Jossey-Bass, 2012).

James A. Davis is Professor of Musicology and Chair of the Music History Area at the School of Music, State University of New York at Fredonia. His primary research focuses on the music and musicians of the American Civil War. He has also worked in the areas of music history pedagogy, American popular music of the nineteenth and twentieth centuries, and the history of bands. He is the author of *Bully for the Band! The Civil War Letters and Diary of Four Brothers in the*

10th Vermont Infantry Band (McFarland, 2012) and *Music Along the Rapidan: Civil War Soldiers, Music, and Community* (University of Nebraska Press, 2012). His historical articles have been published in *American Music*, *Journal of Military History*, *Nineteenth Century Studies*, *Journal of the History of Ideas*, *Journal of Band Research*, and *Journal of American Culture*. His pedagogical work has appeared in the *Journal of Aesthetic Education*, *Philosophy of Music Education Review*, *International Journal of Teaching and Learning in Higher Education*, and *Journal of Music History Pedagogy*. He is the founder of the Master Teacher Session at the annual meetings of the American Musicological Society.

William A. Everett is Professor of Musicology and Associate Dean for Graduate Studies and Curriculum at the University of Missouri-Kansas City Conservatory of Music and Dance. He is the author of *Sigmund Romberg* (Yale University Press, 2007), *Rudolf Friml* (University of Illinois Press, 2008), contributing co-editor of *The Cambridge Companion to the Musical* (2002; 2nd ed., 2008), and a contributing editor for musical theater for the *Grove Dictionary of American Music*, 2nd edition. His research specialties include American musical theater, particularly operettas of the early twentieth century, and the relationship between music and national identity. At UMKC, Everett was a FaCET (Faculty Center for Excellence in Teaching) Fellow from 2008 to 2010, where he helped develop programming and organized symposia on teaching and learning. He was reviews editor for *College Music Symposium* from 2000 to 2006, and is a member of the editorial board for *Studies in Musical Theatre*. He served as Program Chair for the College Music Society's 2009 International Conference in Croatia, and was CMS national vice-president from 2011 to 2012.

Jessie Fillerup is Assistant Professor of Musicology at the University of Richmond, where she studies music, narrative, aesthetics, and philosophy through interdisciplinary methods of inquiry. She has written articles and reviews on the music of Maurice Ravel, fin-de-siècle French music, music history pedagogy, and the relationships between music, temporality, and theatrical magic. As a teacher she emphasizes collaboration as both subject and process, encouraging interaction between her students and the interdisciplinary study of the arts. She has explored the creative and scholarly challenges of teaching through presentations, articles, and professional leadership, serving as Chair of the American Musicological Society's Pedagogy Study Group and Review Editor of the *Journal of Music History Pedagogy*. Currently she holds an NEH "Enduring Questions" grant, which supports the development and teaching of a course that explores a pre-disciplinary question in the humanities.

Melanie Lowe is Associate Professor of Musicology and Chair of the Department of Musicology and Ethnomusicology at Vanderbilt University's Blair School of Music. She is also affiliated faculty in the Programs in American Studies and Women's and Gender Studies. She is the author of *Pleasure and Meaning in the*

Classical Symphony (Indiana University Press, 2007) as well as articles on other eighteenth-century topics, music in American media, classical recording, and early adolescent girls and teen pop culture. Professor Lowe is the recipient of numerous grants and awards, among them several teaching honors: the Lawson Lectureship for Service and Leadership (Vanderbilt, 2008), the Madison Sarratt Prize for excellence in undergraduate teaching (Vanderbilt, 2001), and the Princeton Graduate Alumnae Excellence in Teaching Award (Princeton University, 1993).

Susan McClary (Ph.D., Harvard) is Professor of Music at Case Western Reserve University; she has also taught at the University of Minnesota, McGill University, and UCLA. Her research focuses on the cultural analysis of music, both the European canon and contemporary popular genres. In contrast with an aesthetic tradition that treats music as ineffable and transcendent, her work engages with the signifying dimensions of musical procedures and deals with this elusive medium as a set of social practices. Best known for her book *Feminine Endings: Music, Gender, and Sexuality* (1991), she is also author of *Georges Bizet: Carmen* (1992), *Conventional Wisdom: The Content of Musical Form* (2000), *Modal Subjectivities: Renaissance Self-Fashioning in the Italian Madrigal* (2004), *Reading Music: Selected Essays* (2007), *Desire and Pleasure in Seventeenth-Century Music* (2012), editor of *Structures of Feeling in Seventeenth-Century Expressive Culture* (2012), and co-editor of *Music and Society: The Politics of Composition, Performance and Reception* (1987). Her work has been translated into at least thirteen languages. McClary received a MacArthur Foundation Fellowship in 1995.

Michael Markham is Assistant Professor of Musicology at the State University of New York at Fredonia. He joined the faculty there in 2008. The previous two years he served as Mellon Fellow in Music and Cultural History at Stanford University. In 2006 he received his Ph.D. in Musicology from the University of California, Berkeley with a dissertation entitled "The Heritage of Campaspe: Oral Tradition and Giulio Caccini's 'Le nuove musiche' (1602)." His research touches on theories of performance and space in early seventeenth-century Italy and the problem of text and Italian solo song in the Renaissance. His work on Monteverdi, on Giulio Caccini, on the spaces and images of solo singing in the Renaissance, and on Bach has appeared in the *Cambridge Opera Journal*, *Opera Quarterly*, *Repercussions*, and *Seventeenth-Century Music*. His most recent publication on the nature of performance space and noble/professional identity in late-Renaissance Florence will be appearing in *Sound, Space and Object: The Emergence of Music Rooms in Early Modern France and Italy*, a volume edited by Deborah Howard and Laura Moretti and to be published by the British Academy in 2012.

Mary Natvig is Professor of Music and Assistant Dean of the College of Musical Arts at Bowling Green State University. She taught part-time at the Eastman School of Music from 1987 to 1990 and was a Visiting Assistant Professor of Violin at Hope College from 1982 to 1984. Her areas of research are the music of fifteenth-century Burgundy, women in music, and music history pedagogy. Her publications include an edited collection entitled *Teaching Music History* (Ashgate, 2001), as well as chapters and essays in books published by Oxford University Press, the Alamire Foundation, and the University of California Press. Her articles have appeared in *College Music Symposium, Women in Music, New Grove Dictionary of Music and Musicians, New Catholic Encyclopedia, Women of Note*, and *American String Teacher*. She also directed the BGSU Early Music Ensemble (director and performer) for twenty years, and has freelanced on Baroque and modern violin. For sixteen years Natvig taught Suzuki violin through BGSU's Creative Arts Program. Her Ph.D. is from the Eastman School of Music (1991).

Edward Nowacki is Professor Emeritus at the College-Conservatory of Music, University of Cincinnati. He earned his Ph.D. at Brandeis University in 1980 with a dissertation on the Office Antiphons of the Old Roman manuscripts. His research has focused on theories of orality in the composition and transmission of Gregorian chant, and on liturgical performance practices in Christian Antiquity and the Middle Ages. He has taught at Brandeis University, Indiana University, and the University of Cincinnati. From 1998 to 2008 he lectured in music history to the freshman class of the College-Conservatory of Music and in 2005 was awarded the Ernest N. Glover Outstanding Teacher Award by the college's undergraduate association. He is currently writing a collection of essays on ancient Greek and medieval Latin music theory.

Marjorie Roth earned a DMA degree in Flute Performance from the Eastman School of Music in 1998, and a Ph.D. in Historical Musicology, also from Eastman, in 2005. She completed one year of her dissertation research as a Fulbright grant recipient in Vienna, Austria. She is currently Associate Professor of music at Nazareth College in Rochester NY, where she also serves as Director of the Honors Program. Dr. Roth has recently taught music history courses in Italy and Austria, and since 2004 has read professional papers at conferences in the United States, Canada, and Europe. She has been invited to present a paper at a scholarly conference in June 2012 sponsored by the Library of Alexandria in Egypt. Her research and publication interests include Renaissance music history and analysis, esoteric studies, gender studies, and music history pedagogy.

Scott Warfield is Associate Professor of Music at the University of Central Florida, where he teaches in all areas of music history through the graduate level. As a musicologist, he researches and writes primarily on the life and music of Richard Strauss, and also on American musical theater. He is a frequent presenter at national and international meetings, and his articles and reviews appear in a wide range of scholarly journals, including the *Richard Strauss-Blätter, Fontes artis musicae, Journal of Musicological Research, Journal of the Society for American Music, Kurt Weill Newsletter*, Music Library Association *Notes*, and *Nineteenth-Century Music Review*. He has contributed chapters to both *The Cambridge Companion* *to Richard Strauss* (2010) and *The Cambridge Companion to the Musical* (2002, 2008). In addition to his scholarly work, Warfield was for nearly twenty years the chief program annotator for the North Carolina Symphony, and he has also written for other venues including Carnegie Hall. He has also been a classical music critic for the *Orlando Sentinel* and for the *Raleigh News & Observer*.

Elizabeth A. Wells earned a Bachelor of Music degree from the University of Toronto with a concentration in History and Literature of Music and completed her doctorate in musicology at the Eastman School of Music. Her dissertation, entitled *West Side Story: Cultural Perspectives on an American Musical*, was supported by the Presser Foundation, the Elsa T. Johnson Dissertation Fellowship Susan B. Anthony Institute for Gender and Women's Studies, and the AMS-50 Dissertation Fellowship and was published by Scarecrow Press in 2011. She is now Associate Professor and Head of the music department at Mount Allison University in Sackville, New Brunswick, Canada, and has taught music history at Mansfield University in Pennsylvania, the State University of New York at Geneseo, and the Eastman School of Music. She has won the Tucker Teaching Award, the Association of Atlantic Universities' Distinguished Teacher award and the 3M National Teaching Fellowship. Her research interests include twentieth-century music, opera, musical theatre, feminism, and the scholarship of teaching and learning.

Foreword

The Master Narrative and Me

Susan McClary

A former graduate student contacted me recently to report that he had looked online and was relieved to discover that I was no longer saddled with the burden of teaching the music history survey. I had to disabuse him of this misconception: the department had merely changed the course number, and I was now teaching the entire sequence all by myself. I was doing so, moreover, by choice.

I have never been able to understand why so many of my colleagues scramble to offer only seminars and avoid teaching the undergraduate history survey like the very plague. At my advanced age and relatively high rank, I could easily refuse this assignment for the rest of my career. But in fact I love teaching the history survey. I might even go so far as to say that everything I know I learned my forty years of guiding undergraduates through the labyrinth starting with Plato and ending—in Spring 2011, in any case—with Kaija Saariaho's Émilie (2010).

Yet I also serve as a mentor to young composers and therefore realize all too acutely how heavily the burden of that tradition (what postmodernist theorist Jean-François Lyotard would call "the master narrative") weighs upon them.[1] For better or worse, musicians used to learn their craft without having had to absorb a thousand years worth of previous styles and achievements. The music history sequence itself has a history—and quite a recent one, at that. Like many others, I have begun to wonder if this compulsory trot through a cobbled-together history of Western music benefits students as much as musicologists wish to believe.[2]

When Jim Davis invited me to contribute to this project, I started pondering these issues in earnest. I would hate to give up teaching the undergraduate music history survey, but I worry about how to justify subjecting music students to this regimen. Given all their other pressing commitments (private lessons, ensembles, training in musicianship and theory, distribution courses in the liberal arts, degree recitals, concerts), why should they also have to wade through obscure repertories perhaps irrelevant to their immediate futures? And if the history survey continues

---

[1]   In the original French, "grand récit." Jean-François Lyotard, *The Postmodern Condition: A Report on Knowledge*, trans. Geoff Bennington and Brian Massumi (Minneapolis: University of Minnesota Press, 1984).

[2]   For more on the "cobbled-together" problem, see Robert Walser, "Eruptions: Heavy Metal Appropriations of Classical Virtuosity," *Popular Music* 2 (1992): 265, and the response by Richard Taruskin, *The Oxford History of Western Music*, vol. 1 (Oxford and New York: Oxford University Press, 2005), xiv.

to be taught, how might the teacher present those repertories in such a way as to make them relevant—or at least interesting and enriching?

Those who regard the music history survey as a necessary evil frequently present it in an "eat your vegetables!" fashion. I recall staying up nights before exams memorizing the particular sequences of As and Bs that differentiate the *rondeau* from the *virelai* and *ballade*, only to forget them promptly after the test. In those days of positivistic dogma, such formulas were highly valued as hard facts and were thus deemed worthy of rote learning. Lacking was any sense of why the formulas had ever mattered aesthetically or culturally, for addressing those issues would have led to illicit speculation. And so, while practicing the final two pages of Beethoven's Op. 110 in the practice room for my junior recital, I would chant to myself: "ABaAabAB …."

When I reached graduate school, I discovered that any factoid in the storm was considered fair game; I failed the first iteration of my general examinations because I could not say when the valve on the French horn was patented or what "primitive" tribe improvises canons. (I never bothered to hardwire into my brain the date for the valve, though I could easily Google it, but the never-to-be-forgotten answer to the second question is "Pygmies.") Experiences like this taught me to distrust fact-hoarding. So long as the music history survey focuses on dates and technical terms, it will fail to spark interest and will quite frequently enrage. It is always possible to hold someone else hostage to a nugget of information you happen to have, and I do not consider this education.

So what, then, is education? What do we really want students to bring away from their first (and frequently their last) sprint through the history of European and North American musics? Occasionally a student will become hooked and sign on for a career in musicology. I, for example, was so entranced by my initial exposure to Monteverdi's *Orfeo* that I decided to abandon the practice room and devote my future to figuring out how his music works. But such students (thank God!) always count as exceptions. For the most part, musicologists concern themselves with instilling some concept of history in tomorrow's performers and composers. How can we pitch the master narrative so as to make it valuable to this constituency?

Like any novelist plotting a large-scale narrative, the music history teacher should have some major themes that can resonate from period to period across the entire span. I am not suggesting that we resurrect the teleological tale of increasing progress that used to circulate; quite the contrary, we have to work hard to prevent students from dismissing as incompetent those earlier repertories that do not yet operate according to eighteenth-century standards of tonal logic. But I do recommend that a few important issues appear already in the opening lecture and that they continue to surface throughout the entire course.

Several of my own themes have developed from the questions posed urgently in the culture of our own time. For the last hundred years, musicians and critics have debated fundamental premises defining musicking in the West.[3] As it turns out, those debates have occurred in various guises all the way through history. If musicologists cannot hope to resolve those contentious issues, they can show students how to think actively about their own moment and futures by teaching through the debates themselves. And who could serve as a better guide for sniffing out controversies than my long-time friend and interlocutor Richard Taruskin, who—together with the late Piero Weiss—compiled a convenient and brilliantly annotated collection of documents for precisely this purpose.[4] I cannot imagine teaching the music history survey without requiring this as a textbook.

We can find many of the principal debates—including the following—already posed right from the outset:

- *The purposes of music.* Human beings engage in musicking for a wide variety of reasons: for religious devotion, for bearing witness to the order of the universe, for entertainment or relaxation, for disinterested contemplation, for subjective expression, for communal coherence and survival. Powerful arguments for each of these positions have appeared throughout history, and they continue to motivate our aesthetic controversies today. Indeed, any consideration of what to include on the syllabus or what analytical tools to use hinges on how we respond to this question. Does hip-hop belong in a course on Western music? What does set theory seek to accomplish? Students who have read Plato's *Republic* or Johannes de Grocheo will know how to grapple with such issues when they arise in the last segments of the survey.
- *The economics of musicking.* Although musicians should know better than anyone how expensive musicking is, we still often pretend that commercial interests arose only recently to contaminate what had been a pure, authentic medium. But someone always pays the piper, whether political institutions (including the Church) or the market. And given the choice between institutional authority and the market, I usually side with commercial enterprises, which prove more responsive to changing tastes and more conducive to innovation— even if only for making a buck. If students know about freelance musicians in twelfth-century Paris, the printing press that made an international star of Josquin, and the public theaters in Venice that turned opera into a viable genre, they will be less likely to raise knee-jerk objections to the recording industry. Music has been commercial for a very long time.

---

3   The late Christopher Small— a giant in the field of music education, broadly conceived—introduced the term "musicking" as a way of shifting the focus from a noun denoting objects to a verb pointing to human activity. His concept has had a profound effect on music studies. See his *Musicking: The Meanings of Performing and Listening* (Middletown, CT: Wesleyan University Press, 1998).

4   Piero Weiss and Richard Taruskin, eds., *Music in the Western World: A History in Documents*, 2nd ed. (New York: Schirmer, 2007).

- *Music and social values.* Those of us associated with Critical (or "New") Musicology came of age in the 1960s, when the power of music to effect change appeared self-evident, and the rapid transformations of musical style during that decade testified to the ability of musicians to pick up on, articulate, and broadcast each successive ideological wave. That life experience shaped the research projects pursued by Lawrence Kramer, Rose Rosengard Subotnik, Richard Leppert, and I when we later established ourselves in the field. It was not to sully the canon that we sought to connect it to its cultural contexts but rather to demonstrate that music had always maintained those powerful interrelationships with society. As usual, Plato got there first. In his words: "the modes of music are never disturbed without unsettling of the most fundamental political and social conventions."[5]
- *The impact of technological innovations on music.* The last decade has witnessed a stunning revolution in the ways information circulates. Who could have predicted the ubiquity of iPods, iTunes, or YouTube, and who knows what influence these and successive digital technologies will have on reading and writing, listening and composing? My undergraduate students know they have to be able to work within the new media: to edit their own performances with ProTools and to position them to best advantage on the internet. Yet many schools resist offering training in these new-fangled processes, fearing such additions to the curriculum will dislodge the learning of traditional skills. But students who know how Guido d'Arezzo was thrown out of the monastery by resentful monks fretting that they would be rendered obsolete by his new notational devices will see this as just the latest round in the trials and tribulations of technological innovation.
- *Class, race, gender, sexualities.* I have to answer this one for myself, as a prime offender. My favorite review of my book on Bizet's *Carmen* was titled (and not as evidence of approval!) "Sexy, Racy, Classy." But such issues arise in the survey not because I drag them in but because they have always been there: in Plato's desire to exclude the musics of ethnic groups such as the Lydians, in John of Salisbury's homophobic rant against polyphony, in the struggles of Hildegard von Bingen to have her voice heard in a culture that demanded the silence of women. Nineteenth-century German aesthetics managed to make us forget how pervasive these themes have been throughout history—and also how this aesthetic base justifies itself by universalizing its particular privileges of gender, ethnicity, and class.

* * *

[5]   Plato, *The Republic*, *The Collected Dialogues of Plato Including the Letters*, ed. Edith Hamilton and Huntington Cairns (New York: Pantheon, 1961), 665-66.

When I teach the music history survey, I try to bring the students into the active process of piecing this story together from documents and scores. I explain my inclusions and exclusions, and I invite them to argue for alternatives. Whenever possible, I perform myself to show them the difference analysis and cultural knowledge can make to the rendering of bare notation into sound; performing also helps me establish credibility and rapport with young musicians. By the end of the course, I hope to have made them aware of the legacy they have inherited and of their responsibility for making sense of their own present moment and futures. I am delighted, of course, if I have led them to appreciate Perotin or Strozzi or C. P. E. Bach or Gubaidulina along the way. But I want more than anything to pass critical and interpretative skills on to generations of productive musicians who will come after me.

At the end of my year-long course in 2010-11, I asked the students—all of them music majors—whether or not they believe the history survey should still be required. Even taking into account the fact that my customers were not likely to express themselves with full candor (given our unequal power relationships), I was astonished at their responses. The performers reported that they had developed the habit of researching the pieces they intended to play or sing on their recitals, because they realized that doing so would allow for more vivid experiences. The composers claimed to have a much better grasp of their own moment in history and of the horizon of possibilities available to them. In the end, they complained only that too much had been crammed into a single year. They wanted more!

The music history survey will continue to matter as long as we can make it relevant to the musicians of today and tomorrow. And with such fabulous material, we ought to be able to accomplish that goal without too much difficulty.

Preface

The first time you stand in front of a music history class—*your* class, as instructor of record—is an intimidating and exhilarating experience. Having taken innumerable history classes in pursuit of this honorable position, it may seem that you already possess the requisite knowledge and experience to slide into your new role with minimal stress. Your own education provided plenty of examples to draw from and it may seem that the structure and content of a college course is almost second nature to those who have spent the majority of their lives sitting in classrooms.

Then comes planning each week of the semester, creating a few assignments, writing the syllabus … eventually what had appeared to be a fairly obvious process from the perspective of a student grows increasingly complex. You begin to see how all elements of a class are interrelated; how deciding when to schedule an exam depends on your school's holiday schedule, which may require you to change the amount of time you were planning on spending on certain topics, which then alters the amount of homework assigned, which forces you to raise the percentage of the final grade given to the research paper—and on and on.

I remember my first semester as a tenure-track professor. The first classes were as exciting as I had imagined they would be. In fact, the first few weeks were a great deal of fun, and I felt confident that I had prepared well and that I knew what I was doing. It was not until the third or fourth week that this began to change. The first exam turned out to be too long and almost impossible for the students to finish in the time allotted. Then a student politely questioned why I had given her the grade I had on her paper, and I found my answer to be less than convincing. Little things, to be sure, but nonetheless indications that I was not quite as in control as I had thought I was. Then by mid-semester I realized I was never going to cover all the material I had intended and my panic grew as I fell further and further behind. Somehow my students and I survived that semester, thanks in no small part to their patience with a neophyte teacher. Though the course ended up being relatively successful, there were so many factors that needed fixing that it was almost two years before I felt that the basic structure of the course was solid. The revised version of the syllabus barely resembled my first attempt.

Why were there so many issues that first semester? Hadn't I seen any number of good syllabi, creative assignments, and inspiring lectures? The problem, I believe, was that while I had experienced all the elements of good teaching, I had never considered what made them good. I knew what a good syllabus looked like, but not *why* it was good. In addition, my graduate studies had been so focused on advanced topics and materials that I took for granted the pedagogical framework in which that material was presented. And my days as an undergraduate student were long gone and not easily remembered, so my understanding of how the undergraduate classroom functioned was hazy at best, despite having spent time teaching undergraduates during graduate school. What I needed that summer when I prepared my first classes was advice from experienced teachers on the basic mechanics that make up a successful college course, the "nuts and bolts" of teaching. Thus the genesis of this book.

The Music History Classroom contains essays written by experienced music history teachers that provide graduate students, adjunct instructors, and full-time faculty a resource for designing, implementing, and revising college-level music history courses. While this largely refers to the music history survey for music majors, the ideas and materials presented here are applicable to other music history courses such as period classes, composer or repertory courses, and special topics seminars. In addition, most of the materials and discussions found in *The Music History Classroom* translate easily for use in general education courses on music.

All the essays in this collection work from a basic premise: that teachers are passionate about their subjects and will spend much of their professional lives refining and reexamining the content they teach; yet no matter how knowledgeable the teacher or how fascinating the material, successfully transmitting that content will always fall short without a considered, coherent, and effective pedagogical framework. You need to learn *how* to teach before worrying about *what* you teach.

There are many useful texts dealing with the mechanics of college teaching such as those by Barbara Gross Davis, Joseph Lowman, and Wilbert J. McKeachie. This book does not seek to supplant these texts so much as to bring current thought on the scholarship of teaching and learning within the unique environment of the music history classroom. Many of the issues confronting teachers in other disciplines are pertinent to musicologists, but there are differences that complicate the transference of basic pedagogical principles. A key distinction lies in the unique nature of musical materials (such as scores and recordings) and the pitfalls involved in negotiating between historical information, admittedly complex technical musical issues, and the aesthetics of performing and listening. In addition, those who work with music majors must contend with the attitudes and eccentricities common to young musicians immersed in the unique culture of the music department.

The Music History Classroom draws on the talents of many different teachers with a variety of experiences and philosophical backgrounds. This suits the diverse nature of the teaching craft. Just as there is no single learning style appropriate for all students, there is no single way to teach. Teaching is a very personal activity; we all have idiosyncratic strengths and weaknesses that dictate how we present ourselves to our students or what types of assignments we favor. Some are born lecturers. The animation and integrity they bring to a lecture inspires students and successfully communicates information and ideas more intimately than any other way. Others, however, might be gifted writers or, more properly, gifted editors. To them the written assignment and the process of working with a student to find their own voice creates a life-changing educational experience. Neither is better or worse; they are simply different. But knowing yourself as a teacher—where you excel, and where you feel less confident—is critical when constructing an effective learning environment. We should not hesitate to play to our strengths, but we should know where our deficiencies lie and not allow personal aversions to keep us from investigating and implementing other teaching approaches. Never tried small-group discussions in your classes? Maybe it is time to try, and if it doesn't work, then move on. Not confident about recent trends with the internet? Then ask your students to show you—and turn it into an active learning experience for both you and your students.

It must be remembered that not all teaching techniques work in all situations. A marvelous writing assignment from a small seminar may be unsuitable for a class of 100 students, while a set of carefully crafted exam questions for senior music majors would likely baffle a class of freshman non-majors. Yet all the topics addressed in this book provide a proven basis from which to build. Even though a particular type of classroom activity may not transfer immediately to every class, it does offer an example of how such activities are created. It falls upon the individual teacher to examine how such examples, and the theories behind them, can be modified to fit existing circumstances, and how such approaches fit within that teacher's pedagogical philosophy.

This act of reflection, of examining how we teach as much as what we are teaching, is undeniably one of the most important steps in growing as a teacher. While it is hoped that *The Music History Classroom* is beneficial to those new to a music history course, it is also hoped that it lays the foundation for critical thinking and self-examination long past the first year. The better informed we are of teaching methodologies and the more aware we are of our own teaching style the more we will continue to evolve and improve as teachers.

My sincere thanks to the contributors to *The Music History Classroom*, not only for offering their invaluable insights but also for sharing my vision of a work that would benefit future generations of teachers. My thanks also to Heidi Bishop and Laura Macy of Ashgate for recognizing the value of this book and working so hard to see it come to fruition. And finally I would like to thank my teachers, whose knowledge, abilities, and enthusiasm led me to follow in their footsteps; and my students, who have shown remarkable patience while I have tried to learn how to teach.

Jim Davis
Fredonia, New York

Chapter 1

Creating a Music History Course: Course Design, Textbooks, and Syllabi[1]

William A. Everett

Teaching music history is an extraordinary experience, one filled with awe-filled moments, exceptional opportunities, and certainly its share of challenges. Especially in a survey course, covering many centuries of music in a very short fifteen weeks while providing some level of understanding and a meaningful learning experience can be daunting. But it is also eminently doable.

A large part of the success of a music history course results from careful planning and design. A well-constructed course, where the instructor has thought about both content and pedagogy, can result in a highly successful learning experience for students. But how does one design an effective course? What parameters need to be considered? What about textbooks? What is the role of the syllabus? How do all of these elements connect? This chapter will address these and other issues related to planning and implementing a music history course.

Determining Course Goals

When designing a course, whether it is an undergraduate music history survey, something more specialized, or an offering geared toward a particular student population, the first consideration should be what students are supposed to gain from the course. These goals can include, for example, familiarization with composers and repertory, a depth of knowledge about a particular topic, a practical application of archival research, or becoming more knowledgeable listeners and performers. One can also think on a broader scale; after taking this course, what should students be able to draw upon and use during the next semester, at the end of their undergraduate or graduate studies, and looking beyond the current curricula, five, ten, or even more years later? Thinking in the broader way when envisioning a course and all its components certainly can, according to those involved with the Scholarship of Teaching and Learning (SoTL), shift the focus from what could be an exercise in data-driven short-term memory to a truly meaningful life- and career-enhancing experience.

---

[1]   I would like to thank Andrew Granade, Paul Laird, and Jonathan Borja for their insights regarding earlier drafts and portions of this chapter.

Once these large-scale goals are in place, all aspects of the course should be focused on achieving these purposes. Learning objectives, assignments, classroom activities, and even course materials such as textbooks and anthologies can be tied to these overriding concepts.

Starting with the "big picture" in a music history class, what aspects of the course should students be able to access years later—core repertory, stylistic features, socio-economic factors affecting music, or something else? What other skills can be developed in the class? These can include the use of technology, scholarly writing about music, writing reviews, or speaking about music to a non-specialist audience. The recurring question as to "why study music history" needs to be considered here.

These large ideas can then be transformed into course goals and learning objectives. Course goals tend to me more abstract while learning objectives are measurable. For example, a course goal could be "to possess a deeper understanding of the socio-cultural dimensions of music" while a learning objective could be "to be able to articulate how different socio-cultural elements relate to particular musical genres." Many educational specialists advocate using active verbs, instead of static nouns, when stating goals and objectives. Verbs encourage active learning and invite students to engage in the class; they also remind the instructor that learning is a kinetic process. Thinking about course goals can also help teachers venture beyond the traditional survey or chronological approach to design fresh new courses driven not only by material but also perhaps by concepts, controversial issues, a particular repertory, or specific skill sets.

When determining learning objectives, several acronymic designators can prove useful, such as SMART. Is the objective Specific, Manageable, Assessable, Realistic, Time-achievable? Is it Succinct, Measurable, Achievable, Results-driven, and Time-manageable? Such markers help keep the learning objectives in focus.

This concept of *Backward Design* or *Universal Design* has many advocates, and Grant P. Wiggins and Jay McTighe describe the approach in their *Understanding by Design*.[2] They offer a three-stage sequence: Stage 1—Identify desired results, Stage 2—Determine acceptable evidence, and Stage 3—Plan learning experiences.[3] L. Dee Fink, in *Creating Significant Learning Experiences: An Integrated Approach to Designing College Courses*, offers a related tripartite model: 1) Learning goals, 2) Teaching and learning activities, and 3) Feedback and assessment processes.[4] (Notice the use of verbs in the former and nouns in the latter.) Both triads include learning goals and related learning experiences/activities. Wiggins and McTighe emphasize the identification of evidence to show that learning is taking place, while Fink advocates assessment as a central component of effective course design.

---

[2]   Grant P. Wiggins and Jay McTighe, *Understanding by Design* (Alexandria, VA: Association for Supervision and Curriculum Development, 1998; expanded 2nd ed., 2005).

[3]   Wiggins and McTighe, *Understanding by Design*, 17-21.

[4]   L. Dee Fink, *Creating Significant Learning Experiences: An Integrated Approach to Designing College Courses* (San Francisco: Jossey-Bass, 2003), 62-66.

Taxonomies of Learning

In moving from the macro-level aspect of course design—the ultimate goals of the course, which as a teacher you may never see—to designing ways to accomplish these ideals, it is helpful to reflect on what it means to understand and to learn. "Bloom's Taxonomy," in both its original 1956 version as developed by a group of educational psychologists led by Benjamin Bloom and its 1990s revised version updated by a group of cognitive psychologists under the leadership of Lorin Anderson (one of Bloom's students), provides a viable and valuable model for the different levels of understanding. Related to this, L. Dee Fink offers his own "Taxonomy of Significant Learning." When viewed in tandem (see Table 1.1), these models all demonstrate ways in which the consequences of instruction can achieve an ever-increasing depth of understanding.

Table 1.1   Bloom and Fink taxonomies in tandem

Bloom 1956	Bloom 1990s	Fink
Knowledge	Remembering	Foundational knowledge
Comprehension	Understanding	
Application	Analyzing	Application
Analysis	Analyzing	
Synthesis		Human dimension
		Caring
Evaluation	Evaluating	Learning how to learn
	Creating (synthesizing)	

While space does not permit an exhaustive discussion of each of these taxonomies, they all suggest ways in which learning beyond the acquisition of knowledge and subsequent memorization can take place. In music history classes, this challenges instructors to find ways to have students do more than memorize data for tests. These taxonomies provide frameworks that allow teachers to think creatively about helping students truly understand music history and have significant learning experiences in their music history classes.

Looking at just one of these approaches in more detail as it relates to music history, Fink's "Taxonomy of Significant Learning" can have direct applications in our field. Each of his six components is eminently translatable to this domain and can be useful in strategizing a syllabus and determining the overall layout of a course.

The first, *foundational knowledge*—specific points and concepts—underlies Fink's entire model. As Fink asserts, "Foundational knowledge provides the basic understanding that is necessary for other kinds of learning."[5] Students (and teachers) cannot ignore basic facts of music history, such as repertory, composers, performers, forms, genres, stylistic features, and key terminology. These are fundamental for educated musicians.

Application allows students to engage with the material through developing various skills (such as writing and public speaking) and also to invite them to experience critical, creative, and practical thinking. Critical thinking involves analysis and evaluation, skills that emerge out of pre-existing foundational knowledge. Creative thinking encourages new interpretations and perspectives as well as innovative ways of expressing these fact-based ideas. Finally, practical thinking encourages problem solving; students are given the opportunity to apply their knowledge in new situations. By applying foundational knowledge to projects inside and outside of the classroom, students engage with the course material on their own terms.[6] Creative ways exist for music history students to apply their knowledge and use their critical, creative, and practical thinking skills; these can include such diverse activities as evaluating a Wikipedia article, investigating a facsimile of the Squarcialupi Codex, or performing a role in a Baroque opera.

Integration can also take place in various forms. Students should be encouraged to look for and find connections of various sorts. How does what is covered in week 2 relate to what is covered in week 9 of the semester? How does music history relate to their experiences in ensembles, in their private lessons, and in their individual listening practices? When students discover these connections, the relationships become much more meaningful and, importantly, students achieve a sense of ownership for these connections because they found them. Students can likewise draw connections between what they discover in music history classes and what they learn in World, European, or American history classes. Art history can be especially useful here. When students look at portraits of musicians, they can create their own multi-disciplinary integrative experience as they discern why the subject is portrayed in a particular way.

Students (and teachers) are human beings and experience first hand the subjective *human dimension* of their art. Using music history, students can identify their own musical tastes and discover new repertories that appeal to them directly. Students may discover hitherto unknown riches in music history classes. It therefore can be extremely valuable to allow time for students to reflect on the music they experience in the course.

Developing a *caring* attitude is another dimension with immediate resonance in a music history class. Many students are already passionate about music they know; this passion can be applied to other styles of music, perhaps a repertory with which the student has had no previous exposure. If a school has a community engagement initiative, students can certainly find creative ways to bring their music history skills into this realm.

---

[5]   Fink, *Creating Significant Learning Experiences*, 31.
[6]   Fink, *Creating Significant Learning Experiences*, 38-42.

Finally, Fink advocates the concept of *learning how to learn*. A finite amount of material can be covered in any music history course, whether it is a survey or a focused seminar. By modeling one approach to the task of learning music history, students can apply this system to learning about any topic they desire. This is perhaps one of the greatest outcomes of any learning experience.

Developing Course Content

Once large-scale goals have been determined and taxonomies of understanding and learning have been considered, more detailed course planning can begin in a meaningful way. First, how will a teacher know that students understand the material, whether at the foundational level or at more advanced levels? It is useful to recall Wiggins and McTighe's second stage, "Determine acceptable evidence." To accommodate a diverse set of students, various assessable activities may be used, including—but certainly not limited to—examinations (written, oral, listening), short quizzes, research papers, program notes, creative projects, role plays, online discussions, and in-class performances. Subsequent chapters in this book provide additional information on many of these activities; what is relevant here is to think about these topics within a global framework for the course.

Next comes the planning of the learning experiences. How will students acquire demonstrable knowledge? How will you, as a course facilitator and leader, use such activities as lectures, student presentations, library assignments, performances, discussions, and the like to create a learning atmosphere that exists not only inside the classroom but also potentially outside a formal academic space?

When creating this three-level framework of large-scale course goals, means of assessing student learning, and learning experiences, it is important to continually consider how the levels will intersect and reinforce each other. Recalling the SMART elements articulated above can be especially useful at this point in course design—how will the measurable course objective actually be measured? How will you assess a student's understanding of Baroque opera? It may be worthwhile to create a flowchart for every assignment and class session in order to ensure that all course activities support at least one learning objective or course goal. If a particular assignment or lecture topic does not feed into the integrated web of the course, it probably can be left out. This is like a well-written research paper— one that is governed by a focused and well-defined thesis statement generally fairs better than one that is not. An integrated, well-planned course can often be much more effective for long-term learning than a series of (potentially seemingly unrelated) lectures.

Especially when teaching a new course for the first time, it is all too easy and extremely tempting to include too much information. It is impossible to cover everything on a topic, or to address every page in the textbook and every work in the anthology. Choosing what to leave out is difficult, but keeping the overall goals of the course in mind provides one set of criteria for determining course content.

Fink advocates building a feedback and assessment system into course design. During and at the end of the semester, student feedback can be extremely useful. Reflect on your practices. Did that project on Machaut *really* work as well as you had hoped? What could you change next time to make it more effective? This type of self-assessment keeps the course vibrant and fresh, and by corollary does not allow it to become stale.

Planning the Semester

When outlining the course, it can be useful to conceive of a pyramid: a significant topic at the top supported by middle levels of ideas built upon an even larger foundational base. For example, your class may be intended to cover music of a particular era. The top part of the pyramid would be the overarching aspects of music at that time. The middle sections would support the uppermost aspects and consist of central topics relevant to that era. The bottom part would include specific case studies and learning activities that validate the middle levels that in turn buttress the top of the pyramid (see Figure 1.1).

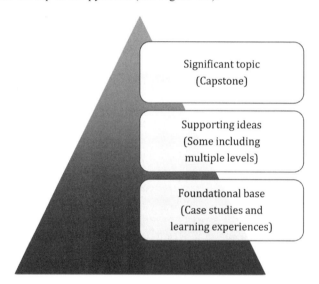

Figure 1.1   A pyramid of course planning

The top part governs the semester plan; it holds everything together. If you are teaching a two-semester survey divided at 1750, what will unify each part of the course? What is the overriding theme—the capstone—in your approach to the class? If you are teaching a more specialized topic, what is the significance of that topic?

A middle level of supporting ideas needs to reinforce the capstone. Some of these may have more than one dimension; in other words, ideas can be subdivided.

For example, in a class devoted to music before 1750, it would make sense to create a tripartite division of ideas according to medieval, Renaissance, and Baroque. What makes each era distinctive? In this example, each era would then need to be subdivided, perhaps chronologically, perhaps according to genre. Oftentimes, a textbook does this, since most arrange material into sections, then chapters.

The lower stones of the pyramid, the ones that support all the ideas of the levels above them and therefore the capstone, constitute a foundational base of case studies (often accomplished during class meetings as lectures) and learning activities. These can be either self-contained entities or part of a serial story, depending on how one approaches the course. Again, a textbook can provide solid guidance here. What topics need to be covered and how long should be spent on each? What should students gain from each lecture? Utilizing Fink's notion of integration, it can be useful to have students discover connections between the individual lectures, the various middle levels and structural units, and the capstone. A discussion of Mozart's operas, for example, could fit into the general coverage of the Classical era, which in turn forms the first part of a survey of music from 1750 to the present. It could also be part of a unit on staged dramatic forms in a class on music and gender. Keeping these various levels in mind when creating and preparing individual lectures can greatly enhance the overall effectiveness of the course.

In this regard, one can also make an analogy to a mosaic. The individual lectures are the unique tiles that when assembled in a certain way create images that in turn form part of the complete artwork.

Once these conceptual parameters have been determined, practical considerations must be addressed. Holidays, audition days, touring dates, convocations, master classes, and other activities can and will affect your course planning. These dates are often announced well in advance and can therefore be built into your semester schedule. Knowing, for example, that the wind ensemble will be on tour for a particular three days and that students will be missing class means that you probably do not want to focus on wind repertory at that time. It is also a good idea not to schedule examinations on dates when you know students will have to be gone. Remember that fall and spring breaks will affect the overall flow of the course.

After considering conceptual and practical considerations, create a course calendar. Consider how the individual lectures will fit together into larger units and ultimately relate to the learning objectives of the course. Again, a well-chosen textbook can be of tremendous benefit here.

When plugging particular activities (for example lectures, examinations, students presentations) into a course calendar, think about how the variety of activities flows together. Carefully determine how much material will be covered on each exam. Plan due dates for projects after estimating how much time it will take students to complete them. Think about other demands on students' time and how many hours they will need to complete your assignments. If you are incorporating any type of peer review, consider the time it will take students not only to complete their own project but also to review those of their colleagues.

During the planning process, consider your schedule as well. How much time will it take for you to assess and return projects to students in a timely manner? Be realistic in your expectations of yourself.

A solid course calendar should include, in addition to the topics covered, all readings and other preparations, examination dates, and due dates for all assignments. Students, especially music students, juggle many activities and part of their success depends on their ability to plan ahead. Providing solid guidance on a syllabus does a great deal to ensure student success.

A course calendar can be arranged in different ways. It can include details for each lecture or for each week. Depending on the nature of the course, the amount of interaction and discussion you want to achieve, and the types of classroom activities you plan to include, a weekly plan or a daily plan may be most effective. A weekly plan allows a bit more flexibility and implies a larger grouping of topics, while a daily plan emphasizes more discrete topics.

Regardless of the weekly or daily approach, it is important to adhere as closely as possible to the course calendar. Getting behind can have dire consequences at the end of the semester, where significant information (for example, Bach and Handel in a pre-1750 survey or the music of living composers in a post-1750 survey) might be excised from the course due to a lack of time. When one gets behind, it is imperative to slightly abridge material in the lectures that immediately follow in order to return to the schedule as quickly as possible.

Make contingency plans. Unexpected things will happen that will have an impact on the course. If you live somewhere where the campus may close due to inclement winter weather, realize that this is a reality and that you may well lose lectures in December, January, and February. Think about how you will need to redistribute lectures should classes be cancelled. Several teachers include topics of secondary significance throughout the semester that can be expanded or condensed as necessary.

Plan when things are due. Put calendars for all the classes you are teaching next to each other and stagger major due dates. Avoid, if possible, having papers for three or four classes coming to you the same week, with students expecting a quick turnaround. This will create less stress for you and less anxiety for students. If you are a performer as well as a music history teacher, try to not have students submit papers around the time you have a major performance and are atypically busy with rehearsals. Look at your own professional schedule when determining due dates for assignments in your classes.

Textbooks and Anthologies

Choosing a textbook is another challenging task. A textbook, in many instances, drives the syllabus for a class and indeed can often become the syllabus. Fortunately, several outstanding textbooks exist for teaching undergraduate music history.

In selecting a music history textbook, several factors need to be considered. How does the book match the needs for your curriculum and your particular classes? Part of this depends on how many semesters you have to teach undergraduate music history and the number of contact hours. What works for a survey consisting of two three-hour courses may not work for one that includes three two-hour courses. Does the organization of the potential book match your curricular needs?

At which point in their studies students take music history needs to play into the selection process: fourth-year students generally have a firmer grasp of technical aspects of music and have performed more repertory than second-year students. Student experience and expertise should be factored in to the choice of textbook.

The type of institution must also be taken into account. How broad is your students' knowledge of history, philosophy, and cultural studies? Consider how these topics are considered in various music history textbooks and how this coverage corresponds to what students already (may) know.

The potential use of ancillary materials, including online resources, is yet another aspect. When such things exist, how could and would you use them in the course? A textbook and its supplemental materials should support teaching, not replace it.

When one considers *Backward Design*, a textbook becomes not the focal point of the class but rather a resource and tool whose fundamental purpose is to achieve the overarching class goals. In short, a text should help the instructor realize what students need to take away from the course. Do you want to focus on repertory and give students a solid foundation in this area? If so, choose a text that does the same. Are you more concerned with the socio-cultural role of music and relationships between the arts? If this is your fundamental goal, find a book that aligns with this approach. Allow the text to serve your needs.

While it is possible to teach without a textbook, relying instead wholly on other resources, students and teachers (especially those early in their careers) typically relish the security of having a textbook. Especially in an undergraduate music history class, having a textbook's systematic approach to which students can refer readily at hand can reinforce and support other course activities.

The criteria one uses to select a textbook also apply to choosing an anthology. In many cases, textbook and anthologies appear in tandem. It is generally advisable to choose the anthology that aligns with the textbook of choice.

A teacher does need to decide how to use the anthology. Referring again to *Backward Design*, how will the anthology support large-scale course goals? Is it the basis for the music that happens in class, or is it something students explore on their own?

One does not have to rely exclusively on a textbook and anthology for course content. Supplemental materials, such as readings, podcasts, recordings, and websites, can provide additional insights for students. To maximize their effectiveness, all readings and other information-gathering assignments should relate to the overarching course goals and objectives.

Technology

Although technology is the focus of Chapter 6, it bears at least a brief mention in this context. Technology can be used to help accomplish course goals. Whether students use or even create podcasts as part of the learning process, participate in online discussions as a way to deepen their understanding of course materials, or build websites as part of the course, technology can facilitate the learning process.

It is also possible to include technology among the course goals and objectives. One learning objective for the course could relate to the evolving role of technology in the humanities. Not all learning objectives need to be directly related to content. Indeed, it may well be that a new technology students explore in the context of music history is the aspect of the course they will continue to use the most after the class is over.

Technology can also be used for assessment feedback throughout the course. Using online surveys and clickers, for example, students can provide valuable information to the instructor about their learning experiences.

Mechanics of the Syllabus

The syllabus is in effect the course contract between you and the students. It outlines the expectations each of you has for the other. It should facilitate a positive course experience for everyone involved. It allows students and the teacher to plan accordingly throughout the semester. In the case of a grade appeal, the syllabus becomes a central document in achieving resolution. For new teachers, it may be worthwhile to have the department head or a senior colleague review your syllabus to make sure it contains all the information the institution requires; many schools have institutional policies about items that must be included on all syllabi.

While every syllabus is different, and surely should be, certain items need to be included. Basic information about the course—its title, course number, meeting time and place—should be immediately evident, as should the instructor's name and contact information. Other fundamental items include course goals and learning objectives, grading criteria, due dates and descriptions of all assignments, a course calendar, and general classroom policies.

The instructor's name and contact information, in addition to office hours, should be prominent. Students need to know how to contact the instructor. If you have a preferred mode of communication (email, in person during office hours, for example), this needs to be stated as part of the syllabus. It is generally preferable to have at least two modes of communication; for instance, students may have class or rehearsal conflicts with your office hours and will therefore need to communicate with you either at a different time or in a different way.

Include course goals and learning objectives. Be explicit about what you want students to gain from your course. This can be done as a series of bullet points or as prose.

Likewise, be clear about grading and how different forms of assessment will be factored into the final grade for the course. Determine the relative importance of each assignment. It is good to consider factors such as length, substance, and the time you expect students to spend on the project when determining its relative importance in determining grades.

One newer approach in this regard is to present the various assignments to the students and have them collectively determine the relevant percentages. This is not only an active learning experience but also gives students a sense of course ownership. It constitutes a strong exercise in group decision making and coming to consensus. It also provides insights to the faculty member as to where the students feel confident (reflected by a higher percentage value) and less confident (where they want a lower percentage value). The instructor can then address these points, encouraging students in the dimensions of the course where they themselves have articulated insecurity.

Be sure to include all assessment activities on the syllabus. Consider this binding. Avoid adding requirements to the course after the syllabus has been distributed; plan ahead in this regard. Be sure to include any activity for which students will be assessed—examinations, projects, journals, quizzes, class participation, and so forth. The importance of this aspect cannot be stressed enough.

Along with a list of assessment activities, it is good to offer a brief description of each assignment. What kinds of examinations will be given in the class—short answer, essay, multiple choice? What is expected on a listening exam? What are parameters for the research paper in terms of length, appropriate topics, citation style, minimum number of sources, and the like? How will it be graded? Again, students appreciate these sorts of details as they plan their semesters.

Rubrics for grading may also be included. Concrete information on grading criteria in terms of content, organization, having a strong thesis statement that is supported throughout, writing style, grammar, and so forth can put everyone at ease. Students and the teacher should know what to expect from each other.

The syllabus should also include a course calendar, as discussed above. Having dates set at the beginning of the semester greatly enhances the students' learning experiences and their potential for success in the course. It is possible to encourage students to attend events not on the syllabus once the semester has begun, but requiring them to do so can cause problems at many institutions.

As a contract, policies regarding the course must also be articulated, including those on the definition of an excused absence, the effect of unexcused absences on the final grade, late assignments, and missed examinations. These are inevitable occurrences. You may also want to include information regarding incompletes, what happens if a student submits the same "original" paper in more than one course, and your policy on what constitutes an "audit." These, and other issues, continually arise.

If more than one person is teaching the same course, it may be worthwhile for everyone who teaches that course to develop a common set of policies. Indeed the entire music history area could come up with a shared policy statement. This can be amended as new policies are developed to plug the inevitable loopholes that a small percentage of students always seem to discover.

Most universities have clearly defined catalog statements covering topics such as academic integrity, plagiarism, sexual harassment, non-discrimination, and grade appeal. It is possible to either include these in your syllabus directly or include a statement to the effect that the university catalog policy will apply for topics not explicitly covered in the syllabus.

When assembling a syllabus, it can be very useful to look at syllabi from colleagues in music as well as outside of music. How a chemistry professor addresses learning objectives and plans course activities can give the music history professor valuable ideas about how to create an integrated course that will benefit students long after it is over. How a European history professor organizes a survey class can likewise stimulate ideas as to how a music history teacher can, like the history colleague, cover a wide expanse of time in a single semester.

Summer School and Special Sessions

Summer school and various special sessions, such as intersessions, have their own distinctive characteristics. Most notable is the intensity and speed of the course. What typically occurs in one week during a regular term now takes place in one day. Time is condensed, and this is an extremely important factor to consider. Learning goals, assessments, and class activities need to be adjusted. If a class has four exams throughout a sixteen-week semester, in summer school, this becomes one exam per week. Reading assignments need to be carefully considered, as do research-oriented projects. The possibilities of students being able to access and process the requisite course material in a four-week period are very different than in a sixteen-week class.

While summer school and intersession courses certainly have their challenges, they also have tremendous rewards and provide extraordinary opportunities. Typically, this would be the only class a student would take at the time. The ability to focus on a topic without other demands that are characteristic of the regular semester (recitals, ensemble performances, other classes) can allow for a dedication to the topic that is not generally available. Students can luxuriate in the world of music history, though it will certainly be an intense experience.

One should carefully consider the type of class to be taught during the summer or in a special session. While undergraduate survey courses certainly can and do work in such contexts, more specialized topics can flourish. These can include local music explorations, complete with field trips, since class times are extended; focused topics, such as the work of a single composer or even a single work; and study-abroad experiences.

The First Day

The first day of a new semester is almost always ridden to some degree with anxiety. Being prepared is the key to success. The first few minutes of the class (even the time before the class actually begins when students are arriving into the classroom) will set the tone for the entire semester. Students will discern the entire approach to the course—what type of content will be emphasized, how the instructor relates to the class, pedagogical approaches, and the like—in these opening moments. They will determine the entire learning environment and teacher effectiveness almost immediately. Malcolm Gladwell, in his book *Blink: The Power of Thinking Without Thinking*, relates a study by Nalini Ambady in which students were given videotapes, with no sound, of a teacher and asked to determine that teacher's effectiveness. The results from watching ten-second clips, five-second clips, and two-second clips were extremely consistent. Furthermore, these quick impressions were essentially the same as that professor's end-of-the-semester student evaluations.[7] An initial two-second impression has an enormous effect and needs to be carefully considered.

It may be prudent, therefore, to delve immediately into content. Content, after all, should be the focus of the course, not policy. The syllabus can be covered either before the semester begins (by posting it on the course website) or later in the class period. What happens in the first minutes of the class will set the tone for the entire term. If an interactive approach is desired, the class should begin this way. If the course is going to focus on repertory, start with this. If critical listening is central to the course, engage students immediately with a practical example.

The fundamental premise is to be prepared. Students will sense this. If the instructor is obviously prepared on the first day, the students will feel obliged to be similarly prepared. Bring all required textbooks and anthologies to class to physically show them to the students. Some students will have already purchased them; others will wait until after the first day of class. Having the semester planned according to a course calendar will also instill a sense of confidence in the instructor and the course among the students.

Some instructors arrive early on the first day and introduce themselves to the students as they enter the room. This helps the teacher and students get to know each other before the class formally begins.

Preparing for Class

A well-planned course calendar does not just help the students; it also provides guidance and structure for the instructor. Preparing class materials in advance is essential. Planning lectures a week in advance is advisable, especially when

---

[7]   Malcolm Gladwell, *Blink: The Power of Thinking Without Thinking* (New York: Back Bay Books, 2005), 12-13.

technology and audio-visual materials are being used. Locating specific excerpts from audio and video recordings takes time, as does choosing the most effective performance to illustrate the points being made. If a library recording is desperately needed, it is almost certain that that particular recording will be checked out if it is needed for class within a matter of hours. (And it may be a proactive student in the class who checked it out!) If one plans ahead, an alternative can be located and the students will be none the wiser.

Just as class preparation time should be built into an instructor's schedule, so should grading time. It takes time to assess assignments, and students expect a quick turnaround, especially if a similar assignment is due later in the semester. Students desire timely feedback on their work, and their success and interest in the course is related to the professor's interest, demonstrated at least in part by timely feedback.

Graduate Teaching Assistants

Many schools have Graduate Teaching Assistants (GTAs) assigned to music history survey classes. Such advanced students can be extremely useful. They can lead discussion sessions to reflect on the topics at hand, guide focused listening activities, and help students review for examinations. It is important that GTAs understand the instructor's approach to the course so that they can help achieve the fundamental course goals. It may be good to require GTAs to attend the main lectures in order to keep a consistent flow of information.

Working in consultation with the instructor, GTAs can develop their own *Backward Design* models for their activities, focusing on large-scale issues and creating meaningful learning experiences for their students.

A Rewarding Challenge

Teaching music history is indeed a rewarding challenge. Conceiving and implementing a course is a creative process that requires continual assessment and renewal. Students change, their musical experiences change, and the teaching of music history likewise needs to change. Although teaching music history requires a great deal of time and energy throughout the semester, effective planning and design before the course begins can make the experience even more rewarding for everyone involved. It can also allow for a more efficient use of time during the semester. An integrated course focused on overriding course goals and learning objectives provides an efficient and effective model for teaching music history in a variety of contexts.

Chapter 2
Classroom Activities

Mary Natvig

Teaching music history can be daunting. Some of us have 100 or more students in the classroom and often only two semesters to "cover" the entire history of Western art music—plus some popular music, jazz, and world music thrown in at the end. In some programs, music history is the most difficult academic class music students will take—perhaps the only course in which they are required to write a paper. Instructors are often responsible for teaching library skills, writing skills, study skills, and critical thinking to students whose pre-college experiences are vastly different.

Instinctively, or because of previous training, some students learn effectively by reading the text and attending lectures. These students make connections on their own, see the big picture, and retain information. (Many of us now in academia are probably older versions of this kind of student, which likely contributed to our eventual careers in higher education.) But what about our students who come to college with decreasing academic preparation and often little desire for intrinsic learning? It's both heartbreaking and alarming to come across a student who can barely comprehend the textbook—and frustrating to look into the classroom and see no one taking notes.[1] The most conscientious of our students will dutifully plow through the reading, copy and memorize PowerPoint slides and/or detailed review sheets (that we've distributed in advance) in order to prepare for exams. These students will pass the course. Others will simply stop coming to class, fail, and will re-take the course or find another major.

The question is: will any of our students (even the good ones) learn anything—really learn—as in some years later be able to place composers, genres, and

---

[1]   See John Biggs, *Teaching for Quality Learning at University*, 2nd ed. (Maidenhead: Open University Press, McGraw-Hill Education, 2003), 3-5. Biggs identifies two archetypal students: "Susan," who is bright, interested and motivated. She reads her text, has a good background, and is able to reflect on what she hears in class. "Robert," however, has little motivation for college level work. He's in school to get a good job after graduation. He just wants to pass the course and will do the minimum amount of work to achieve his goal. Biggs points out that the Roberts of the world have become increasingly more prevalent in the last twenty years, citing "expansion, restructuring and refinancing" in higher education as key reasons for the change in student demography. See also, "Study: Most College Students Lack Skills," *USA Today*, posted January 19, 2006, accessed September 20, 2011, http://www.usatoday.com/news/education/2006-01-19-college-tasks_x.htm.

musical styles in history? Will they be able to hear and identify the differences between Beethoven and Mahler? And most importantly, will our students have the ability to communicate both the meaning and importance of music in multiple ways, including through its social and historical context?

If these are our goals (and shouldn't they be?), we might best examine how we are teaching and consider Dr. Phil's pithy question, "how's *that* working for you?" Or, we can figure out a way to teach better, so that as many students as possible are really learning.

Student Learning Research

> The goal of research-based education is to structure lessons to ultimately rely less on inefficient and tedious rote memory. Helping students access and use more effective types of memory storage and retrieval will literally change their brains.[2]
>
> —Judy Willis, M.D.

The scholarship of teaching (known as student learning research)[3] offers strategies to enhance student achievement. Over the past twenty years, much of the research in teaching and learning has been informed by medical neuroimaging that captures where and how learning takes place in the brain. Scientists tell us that the brain's connecting cells (dendrites) continue to grow and develop throughout life as learning takes place. The more information we gather or the more skills and new experiences we take in, the more connecting pathways our brain develops and the more easily we learn and retain information. Conversely, the less we exercise the brain, the more these cells atrophy.

Neurological research tells us the following about how we learn and retain information:[4]

- New information (or a new skill) enters the brain through the senses or emotions. The information is eventually sent to various storage areas where it stimulates and connects to related information previously stored, thus reinforcing the brain's connecting cells. This juxtaposition of old and new information, called "relational memory," takes place when students build on what they already know. The more ways information can be connected to what students know and are interested in, the better students will learn.
- Multiple interconnected regions of the brain are employed when retrieving and storing information. As with the process of entering new information, sensory and emotional stimuli activate the storage regions as

---

[2]   Judy Willis, *Research-Based Strategies to Ignite Student Learning* (Alexandria, VA: Association for Supervision and Curriculum Development, 2006), 6.

[3]   Biggs, *Teaching for Quality Learning*, 11.

[4]   Willis, *Research-Based Strategies*, 1-7.

well. Therefore, the more ways something is learned and the more senses involved, the better the information is remembered.

- Information coming from the sensory receptors goes through the amygdala before it is sent to the hippocampus and on to the memory storage areas of the frontal lobe. The amygdala plays a role in processing emotions and is linked to both fear and pleasure responses. PET scans show that when the amygdala is hyperstimulated from stress or fear, the pathways to memory storage are blocked. Students who are under stress in the classroom will not learn or retain new information.
- Neurotransmitters (chemicals such as serotonin, dopamine and others) transport information across synapses (gaps) between nerve cells. When too much information is being transported, neurotransmitters work less efficiently: processing information slows down and retention is negatively affected. Varying classroom activity and the pace of delivery helps students to process and retain information.
- When new information is acquired, large regions of the brain are activated. But as that information is used in a variety of ways (or practiced) less brain activity is needed to process the information. The brain's connecting transmitters become more efficient and more pathways are developed to retrieve stored information. Repetition in a variety of ways helps students to learn and retrieve information more efficiently.

The research on how the human brain works has led to reams of scholarship on how to best reach/teach students at all levels. Like any academic discipline, student learning research comes with its own particular jargon—terms that get bandied about at university curriculum committees that render many older generation faculty clueless and irritated—clueless because many of us with Ph.D.s in musicology (and other fields) have usually had no pedagogical training—and irritated because often those who use these terms with utmost confidence appear to aim their teaching at poor students or care little about course content. When I first began attending these types of meetings, I considered myself to be a faculty member who stood for rigor and high standards (and still do), yet one who was committed to teaching well and ultimately concerned with student learning. So, I began to sort through the terminology of student learning research. What follows is a brief summary of the most common methodologies that contextualize the classroom activities suggested later in chapter.

Learner-centered Teaching

In learner-centered teaching the ultimate responsibility for learning is on the student.

> [This pedagogy] focuses attention squarely on learning: what the student is learning, how the student is learning, under what conditions the student is

learning, whether the student is retaining and applying the learning, and how current learning positions the student for future learning.[5]

In this model, power is shared between teacher and students. Students have a say in policies, due dates, what assignments to do, even textbooks. Power sharing, however, needs to be gradual: what's appropriate for a freshman class will not be appropriate for seniors or graduate students. This approach helps students move from dependent to independent learning, mirroring our own scholarly path, from undergraduate years of writing papers on an assigned topic, to seminar papers on a topic of our own choosing, to the advised dissertation, and finally to independent research.

Inquiry-based Teaching

Inquiry-based teaching is founded on the premise that learning works best when students have a need or desire to know something—a question they want answered. This way, students value the outcome of their learning experience. N. T. Feather calls this the "expectancy value theory," "particularly important in the early stages of learning."[6] Reciprocal questioning, especially when it relates to student concerns, can be a way to spark desire for learning.[7]

Many students today attend college to prepare for the work place; they think of a university education as job training. I've found that connecting what students will learn in my courses to future employment is a way to engage the "expectancy value theory." Even in classes for non-majors, I remind students that employees are looking to hire people who can read, write, think critically and creatively, and make connections—and that we will be practicing these skills in this course.

Problem-based Teaching

Problem-based teaching is similar to inquiry-based learning in that it begins with a problem or question that the student needs to solve. It mirrors how we learn in real life whereby we begin with something we know and build that knowledge to learn something new (as in every time we upgrade operating systems or purchase a new phone). Problem-based learning, first used in medical schools in the 1960s and 1970s is founded on an axiom attributed to William Glasser (Table 2.1).[8]

---

[5]   Maryellen Weimer, *Learner-centered Teaching: Five Key Changes to Practice* (San Francisco: Jossey-Bass, 2002), xvi.

[6]   N. T. Feather, ed., *Expectations and Actions* (Hillsdale, NJ: Erlbaum, 1982), cited in Biggs, *Teaching for Quality Learning*, 58.

[7]   Biggs, *Teaching for Quality Learning*, 92. Reciprocal questions include: What is the main idea here? How would you compare this with …? How is that different from …? Now give me a different example. How does this affect…?

[8]   *Association for Supervision and Curriculum Development Guide* 1988, cited in Biggs, *Teaching for Quality Learning*, 80.

Using this principle, medical students were first given real-life scenarios and then guided toward the acquisition of knowledge in order to make a diagnosis and proper treatment.

Table 2.1   Glasser's axiom

Most people learn:
10% of what they read
20% of what they hear
30% of what they see
50% of what they see and hear
70% of what they talk over with others
80% of what they use and do in real life
90% of what they teach someone else

Active Learning

Active learning opposes the idea of passive learning (i.e., listening to a lecture) and promotes students' active engagement with course material. It was popularized by Bonwell and Eison in the 1980s and 1990s and according to my unscientific observations it is probably the most touted pedagogy among college centers for teaching and learning. Active learning takes the standard post-secondary method of instruction, the lecture, and incorporates ways for students to engage cognitively with the course content, thus stimulating higher order thinking.

> Students are involved in more than listening, less emphasis is placed on transmitting information and more on developing students' skills, students are involved in higher-order thinking (analysis, synthesis, evaluation), students are engaged in activities (e.g., reading discussing, writing), and greater emphasis is placed on students' exploration of their own attitudes and values.[9]

---

[9]   Charles C. Bonwell and James A. Eison, "Active Learning: Creating Excitement in the Classroom," *The National Teaching and Learning Forum*, 1991, accessed October 1, 2011, http://www.ntlf.com/html/lib/bib/91-9dig.htm.

The techniques of active learning are many and often include teaching study skills: reading, writing, taking notes, synthesis, and teaching others. M. C. Wittrock reports a study in which "students were required to learn from a text in increasing forms of activity: reading silently, underlining important words, writing out the key sentences containing those words, rewriting sentences in one's own words, to the most active, teaching somebody else the material. There was a strong correlation between extent of activity and efficiency of learning."[10]

Applying Student Learning Research in the Music History Classroom

Effective learning, that is, learning that changes what a student knows and how he or she functions in the world, is dependent on six criteria:

1. The student's desire to learn
2. The student's background knowledge and skills
3. A positive classroom atmosphere
4. An appropriately paced presentation of new material
5. Engagement with the material using a variety of the senses
6. Synthesis and reflection

Student learning research can help instructors address each of these factors. First, we need to help our students acquire a motivation to study music history by leading them to discover the importance of the subject to their lives as musicians.

Initially, the most practical way to motivate students is to relate the study of music history to their future success as employed musicians.[11] For instance, ask music education students what they would do if, in the first year of teaching, they were asked to collaborate with the high school history teacher to provide music for the school's Renaissance fair (or a unit on the Civil War or the Civil Rights movement, or suchlike). Ask them to write down the pieces they will choose to highlight, why, and where they will find scores for their high school woodwind quintet (or choir, or string group) to perform. Or ask performance majors what they might do if asked to perform a recital for the local library's Women's History Month celebration. Ask what will they play and why. How will they introduce the works? Or perhaps their symphony contract includes giving pre-concert lectures to community groups. The concert they have to talk about is titled "The Devil is in the Details," and the orchestra is playing a violin concerto by Paganini, the Faust

---

[10]   M. C. Wittrock, "The Generative Processes of Memory," in *The Human Brain*, ed. M. C. Wittrock (Englewood Cliffs, NJ: Prentice Hall, 1977), cited in Biggs, *Teaching for Quality Learning*, 79.

[11]   Regarding the music appreciation class, connecting the kinds of skills that are learned in class to the skills that employers desire (an ability to write, communicate, problem solve, and so on) is a first step toward motivating students in general education courses.

Symphony, and *L'Histoire du Soldat*. Ask them to outline their talk and explain the reason behind the title. If these tasks prove to be difficult, then ask the students to consider the idea that a music history class might be practical and useful to their future lives as musicians and that they might actually *need* this class to succeed professionally. It is then crucial to continue to point out practical applications for what students are learning in class and to have at least some of the assignments relate to possible real-life situations. Students need help connecting the abstract to the practical and the past to the present.

The second necessity for effective learning is a student who has had a good academic background and is prepared to learn—a student who knows how to read a text, take notes, pay attention in class, and study. Every incoming college student can improve in these areas, though some need more guidance than others. There are different ways to deal with the less academically prepared student. One way is the "sink or swim" approach—"they're in college now and if they can't cut it, they don't belong here." The problem with the approach comes when a significant percentage of the class fits that profile. We all have to develop our own way to cope with students not yet prepared for college, but my own approach is to insist upon, and if necessary teach, good study habits, especially for students in their first music history course. But the students need to know why, for instance, I ask them not to text during class and why I require them to take notes. They need to know that it's because I want them to succeed, not only in the course, but in life. If students think of these policies as restrictive rather than caring, the results are disastrous, which leads to the next requirement for effective learning: a positive classroom atmosphere.

No matter what kind of pedagogy we employ in our classrooms or how hard we try to motivate our students, if they feel uncomfortable or threatened when entering the classroom, we've lost them. The brain is not ready to learn. Knowing students' names and providing opportunities for students to get to know one another helps students feel welcome and part of the learning community. The first day of class is crucial and sets the stage. Make time for "ice breakers" where teacher, TAs and students introduce one another and say something about themselves: their hometown, musical backgrounds, favorite music, and so on. In a large class, it may be impossible for every student to speak individually, yet instructor and TAs can introduce themselves publically and students can make introductions in small groups. I often have students in a large class write out cards on which they provide basic information (name, major, hometown) and any concerns they have about the class or personal circumstances they might want me to know about (optional). I respond via email to students who express particular concerns or potential problems such as an illness in the family, a learning disorder, or other difficulties. All of this takes time away from content. While I used to feel these were "touchy-feely" activities and affected the rigor of the class, I've seen the positive results over and over—students are more apt to participate in class discussions and are more invested in learning. Even venerable institutions such as

Harvard's Bok Center for Teaching and Learning stress the importance of teachers and students getting to know one another from the very start.[12]

The fourth factor in effective learning is appropriately paced delivery. Donald Bligh suggests that no lecture should last longer than twenty to thirty minutes without periodic changes in activity.[13] Graham Gibbs suggested setting a timer every fifteen minutes to let students swap notes, discuss missing points, or compare main ideas with student next to him/her.[14] Those of us who teach music history are probably already changing activities every ten to fifteen minutes or so (examining a score, listening to music, watching a video), thus providing a rest from the continuous lecture. Although I've never set a timer (nor can I imagine doing so) I have found it effective to provide an activity at the beginning, middle, and end of a fifty-minute lecture—activities that are supplemental to listening exercises or questions I might ask the students to respond to orally. Biggs especially advocates what he calls a "brief period of consolidation" at the end of the lecture where students summarize the main points of the class with a neighbor or write a short paragraph about the material presented.[15]

The last two elements important to effective learning—engagement and synthesis/reflection—are often addressed through in-class activities and discussion that takes place in class and online.

Discussion

The most traditional, yet often difficult, way of incorporating engagement and reflection into a course is classroom discussion. We've likely all had the uncomfortable experience of asking a well-crafted, interesting discussion question that results in stony silence. The reasons for such a response are many: lack of preparation or motivation on the students' part, lack of camaraderie or trust among the students or between students and teacher (a good reason to provide

---

[12] James R. Dawes, "Ten Strategies for Discussion Leading," *Derek Bok Center for Teaching and Learning, Harvard University*, accessed October 7, 2011, http://isites.harvard.edu/fs/html/icb.topic58474/Dawes_DL.html. See also Jennifer Barton, Paul Heilker, and David Rutkowski, "Fostering Effective Classroom Discussions," accessed October 7, 2011, http://www.mhhe.com/socscience/english/tc/pt/discussion/discussion.htm; "Suggestions for Leading Small-group Discussions," prepared by Lee Haugen, *Center for Teaching Excellence, Iowa State University*, accessed October 7, 2011, http://www.celt.iastate.edu/teaching/small_group.html.

[13] Donald Bligh, *What's the Use of Lectures?*, 5th ed. (Exeter: Intellect, 1998), 61. See also Part 4 of this book for suggestions on how to vary activities.

[14] Gibbs, Graham and Alan Jenkins, eds. *Teaching Large Classes in Higher Education* (London, Kogan Page Limited, 1992) cited in Biggs, *Teaching for Quality Learning at University*, 4th ed (New York, NY: McGraw-Hill, 2011) 146.

[15] Biggs, *Teaching for Quality Learning,* 101.

a comfortable classroom atmosphere), a culture of anti-intellectualism (it's not cool to be smart), or simply time of day. Whatever the reason, having counted on a discussion session and being met with blank stares is a novice instructor's nightmare, and it's not much fun for the rest of us.[16]

Before any discussion takes place, know what you want the students to learn or be able to do as a result of the dialogue. Are you reviewing for a test and eliciting basic content, or are you asking students to make connections or argue a point? Are you eliciting intellectual responses, emotional responses, or are you trying to develop critical thinking?

Building on the principle that we learn best by connecting new knowledge to something we already know, the best way to begin a discussion is to ask students what they think about something or to make connections between the course content and their own lives: the latest campus issue, something in popular culture or a YouTube clip. (Unless specifically reviewing for a test, avoid questions with right or wrong answers.) It may seem a stretch to get from the latest Lady Gaga video to the Renaissance chanson (or Pink's *Stupid Girls* to Hildegard's *Ordo Virtutum*), but try asking students to identify what does (or does not) make Lady Gaga innovative. "How and why does she use borrowed material?" (Or how might *Stupid Girls* be considered a modern version of *Ordo Virtutum*?) The same concepts can, of course, be applied to many other genres that students will encounter in a music history class. If you don't want to take the Lady Gaga/Pink route, any open-ended questions that ask students to "interpret, analyze, compare, or evaluate" are conducive to participatory discussions: "What do you think was the most important point in the textbook's discussion of nineteenth-century Nationalism?" "What do you think you *will* remember most about Beethoven; what do you think you *should* remember about him?" How would you explain the reasons for the Classical period's emphasis on formal clarity to your political science professor?" The level of these questions should, of course, be adjusted to fit the student profile at your institution. The point is to grease the wheel, to get students thinking about a topic and sharing ideas with each other, and eventually to see them able to engage with ideas across disciplines.

Finally, it is important to have realistic expectations. If the goal is for students to evaluate an argument or idea, know that first-year students may have many opinions but perhaps few or misconceived (or outright wrong) reasons for their assertions. Set up guidelines such as "for every claim that you make be sure to include at least one piece of evidence to back it up." Part of the discussion can (and should) include an evaluation of that evidence. A gentle hand and diplomacy

---

[16] For a more detailed discussion of the use of discussion in the music history classroom, see James A. Davis, "Classroom Discussion and the Community of Music Majors," *Journal of Music History Pedagogy* 1, no. 1 (2010): 5-17, accessed August 10, 2011, http://www.ams-net.org/ojs/index.php/jmhp/article/view/8 and José Antonio Bowen, "Rethinking Technology Outside the Classroom," *Journal of Music History Pedagogy* 2, no. 1 (Fall 2011): 43-59, accessed October 10, 2011, http://www.ams-net.org/ojs/index.php/jmhp/article/view/47.

are needed, however, so that students don't feel embarrassed or squashed when responding poorly or incorrectly, which is a sure way to shut down the discussion, and probably any future discussions. Ways to respond to sketchy or incorrect comments might include: "Sue, can you build on/refine what Sara just said?" or "John, I can see why you might have said that, but let's check that out; Bob, could you look that up on your laptop …." Avoid at all costs the automatic response of "good" to every comment offered, especially if it's *not* good. But do reinforce the students' participation and make the classroom a safe place to make mistakes and explore ideas.

Another way to invest students in a discussion is to ask them to solve problems. A few scenarios were suggested above and these types of questions provide an opportunity to incorporate real-life situations that connect to course material. YouTube videos provide a limitless resource for discussion material. Compare and contrast performances of the same work (i.e., historically informed vs. historical recordings, or contrasting cadenzas—Gilles Apap's Mozart, K. 316 is a good place to start). Which performance is more "historically" accurate—and what *is* historical authenticity? How would *you* approach the work? Or, are the images chosen by X to accompany Beethoven's *Eroica* Symphony appropriate to the historical and cultural context of the work? Do they aid in understanding the structure of the piece? What kinds of images would *you* choose and why?

Other points to keep in mind for successful discussions are:

1. Don't be afraid of silence. At a recent address at Bowling Green State University's Teaching and Learning Fair, Peter Facione[17] suggested telling students to wait eleven to fifteen seconds before answering the first discussion question, giving all students (not just the perpetually eager ones) time to think and respond. Another way to handle this is to ask students to write down their thoughts/reactions to the discussion question before answering out loud.
2. Provide a guideline for what constitutes good discussion participation. My guideline includes the stipulation that poor participation is reflected by both *lack of* participation and *dominating* a discussion.
3. If you have a large class, consider small group peer discussions or think-pair-share exercises.[18] Give them time to confer, then call on representatives to summarize some or all of the groups' discussions. Sometimes students in a large lecture are resistant to active learning, expecting and preferring to sit passively in a lecture. I've found it's important to explain to students the reasons for such activities and that they'll get "more for their money" if they participate.

---

[17]   Facione is author of *THINK Critically* (Upper Saddle River, NJ: Pearson, 2011).

[18]   Think-Pair-Share has been around for about thirty years. Students are given an open-ended question to discuss in their seats with one other person in the class. After a few minutes, the students report the result of their conversations to the whole group.

Active Learning and In-class Activities

James Briscoe's recent book, *Vitalizing Music History Teaching*, presents a number of excellent essays that encourage active learning in the music history classroom: Per Broman's chapter advocates problem-based teaching with practical research projects of interest to general students as well as music majors.[19] James Parakilas, suggests having students make a modern score from historical materials— "anything," he says "that will teach budding performers to find questions and not answers in a score …."[20] And Jessie Fillerup's essay describes a captivating set of classroom activities that ["both" seems awkward here: "set of activities that both teaches?"] teaches content and has students experience, first hand, aspects of John Cage's compositional techniques. These are excellent models for how to use classroom time to engage students actively with the content of the course.

The classroom activities listed below come from a variety of sources, some from my own experiences in various music history classrooms: the music major survey, music appreciation for non-majors, and undergraduate topics courses. Many come from the pedagogical scholarship on student learning research, and others are from generous colleagues who have suggested ideas over the years. The list of activities is long, so I've not presented every single permutation or type of question applicable to the music history course. Just a few examples serve to spark the imagination and allow for adaptation in different courses or for different types of students.

- *Taking notes*: My colleagues and I have noticed that many students no longer take notes in class or they rely completely on the PowerPoint slides by copying every word and nothing else. The physical act of taking and reviewing notes facilitates student learning and in most cases students should be taking notes during class. There are a number of good online resources to help students develop note-taking skills. Worksheets with key words or questions that guide students through the lecture can also help them develop these skills. Taking a few minutes in the middle of class for students to examine each other's notes provides a small active learning break and also allows students to help each other, a good way to reinforce new information.
- *Panel discussions/debates*: Divide students into teams and give each team a position to defend. Have them prepare their arguments outside of class and encourage them to bring in musical examples as evidence. In a large class, where 100 percent participation would be prohibitive, this could be one of

[19]   James Briscoe, ed. *Vitalizing Music History Teaching* (Hillsdale, NY, Pendragon Press, 2010).

[20]   James Parakilis, "Texts, Contexts, and Non-Texts in Music History Pedagogy" in James Briscoe, ed. *Vitalizing Music History Teaching* (Hillsdale, NY, Pendragon Press, 2010) 48.

several options for class projects or extra credit could be given for those students who choose to participate. The results might also be presented in online discussions or blogs.

- *Pre-class video/listening reflections*: At the beginning of the class period show students a video or play a piece that relates to the day's topic. Without any preparation, ask students to write a paragraph about what they hear, what the piece might "mean," and any other initial impressions of the work. These papers might be graded or not, perhaps used for taking attendance or to spark discussion.

- *Worksheets*: Once in a while I turn all of the information from my lecture into questions on a worksheet and have the students look up the information in class (with laptops, usually in groups of two or three). The last few questions on the worksheet ask students to make comparisons or think critically about an issue or work that they have been investigating. In the last fifteen to twenty minutes of class we review the information and discuss how and where the students found the answers. I also use worksheets when showing a documentary or film. The questions highlight important factual knowledge I want students learn from the video and/or ask students to make connections or analyze issues. Worksheets also help to focus attention.

- *One- (or three- or five-) minute paper*: Have students take out a blank piece of paper and write a quick response to an instructor's question.

"How does X relate to (or affect) Y ..."

"Explain why ..."

"What conclusions can I draw from ..."

"What other pieces might demonstrate these ideas and why ..."

- For large classes, these papers can be ungraded or marked Pass/Fail. They also provide a good way to keep track of attendance.
- *Reading/lecture response*: In the last few minutes of class ask students to summarize the main points of the lecture or respond to a prompt. Carol Hess suggests, "after we have studied the gestation of Brahms's First Symphony, I announce (five minutes before the end of class): You are Brahms. It is 1855. Write a letter to Clara Schumann describing some of the difficulties you encounter as you contemplate composing a symphony." [21] Or students might write a paragraph that begins "During today's lecture I was surprised

---

[21]   Carol A. Hess, "Score and Word: Writing about Music," in *Teaching Music History*, ed. Mary Natvig (Burlington, VT: Ashgate, 2002), 195. Hess's article includes a number of such scenarios that can be used for in-class writing. In the same collection, see also Peter

that ..." or "I wondered about ...," "I learned that ...," or "I was confused by ...." The papers can be used to clear up misconceptions, clarify points, or reinforce concepts, either via email to the entire class or at the beginning of the next class period.

• *Quiz questions*: At the end of a unit, have students write down two or three exam/quiz questions appropriate to the content. This encourages students to synthesize the material presented and allows them to feel invested in the assessment process.

• *Dancing, acting, and performing*: If students feel comfortable in the class, these kinds of activities are great fun. More importantly, they facilitate learning by using different kinds of sensory input. Students can quickly learn a Renaissance dance (the *branle* works well) or the basic *minuet* step, while a small group of students plays the music.[22] Instead of using recordings for every musical example, have students perform: string quartet, sonata, and Lieder all work well and often coordinate with what students are doing in their lessons. All students can also sing phrases, themes, melodies, or harmonic progressions from the works being studied. Even students who are not performing musicians (as in a non-major class) can participate in performances using laptops, smart phones, or found objects. I've also, occasionally, asked students to act out scenarios in class: a scene from *The Beggar's Opera*, or pantomimes of opera plots, Lieder, or programmatic works to see if students can guess the work. This is also a good way to provide an active learning break in the class.

• *Games*: I confess that aside from the occasional Jeopardy-style exam review, I've not yet incorporated games into my music history courses.[23] Preparing for this essay, however, I've come across some interesting resources that I am eager to try. José Bowen's article, "Rethinking Technology Outside the Classroom"[24] points to games found through Merlot such as Eftychia Papanikolaou's Beethoven/Berlioz game and his own jazz games. Merlot also links to music history crossword puzzles and a drop the needle quiz.[25] Symphony orchestra sites often have links to games and though their

---

Burkholder's article "Peer Learning in Music History Courses" (205-23) for other ways to incorporate in-class writing and review.

   [22]   To learn the steps, the Library of Congress has excellent dance videos available online: http://memory.loc.gov/ammem/dihtml/divideos.html (accessed May 19 2012).

   [23]   I usually just do a homemade low-tech version of the game, but recently heard about the following sites that provide templates: http://www.point4teachers.com/; http://www.superteachertools.com/jeopardy/ (accessed May 19, 2012).

   [24]   Bowen, "Using Technology Outside the Classroom," 47.

   [25]   Merlot is a wonderful teaching site that has much more than games. It's worth browsing through to discover its many resources: http://www.merlot.org/merlot/index.htm. See also Papanikolaou's game: http://www.academic.muohio.edu/mus189/berlioz/interactive/; Bowen's games: http://faculty.smu.edu/jabowen/; Crossword puzzles: http://

content might be suitable for a non-major class, their packaging is aimed at children.

- *Reacting to the Past*: RTTP is a published curriculum of historical role-playing games that are based on primary texts and focus on the history of ideas and significant historical events. Classes are run by students and include oral presentations, debates, and written work. So far, none of the published games are specific to music, but the concept could easily be transferred to music history scenarios.[26]

- *Invited performances*: Just as engaging as having students in the course play for one other is inviting their teachers or guest artists to play in class. It is especially effective if the performers will work with the instructor to emphasize or demonstrate sections of the music that are being highlighted in class or in the text—thematic transformations, modulations, form, performance practice issues, and so on. Discussion can then ensue about the importance of historical and theoretical knowledge in performance.

- *Invited presentations*: Invite members of other departments to speak to the class, or co-teach certain lessons or units. I've "reciprocal taught" (a euphemism for "you come to my class, I'll come to yours") with art history professors, ethnomusicologists, and most recently a geologist (in a class on music and protest, where the geologist talked about mountaintop removal mining and I spoke on the protest songs).

- *Social activities*: Bring in food from different countries, historical periods, or perhaps music-themed food (Melba toast, Peach Melba, *Mozartkugeln*, Eggs Berlioz, Eggs Bizet, Consommé Bizet, Queen of Sheba Cake, Chicken Tetrazzini, Tournado Rossini[27]). For a large class, this might be limited to candies or snacks, but using all the senses to accompany new learning helps activate the brain—plus it creates a positive classroom atmosphere.

Course Content, Conundrums, and Conclusions

All of the pedagogies reviewed earlier in this chapter can be traced to the educational theory of constructivism, based on the ideas of Jean Piaget. Piaget

---

library.thinkquest.org/15413/history/music-history.htm; Drop the needle quiz: http://www.coastonline.org/megill/skilltests/skilltests.html (all accessed May 19, 2012).

[26] *Reacting to the Past* was begun in the late 1990s by Barnard College history professor Mark C. Carnes. Since then a consortium of forty colleges and universities has adopted the RTTP curriculum. For an overview of the program, see http://reacting.barnard.edu/ (accessed May 19, 2012). For a detailed pedagogical introduction, go to http://reacting.barnard.edu/sites/default/files/inline/reacting_pedagogical_introduction-9-20-2010.pdf (accessed May 19, 2012).

[27] An internet search will get you to most of these recipes, though most are appropriate only for a very special occasion and a very small class!

argued that people learn by constructing their own understanding of the world through experience and reflection. This implies that learning is about conceptual change, not just the acquisition of knowledge. True learning takes place only when the student can *use* the acquired knowledge. Constructivists caution, however, that incorrect pre-conceptions must be addressed before new knowledge can be constructed. Here the importance of foundational knowledge, what we normally term course content, enters into the picture.

Bloom's taxonomy (described in Chapter 1) divides learning into six levels: *knowledge, understanding, application, analysis, synthesis,* and *evaluation.* The bottom category, *knowledge,* is referred to as the lowest level of learning and each level up becomes increasingly more complex. Sometimes it seems that educational reformists advocate avoiding Bloom's lower levels at all cost—aim for the top, make sure students can *analyze, synthesize,* and *evaluate.* Make no mistake: these are important thinking skills. But I often wondered how students could even begin to attempt them if they had nothing on which to base an analysis. What evidence will they use for their analytical claims? When I was first investigating various pedagogies in higher education I came across articles that either aspersed content by emphasizing its "lower level status" or those that ignored content altogether. *Knowledge* may be the "lowest" level of learning, but it is the absolute essential ingredient in any of the higher components. No matter what pedagogies we adopt, fundamental knowledge cannot be forsaken—first, to ensure that the misconceptions brought into the classroom are corrected and second, so that our students have a solid foundation on which to base analyses and evaluations.

The dilemma is obvious. By taking time to apply active learning strategies, to work on learning skills, and to encourage higher order thinking, we have less class time to deliver fundamental knowledge: the skills vs. content conundrum.[28] There are solutions, however. First begin slowly, especially in a large class, and maintain balance. I don't have students acting out skits in every class. Nor do I ask them to fill out worksheets or eat *Mozartkugeln* every day (nice as that would be …). All of the suggested activities should be used with discretion and fit the personalities of both instructor and students. In a very large class, maybe only a few of these in-class activities will be effective. Keep trying even if students balk; you'll eventually find something that works.

Second, find creative ways to ensure that students can acquire the necessary content outside of class. José Bowen maintains that "our job in the classroom is to help students sort through [content]. So creating strategies that will ensure students will be prepared for class should be a primary part of good teaching."[29]

---

[28] Dan Berrett, "Which Core Matters More?," *Chronicle of Higher Education,* September 25, 2011, accessed September 9, 2011, http://chronicle.com/article/In-Improving-Higher-Education/129134/.

[29] Bowen, "Using Technology Outside the Classroom," 44. See also Bowen's "Teaching Naked: Why Removing Technology from Your Classroom Will Improve Student Learning," *National Teaching and Learning Forum* 16, no. 1 (2006): 1-14, accessed

Bowen offers several good suggestions: online practice exams, pre-class quizzes, and not allowing unprepared students to participate in class discussion (they sit on the outside of the circle and take notes). Bowen also advocates sending out pod/videocasts that highlight course content, leaving class time to interact with students in problem solving activities and active learning strategies. After reading Bowen's article, I tried pre-class on-line quizzes and student participation in class discussion (with 120 students) increased markedly.

It may seem like the good old days, when a teacher could walk into a college classroom and deliver a nicely nuanced lecture with a few "overheads" and musical examples to illustrate key points—maybe with an aromatic purple ditto for students to take home. I recall fondly the first music history courses I took as an undergraduate that were delivered in this manner. But when I peruse my freshman notebooks (yes, I kept them), I am surprised to see that the earliest example of organum, according to my now unfamiliar 18-year-old handwriting, was found in a treatise called *Musica Kyrie Deis* and that "*Joskah* was a very important composer of motets in the *Renn*." And so I wonder, did I really read the text before class? (I thought I did.) And then I recall my first year of teaching (pre-Ph.D.), taking hours every evening to prepare the content for my own nicely nuanced lectures, and I realize that this was the year when "music history" finally "took." I would call it the ultimate in "problem solving, inquiry based, active learning" experiences. The realization reminds me that all students can benefit from the kinds of activities mentioned in this chapter and throughout this volume, from the unprepared and unmotivated to the eager and advanced.

October 15, 2011, http://www.ntlf.com/html/ti/naked.htm. See also http://www.npr.org/templates/story/story.php?storyId=111872191 and http://www.openeducation.net/2009/07/31/dean-encourages-professors-to-teach-naked/ (accessed May 19, 2012).

Chapter 3
Lecturing

Edward Nowacki

Challenges and Opportunities

The music history classroom presents the lecturer with special challenges and special opportunities. Of the challenges perhaps the most daunting derives from the nature of the subject. Music history is a constantly changing narrative. Its course cannot be predicted from general principles. Its instances must be learned without the help of general laws. In this respect it differs from other disciplines, like music theory, in which general laws can be used to predict particulars and to invent, or generate, acceptable instances without having to match them with actual historical examples. The instructor of music history must be master of a story whose parts are connected by happenstance. To be sure, generalizations may be possible, but they cannot be assumed in advance. They can only be inferred after the fact from masses of data—data that are apt to be perceived as arbitrary by the student who is confronting them for the first time. Experienced historians, who are able to discern generalities in such data, find the history of music coherent, and that, no doubt, is why musicologists find histories of music to be interesting reading. Students encountering the subject for the first time, on the other hand, are liable to find it daunting, and to regard the reading of music history texts as laborious. Herein lies the first challenge of the music history classroom.

The second challenge—not unique to music history—is the impersonality of lecture courses and the passivity that they may engender in the student. It is a common experience of college teachers, supported by research in the field of educational psychology, that students learn better in small, interactive classes, especially those that require substantial input from the students in the form of discussion, presentations, and research papers. Some observers have gone so far as to maintain that large lectures are categorically deficient as a medium of instruction, and that they are to be resorted to only in cases of unavoidable necessity.

How are we to respond to these challenges? First we should remind ourselves of the obvious. Lectures offer the opportunity to listen to an expert. That has always been their principal attraction. Small classes have their value, to be sure. But programs that assign the teaching of large groups of students to single professors out of necessity should not underestimate the positive value of exposing a large class of students to a seasoned expert. It may be the only opportunity that many of those students have to study with that particular professor and to experience in their own institution one of higher education's celebrated benefits.

But when we tout the benefits of the lecture, do we simply make a virtue of necessity? Does the criticism of lecturing ultimately overwhelm its defense? In fact much of the familiar criticism addresses only the weaknesses of lecturing and none of its potential strengths. Those considering whether to lecture, and how to do so, should put all of that negativity aside and consider what the positive research has shown. The lecture is not intrinsically deficient as a medium of instruction. Large lecture classes are not intrinsically difficult to teach. Lecturing simply entails its own special set of challenges, which if handled in ways appropriate to the medium, can yield effective results that are rewarding to the student and satisfying to the instructor.[1]

Moreover, the challenges are counterbalanced, especially in the music history classroom, by a wealth of opportunities. The first—one could call it a gift—is the deep and enduring love of music that instructors can assume in their students and which they share with them. Promotion and advocacy, while certainly necessary on the fringes of the canon, are not nearly so needed as they are in other fields. The eminent educational theorist Wilbert J. McKeachie has confessed, "I am not as effective a teacher today as I was decades ago because I do not know the students' culture and am thus limited in finding vivid examples of a concept in students' daily lives."[2] In the music history classroom, on the other hand, instructors and students share the same culture for the most part. And while instructors will possess expert knowledge of details far beyond the knowledge of their students, it is a rare detail that cannot be illustrated with an example that is familiar to both the instructor and the student.

The other opportunities of the music history classroom derive from music's unique nature as a nonlinguistic sound medium whose instances can be reproduced for purposes of illustration with live and recorded performance and do not require the room to be darkened while they are sounding. The cognitive and motivational benefits of a lecture illustrated with sounding musical examples give the lecturer in music history an advantage over lecturers in many other subjects.

---

[1]   Heather Dubrow and James Wilkinson, "The Theory and Practice of Lectures," in *The Art and Craft of Teaching*, ed. Margaret Morganroth Gullette (Cambridge, MA: Harvard University Press, 1984), 25-26; Patricia Ann deWinstanley and Robert A. Bjork, "Successful Lecturing: Presenting Information in Ways That Engage Effective Processing," *New Directions for Teaching and Learning* 89 (2002): 19-31; Mark Bland, Gerald Saunders, and Jennifer Kreps Frisch, "Point of View: In Defense of the Lecture," *Journal of College Science Teaching* 37, no. 2 (2007): 10-13.

[2]   Marilla Svinicki and Wilbert J. McKeachie, *McKeachie's Teaching Tips*, 13th ed. (Belmont, CA: Wadsworth, Cengage Learning, 2011), 62.

The Instructor's Demeanor

One of the lecturer's most valuable assets is his or her demeanor in front of the class. Educational psychologists have observed that better learning outcomes occur when students observe their instructor to be enthusiastic. Instruction from an instructor who communicates enthusiasm for the subject increases student motivation, setting in motion one of the chief mechanisms of effective instruction, the transfer of responsibility for learning from the instructor to the student. It should be noted, however, that enthusiasm in the instructor is only a symptom of something deeper and much more important, and that is sincerity. There is nothing more off-putting than false enthusiasm, and not all lecturers have the personality to radiate a constant stream of the genuine thing. Much more effective is the sincerity that even unemotional instructors betray in countless ways by their earnest presentation, by their concern for their students' comprehension, and by their unconscious disclosure of their personal engagement with the subject.[3]

Of course, if the instructor has genuine enthusiasm but hides it, some students may not detect it. Fortunately, there are concrete steps that the instructor can take to communicate enthusiasm. One is simply to make eye contact with the students. If the instructor uses a script—and there are good reasons for doing so—he should use it as a series of cues, not as a text that one might read at an academic conference. Maintaining eye contact with the class and constantly sweeping the room with his eyes will cause the students to see in the instructor someone who is speaking to them personally, and will have the ancillary benefit of giving the instructor stimulating feedback. Other methods of communicating enthusiasm are walking about, gesturing, and varying the pitch and intensity of one's voice. Being stuck behind a lectern and speaking in a monotone make it more difficult for the instructor's enthusiasm to show.[4]

Another way for the instructor to communicate enthusiasm is to place in her lectures examples that she is personally excited about. She might feel obligated to "cover" a canonic narrative in the history of music, but doing so may come at the cost of inhibiting her from teaching what she knows and likes best. To be sure, lecturers have an obligation to the discipline and to their students to cover the main points of the course's subject, but exercising professional discretion in the choice and number of examples in order to emphasize points about which the instructor is personally excited has the potential to communicate the historical lesson more effectively than adhering to a prescribed routine. By disclosing her own personal enthusiasms, the instructor motivates the students to accept responsibility for their own education, because they observe in her not merely an expert transmitter of obligatory learning, but a model of the positive value that the learning contributes to a satisfying life in their chosen field.

---

[3]   Holly E. Long and Jeffrey T. Coldren, "Interpersonal Influences in Large Lecture-Based Classes: A Socioinstructional Perspective," *College Teaching* 54 (2006): 241.

[4]   Svinicki and McKeachie, *Teaching Tips*, 56.

Self-disclosing instructors do not compromise their privacy. The disclosures concern only their personae as students and lovers of music. An effective application of this principle occurs when the instructor is able to put himself in the place of the learner and to make explicit the steps by which he solved a problem or reached a higher level of comprehension. The instructor, in other words, walks the students through each step of a difficult problem as if experiencing the difficulty for the first time. In incorporating that kind of self-disclosure into his lectures, the memory of his student days can be a useful resource. One need only recall the difficulties posed by, say, the medieval polytextual motet, or by Vivaldi's unfair reputation for repetitiousness, or the incomprehensible sensory overload of Stravinsky's *Rite of Spring*. The mature instructor has solved many of these problems by fitting them into logical frameworks that are the fruits of his years of experience in thinking about music. Remembering where he began and being able to share the thought processes by which he came to a higher level of comprehension is one of the best means at his disposal for helping his students along the same path. And it can be done in lecture classes as well as in more intimate instructional settings.

Another way in which the instructor's demeanor can ameliorate the impersonality of lecture classes is her manner of addressing the students. In large lectures, it is often taken for granted that attempting to remember the students' names is a hopeless task. Some instructors have the ability to memorize the names of students in large classes, and their reputation sometimes rises to the level of a local legend. But if one were to be entirely frank, one would have to admit that that ability is rare. Fortunately, instructors need not possess it in order to create an environment in which students feel a personal connection with them. A simple solution is to keep a class roster on the lectern and to call on students by name. Some students will object to "cold calls," but they get used to it, and the effect of this small token of personal recognition on the social chemistry of a large class is incalculable.

Obviously, when the initiative comes from the other side, as students direct questions to the instructor, he may not be able to acknowledge them by name. In that case, if the instructor is comfortable doing so, he should simply ask the student to identify himself. Once the instructor shows that he is willing to recognize the individuality of his students, even at the cost of revealing his own failure to remember their names, he will gain their respect. And any success in breaking down the inevitable anonymity of large lectures has been shown to improve learning outcomes for the simple reason that students who do not feel anonymous are less likely to be passive and more likely to accept the instructor's efforts to shift responsibility for learning onto themselves.[5]

---

[5]   Svinicki and McKeachie, *Teaching Tips*, 273-74; Long and Coldren, "Interpersonal Influences," 241.

How Students Learn

The practice of lecturing is informed by theories of how students learn. Why should they attend the lecture at all, students may ask. Can they not simply read the textbook? The institutional answer is that the lecture provides some added value over and above simply reading the textbook that will increase comprehension, methodological sophistication, and professional growth. But the success of that agenda depends on how it is executed by the particular instructor.

How then do instructors in a lecture class add value to the textbook? By selection, ranking, emphasis, repetition, and illustration. This raises the question whether the instructor should adhere closely to the textbook or offer instruction that is partially or wholly complementary. In my opinion, the teaching of the same subject matter through two media, a textbook read in private and an orally delivered lecture, adds positive reinforcement to the learning process for most learners and is superior to learning from a single medium. This kind of reinforcement may be accomplished in two ways: by assigning the relevant reading before the lecture and using it as a way of preparing the class to assimilate the lecture more effectively, and by using the lecture to prepare the students to comprehend readings performed after the lecture. In either case, the mutual reinforcement will be greatly improved if the instructor gives the students explicit guidelines in the form of questions to be answered or generalizations to be fleshed out. In that way the preliminary half of the exercise will provide a framework for encoding detail transmitted in the complementary half.

But there is a risk in this approach. Some students inevitably suspect a lecturer who merely repeats the content of the textbook. They may find the practice insulting to their intelligence, or a sign of the instructor's unwillingness to give more than routine instruction. It is therefore important for instructors who assign readings preparatory to their lectures to explain this strategy and promote it to the class as a superior way of achieving the course's goals. Of course, the instructor's lecture must involve more than a paraphrase of the textbook. By giving a lumpier version of the textbook's smooth narrative, with self-disclosing advice on the steps that learners need to follow in order to progress from ignorance to understanding, the instructor will persuade even the most persnickety independent learners of the benefit to be derived from this mode of instruction. To be sure, lecturing with no textbook at all or in conjunction with reading assignments that are complementary to the lectures is a familiar and proven method of instruction. The foregoing remarks are addressed only to those who choose to lecture in close coordination with a textbook, perhaps harboring the vague suspicion that it is a less respected method of instruction. In my opinion the value of the method depends on how it is used. In some cases it may be the one best suited to the abilities of the students and to the course's instructional goals.

Visual Media

The availability of multiple instructional media brings us to the question of presentational programs such as PowerPoint. Experts in educational theory have observed that a well-illustrated lecture adds to learning by stimulating the students to encode the material in multiple ways, in a mental network instead of just in a single pigeonhole. This promotes retention and ease of recollection. But there are risks in applying this principle reflexively. It has been shown that when students simultaneously view a PowerPoint presentation and listen to a lecture, they assimilate neither very well. The two media function as distractions to each other. To derive the maximum value from a PowerPoint presentation, it is better when the instructor's verbal presentation and the PowerPoint images are presented successively rather than simultaneously and that they are not permitted to distract from each other. This is especially crucial with PowerPoint, since it often presents alluring visual stimuli that captivate most of the observer's attention. Another disadvantage of PowerPoint is that its slickness and instantaneousness may evoke from the students the same habits of passivity with which they view recreational media. This in turn may give them a false impression of how much discursive information they have really assimilated and thus cause them to be surprised when they begin reviewing for examinations and discover that their comprehension of the course content has been an illusion.[6]

Of course, PowerPoint can be an asset, especially when the images that it presents are too complex to be drawn on the writing board during class. Such images may include scores, graphic analyses, maps, and images of artworks, architecture, and musical instruments. And they have the advantage that they can be distributed to the class by means of digital media. But the old-fashioned writing board is still superior in certain respects. When instructors pause in a lecture to write a personal name or date on the board, the act of writing forces them to slow down so that the writing transpires in the same time that it takes the students to copy it. The importance of such basic written communication cannot be overemphasized. Lectures, even when carefully composed to be easily comprehensible, with short sentences, plenty of repetition, and clear summaries, will inevitably be filled with names, dates, and terms that are difficult to assimilate by those who are hearing them for the first time. Certain things must be written down. Merely projecting them on the PowerPoint screen is less effective.

To Use or Not to Use a Script

One of the biggest questions facing the lecturer is whether to compose a literal script. Whether one's lectures are spontaneous, from an outline, or tightly scripted is, of course, a highly personal matter. One should always lecture in a

---

[6]   deWinstanley and Bjork, "Successful Lecturing," 21.

way that is true to one's abilities and personality. But in lectures, especially to large classes, following a script has several advantages that ought to be given serious consideration. It is commonly observed that students do not like lectures that are read verbatim. Independent learners will appreciate the total precision that a prepared lecture offers, but most students expect spontaneity and take it as a sign of sincerity. Experience has shown, however, that merely preparing an outline often leaves the lecturer tongue-tied and groping for words. A possible solution is to compose a literal script in the very words that one's students will best understand, read it over before class, and then refer to it from time to time in the actual lecture, reading key passages, but otherwise paraphrasing the gist of what one has written and adding spontaneous elaborations.

Particularly in the case of freshmen, writing such a script involves translation from professorial speech to the plain, short sentences that 18-year-old college students will grasp. For some instructors, rephrasing one's usual learned discourse takes considerable thought and effort. It is often remarkably difficult to frame some of the most basic concepts in the history of music in simple, direct language. (What is a mode? What is *musica ficta*? What is romantic about Romanticism?) Yet for a class of freshmen, it is a necessity. A professor's thoughts about the subject are often complex and depend on the help of knowledgeable interlocutors to draw them out, but in a lecture, especially to beginners, one does not have that kind of help. Instructors are well advised to work out such explanations in detail in advance, not necessarily in order to read them, but so that they will have confronted *and solved* the communication problem to their own satisfaction and will not have to grope for words during class.

Dubrow and Wilkinson have suggested that ten single-spaced pages is the maximum for a fully scripted lecture.[7] In my experience, more than three or four such pages is excessive. The reason is that effective lecturers repeat their points using different phrasing, add spontaneous elaborations, pause to write names, dates, and terms on the board, play sound recordings, pose and answer questions, and simply speak more slowly. Empirical studies have shown that students who listen to less densely packed lectures paradoxically retain more of the course's substance.[8] Racing through a lecture in order to cover all the material in an overstuffed script does not promote better learning. The students cannot take it all

---

[7]   Dubrow and Wilkinson, "Theory and Practice," 29.

[8]   See R. B. Kozma, L. W. Belle, and G. W. Williams, *Instructional Techniques in Higher Education* (Englewood Cliffs, NJ: Educational Technology Publications, 1978), 151-52; I. J. Russell, W. D. Hendrickson, and R. J. Hevert, "Effects of Lecture Information Density on Medical Student Achievement," *Journal of Medical Education* 59, no. 11 (1984): 881-89; and M. D. Sundberg, M. L. Dini, and E. Li, "Decreasing Course Content Improves Student Comprehension of Science and Attitudes towards Science in Freshman Biology," *Journal of Research in Science Teaching* 31, no. 6 (1994): 679-93. All of the above are summarized in Bland, Saunders, and Kreps Frisch, "In Defense of the Lecture," 12.

in, and the teacher becomes an impersonal channel of chatter rather than a model of how to learn.

Having written a well-planned script, the instructor may ask herself whether to share it with the class. The general answer to that question is emphatically no. Most scripts, no matter how detailed, are essentially memoranda to the lecturer. Having only the script and not the spontaneous elaborations, repetitions, and illustrations that accompany it will give students a false impression of the course's content. Even worse, placing the script at the disposal of the class may encourage an attitude of passivity that leads them to believe that mere regurgitation is sufficient to earn an acceptable grade. Such low-level learning is quickly forgotten because it fails to promote the growth that enables students to apply the knowledge to new situations beyond the classroom.

On the other hand, instructors should consider the instructional benefit of distributing the headings of their lectures to the class. Studies have shown that distributing or displaying the outline of the lecture before or at the beginning of the class encourages note taking, and making the outline available after the class has the potential to increase learning by helping students to organize their notes, to recall the content of the lectures, and to fill in gaps.[9]

Adopting a textbook as a complement to lectures raises the question whether the lecturer should consider adhering closely to the program presented in the textbook even when it entails simplifications that the instructor himself would not choose as his own. Freshmen tend to be literalists and may become confused when the instructor is cavalier about differing with the textbook or gives the impression that the history of music is arbitrary. To be sure, if the instructor wishes to educate the students about the existence of opposing viewpoints and the criteria for evaluating them, that in itself may be an integral part of the course and should be clearly presented as such. But if differences between the textbook and the instructor's narrative are allowed to pass without comment, the instructor not only foregoes a valuable teaching opportunity, but also risks sowing seeds of cynicism.

Lecture Content

One thing that may not be obvious to instructors in music history is the benefit of incorporating technical and theoretical matter into their lectures. They may be influenced by anecdotal notions circulating in conservatories and schools of music that performance majors have an aversion to music theory. This is a false rumor. When music history professors refer to technical matter, they open up a channel of communication that unites all musicians in a community of fellow-professionals. Especially in schools and departments of music, technical matter is often the best entrée to the current thinking of music students. Consider the following examples.

---

[9]   Svinicki and McKeachie, *Teaching Tips*, 70.

- The instructor explains the church modes as different arrangements of whole- and half-steps (illustrated with an image of a piano keyboard), which cause each mode to have a different character or "feel." She illustrates the differences with examples from the British folksong tradition and recorded examples of various Indian ragas.
- The instructor explains how the plagal modes differ from the authentic by comparing "O Come, All Ye Faithful" (plagal) with "Joy to the World" (authentic), or "Happy Birthday to You" (plagal) with "Take Me Out to the Ballgame" (authentic). He explains that the keynote (tonic, or final) occurs at the bottom of the range in authentic songs and in the middle of the range in plagal songs.
- The instructor explains metric modulation in music of the *Ars subtilior* by comparing it to modern cases of hemiola, using Bernstein's "I Like to Be in America" and the Hornpipe from Handel's *Water Music*. In the process she will have taught a concept, hemiola, that will have a more practical usefulness for most music students even if they forget the obscurities of the *Ars subtilior*.
- The instructor uses first movements of concertos by Torelli and Vivaldi to teach the ritornello principle. He has the students raise their hands when they hear the ritornello end and the episodes begin, reinforcing this architectural point by creating a visual diagram on the writing board as the music progresses.
- The instructor has the students count the passing tones, neighbor tones, and unprepared dissonances in Machaut and compare their frequency to those in Dunstable and Dufay. This will build a bridge to the students' studies of counterpoint while illustrating the most vivid difference between the music of the Ars Nova and the vastly more consonant sound of Renaissance music, which even contemporaries remarked upon.
- The instructor illustrates the principle defined by Rameau's epoch-making claim that the most normative chord progression in tonal music is root motion by falling fifth—most typically vi-ii-V-I—with examples from jazz and pop favorites, such as "Strumming my pain with his fingers, singing my life with his words" in Roberta Flack's hit song "Killing Me Softly with His Song."

Besides containing the narrative of one's lecture, the script also functions as a program, with notes to the lecturer indicating questions to be asked, musical examples to be performed or sounded electronically, and various ad hoc classroom activities. These interruptions of the verbal lecture stream, strategically spaced, are crucial for retaining the class's attention.[10] On the matter of querying the class,

---

[10]   McKeachie and others, lacking the resources of the music history classroom, have recommended the use of the one-minute paper as a device for interrupting the lecture after the class's attention span has been exhausted (no more than twenty minutes into the hour).

it is a familiar practice to throw out anonymous questions, using such phrases as, "Can anyone explain ..." or "Does anyone remember ...." The disadvantage of this practice is that the same students always volunteer while other students never do. Another disadvantage is that the query may be answered with several seconds of silence after which the instructor answers her own question. Students get used to this outcome and simply wait for it. As mentioned earlier in the chapter, it is more effective to call on particular students by name and to take care over the course of several lectures to distribute these cold calls evenly to everyone in the class. In most cases that will guarantee a useful response.

Having heard the answer, the instructor should repeat it for the benefit of the rest of the class. Students answering questions in large classes rarely speak loudly or clearly enough for the entire class to hear and understand the answer, and merely permitting the student's response to become part of a colloquy between the student and the teacher risks shutting out the rest of the class and wasting a valuable teaching opportunity. The same principle holds for questions from the floor. In large classes they will rarely be heard or understood by the rest of the class. If the teaching opportunity is not to be wasted, it is vitally important that the instructor repeat the question in a loud and clear voice so that the Q and A are incorporated into the lecture experience and not allowed to cause everyone else's attention to wander and their interest to flag.

Questions from the floor should be encouraged, but instructors should not allow themselves to be led down a garden path by students with personal agendas. To be sure, such questions are often intelligent and deserving of serious response. But if they are tangential to the subject of the course or require long explanations, instructors should thank the questioner and promise an answer outside of class. Experienced instructors often find that some of their best teaching is in response to questions that raise issues of general or perennial importance that simply happen to be peripheral to the scope of the particular course. Often the instructor would love to answer the question at length but cannot afford the class time. Using a digital teaching utility such as Blackboard to distribute long discursive answers, with links to images and sound files, will satisfy the student who posed the question while giving the whole class the opportunity to benefit from the answer if they choose to do so.

On the matter of naive or thoughtless questions from the floor, the best response is to answer them plainly, without irony, and without betraying impatience. Any hint of sarcasm or annoyance is destructive of the class's good will, and it wastes the instructor's psychic energy on something that ought to be nothing but a momentary distraction. A related issue is what to do when students nod off. The most patient lecturer may feel foolish speaking to a sleeping head even when the rest of the class is alert and participating. The best solution is to gently invite the student to step outside for a drink of water. As in the case of thoughtless questions,

---

The idea is not without merit. See Svinicki and McKeachie, *Teaching Tips*, 63, 70; and Bland, Saunders, and Kreps Frish, "In Defense of the Lecture," 11.

no good is accomplished by embarrassing the poor soul, and few are the professors who have not been in the same position.

Musical Examples

Musical examples play a crucial role in music history lectures. In addition to providing illustrative examples, they relieve the strain of concentration on a stream of purely verbal data and thus provide an antidote to the well-known twenty-minute limit of most adults' attention span.[11] But long musical examples present problems. They consume precious class time, and they risk losing the class's attention while they are sounding. Short examples, on the other hand, are an effective means of illustrating technical points and of helping the students to be attentive to isolated details in the music. Especially useful in this regard is the pause control on the playback equipment, since it permits the instructor to insert comments or questions about each segment of music immediately after it has sounded. Moreover, if the instructor asks a question, say, about the meter, the tempo, or the motivic identity of the example, and no one in the class is able to answer it, a short excerpt can simply be replayed without undue sacrifice of class time. Even when the purpose of the musical example is simply to illustrate a composer's general style, pausing the music after just a few seconds and asking the class some descriptive question is an effective way of reminding the class of the mental effort necessary for attentive listening.

From time to time members of the class may be enlisted to perform musical examples at the keyboard or in some other medium. These may be as simple as playing scales and chords, requiring from piano majors no rehearsal at all. The purpose is simply to impress upon the students a sense of ownership of the class and to persuade them that they share responsibility for its success.

Enactments, Realizations, and Other Performative Activities

Enactments, realizations, and other performative activities that are introduced into the lecture program on an ad hoc basis promote what educational psychologists understand as multiple encoding, causing the brain to encode the lesson in several different ways (e.g., as verbal strings, as musical experiences, as performative routines) whose recall is not dependent on just one kind of cue. Multiple cues are a better guarantee of retention, recall, and later usefulness.[12] An example of

---

[11]   One study places it between ten and eighteen minutes. See J. Hartley and I. K. Davies, "Note-Taking: A Critical Review," *Programmed Learning and Educational Technology* 15, no. 3 (1978): 207-24, cited in Bland, Saunders, and Kreps Frisch, "In Defense of the Lecture," 11.

[12]   deWinstanley and Bjork, "Successful Lecturing," 20-23.

such activity is to have the class create a piece of parallel organum by singing a line of music simultaneously at two pitch levels separated by the interval of a fourth, instead of merely telling them what parallel organum is or playing a recorded performance of it. Having heard the sound of parallel organum in their own voices, the students will also have learned the rule that tenth-century singers followed when they created this musical form. A similar educational benefit can be achieved by having the class realize a simple three-voice fauxbourdon from two written parts by having part of the class sing the upper of the two written voices at the downward transposition of a fourth, thus re-creating the process observed in the fifteenth century and causing the classroom to resonate with the unmistakable sound of parallel six-three chords. Other ad hoc classroom activities that illustrate the lecture may include giving four students index cards with the script of the earliest liturgical drama (translated into English) and having them enact it, or projecting the refrain of a monophonic virelai and having the class join the soloist (provided by a recording) at the appropriate places (A) in the form AbbaAbbaA. This exercise makes immediate practical sense of what is otherwise a meaningless series of ciphers.

One of the most powerful modes of cognitive encoding is what occurs when students actually create the knowledge to be encoded. For example, instructors may wish to show that opera seria consists of a series of arias whose steady states over the course of an act present a maximally varied program of affective types. Instead of merely asserting this fact and presenting illustrations from recordings, it is more effective to have the class decide for each excerpt (it requires only a few seconds of sounding music) what is the tempo, meter, mode, voice type, and affective character of each. To facilitate the exercise the instructor can give the class the expected range of choices for each category. In this way the instructor substitutes a creative exercise for mere passive reception and thus improves the likelihood of comprehension and retention. Exercises like this one can be performed in large lecture classes as easily as in more intimate instructional settings.

Conclusions

The purpose of this chapter has been to offer a balanced view of lecturing, taking both its difficulties and its positive potential into account. To be sure, the ranks of the professoriate are filled with those who have excelled in this medium of instruction by dint of personal brilliance and sheer instinctive aptitude. But others, cognizant of the medium's reputation for difficulty, approach the task of lecturing with misgivings about its potential for success. In my opinion any such pessimism is premature, if not entirely groundless. Lecturing is no more difficult than any other mode of instruction. One need only adapt one's preparation and execution to the distinctive nature of the medium. In the course of the chapter I have suggested several approaches that may assist the lecturer in making those adaptations. They include ways to ameliorate the anonymity of the lecture classroom; ways to help the lecturer disclose his enthusiasm for the subject; ways to communicate the discursive content of the lecture more effectively; ways to make effective use of acoustic and visual media; and ways to enlist the active participation of the class even in large, seemingly anonymous lecture halls. And it goes without saying that the first condition of effective lecturing in music history is a thorough command of the subject. No amount of pedagogical technique will compensate for its lack. With that qualification in mind, no one should hesitate to take up the challenge of lecturing in the confident expectation of a successful outcome.

Chapter 4
Listening in the Classroom

Melanie Lowe

Listening in the classroom, a central activity in any music course, might seem easy. The instructor pushes play, the students remain quiet, and class time is legitimately filled with the course's primary object of investigation—music. But how do we know that our students are engaging *intellectually* with the music we choose to play and not just sitting there listening passively? How can we ensure, or at least increase the chances, that students are *actively learning* from an in-class listening experience? This chapter will outline several pedagogical techniques for encouraging active listening in the classroom, both with and without the use of musical scores. By way of demonstration, I discuss one specific listening exercise for each technique. While the exercises presented here are tailored for the particular musical example, the pedagogical strategies themselves are easily transferrable to other musical repertory. To address writing about listening, I conclude with a brief consideration of broader critical and philosophical questions about listening itself.

Active Listening

We may all agree that "active listening" is the desired listening modality in the music history classroom. But what constitutes active listening? How do we encourage, guide, and achieve it? How might we evaluate student progress during in-class listening activities? How can we respect students' individual listening experiences while at the same time expecting them to hear the specific features we deem essential for musical understanding, or at least required for successful mastery of the content of a given course? These are crucial questions to consider, to be sure, and we will address them in turn in this chapter. But the first and most urgent question an instructor can ask when preparing for in-class listening is: What is the most significant learning goal of this particular listening experience?

The taxonomy of significant learning L. Dee Fink outlines in *Creating Significant Learning Experiences* is especially useful here, as are the questions he provides to help instructors address the six kinds of learning in his taxonomy.[1] Table 4.1 lists the categories of Fink's taxonomy and presents some of the many

---

[1]   L. Dee Fink, *Creating Significant Learning Experiences: An Integrated Approach to Designing College Courses* (San Francisco: Jossey-Bass, 2003), 27-59, 75.

questions he offers to help instructors formulate significant learning goals when designing a course.

Table 4.1   Questions for formulating significant learning goals

Foundational knowledge	What key information (facts, terms, concepts, relationships, etc.) is it important for students to *understand and remember* in the future?
Application	What kinds of *thinking* are important for students to learn here? (e.g., *critical thinking, creative thinking*)?
Integration	What *connections* (similarities and interactions) should students recognize and make between the information, ideas, and perspectives in this course and those in other courses or areas?
Human dimension	What can or should students learn about *themselves*? What can or should students learn about understanding and interacting with *others*?
Caring	What changes would you like to see in what students *care* about—feelings, interests, values, etc.?
Learning how to learn	What would you like for students to learn about *how to engage in inquiry and construct knowledge* with this subject matter?

Note: adapted from Fink, *Significant Learning Experiences*, 75.

The ability to articulate the significant learning goals for a course as a whole will better enable instructors to design meaningful in-class listening activities that serve to advance student progress toward one or more of the course's learning goals.

Indeed, each type of learning in Fink's taxonomy readily suggests a variety of listening strategies. Structural listening, for example, the listening strategy with which instructors are likely most familiar, can be used to build *foundational knowledge*, to apply critical thinking (*application*), and to make connections among the information and ideas presented within a course (*integration*). Likewise, interpretive listening, which builds on a student's foundational work in structural listening, encourages creative thinking (*application*), promotes connections with other courses or subject areas (*integration*), invites relationships of course material with students' everyday lives (*integration*), and ultimately engages the deeply personal, human dimensions of self-reflection and social interaction (*human dimension*). This chapter will illuminate how this taxonomy of significant learning can effectively and efficiently inform instructors in designing in-class listening experiences.

What follows are discussions of five specific learning activities that will demonstrate such tangible connections between in-class listening and significant learning goals. But first, we must consider some basic teaching techniques and sheer practicalities that are essential to promote active listening in the music history classroom.

Teaching Practicalities for Promoting Active Listening

1. Compile all musical excerpts together on *one* audio source.
2. Despite how easy it may seem to switch out a compact disc or to navigate an mp3 player, this unnecessary motion not only wastes precious class time but also creates a delay, however brief, between the set-up of a listening example and the students' engagement with it. With the omnipresence of mobile devices, not to mention how readily distractible college students can be, those few seconds that an instructor fusses with technology provide the opportunity for a quick retrieval of a text or email message, a check of the time, or even simply a glance out the window. The small investment of the instructor's time in assembling a playlist on an mp3 player, burning a compact disc, or setting tabs for streaming audio pays back immediate rewards in terms of the increased student engagement that results from an efficient and streamlined presentation.
3. Ready audio source *before* class starts and do a sound check.
4. Hooking up an mp3 player, inserting the flash drive, or placing the compact disc in the drawer *before* class begins eliminates unnecessary motion and wasted time during class. An audio check safeguards against technological mishaps during class.
5. Set clearly defined tasks for students to do *during* the listening example and communicate them clearly *before* playing the music.
6. Requiring students to perform set tasks *while listening* is the most effective means to encourage an active listening experience. The listening examples that follow will demonstrate a variety of such tasks, but whatever the listening tasks, they need to be doable in the "real time" of one or two hearings of a piece or excerpt. They also need to be articulated clearly and succinctly *before* the instructor pushes play. Further, it is crucial that the tasks or questions be presented *visually* and not merely spoken so that students remember the work they are expected to do while the music is playing. This is easily accomplished by projecting a slide, writing prompts or questions on a white board, or simply using a handout. One advantage to a handout is that it also provides ready space for students to jot down observations and notes while listening. Such ancillary materials need not be pedagogical crutches; if designed creatively and used effectively, they are proactive aids in guiding the process of student learning.
7. Replay the musical example after discussion, if time allows.

8. After discussion of the tasks performed or the questions answered while
    listening, it is helpful for students to hear the musical excerpt again.
    Replaying the musical example provides the opportunity for students who
    were able to complete the tasks to reinforce new learning. For students
    who were unable to complete some or all of the tasks, a second shot at
    the listening experience—this time from the vantage point of knowing
    precisely what the instructor expects them to hear—can help students not
    feel disengaged from the class or disenfranchised by the challenging nature
    of the material.

Structural Listening

A quick survey of the leading textbooks designed for either music majors or
non-music majors reveals that listening for musical structure remains a primary
pedagogical strategy for the acquisition and application of *foundational knowledge*
about Western classical music. If the foundational knowledge in an introductory
music history course includes a basic understanding of such elements and concepts
as melody, theme, repetition, contrast, variation, and so on, then a student's ability
to hear the interaction of these elements and concepts in the articulation of musical
form engages in the active process of *application learning*.

Listening for Formal Structure Without a Score

Tchaikovsky's beloved and widely known *Nutcracker Suite* provides wonderfully
clear and accessible examples of simple formal structures that are perfectly suited
to introduce students to one type of structural listening—listening for the basic
building blocks of musical form. Teaching the ternary form of the opening *March*,
for example, may seem quite straightforward, and to be sure, most students are
able to hear its formal structure quite easily when an instructor writes "A B A"
on the board and points to the letters at the appropriate time as the music plays in
class. But this type of listening is ultimately a passive experience for students: they
simply sit, listen, and (we hope) receive information. For students to listen actively
for formal structure, the instructor needs to be more creative—and patient—in
setting up the listening experience.

By breaking down Tchaikovsky's *March* into smaller sections and setting
specific tasks to be performed while listening to each section (what Fink would call
a *"doing" experience*[2]), students themselves take the lead role in their own learning.
For students who do not know the piece already, and for non-majors especially, the
listening blocks need to be short and the listening tasks small and relatively simple.
One activity that helps students hear the conversation between the brass and the
strings, a defining feature of the A section, is for them to write the names of the

---

[2]   Fink, *Creating Significant Learning Experiences*, 107.

"characters" before each line of the "script" of the opening section as the music plays. This task assumes that students can identify the instruments of the orchestra, and therefore builds on prior learning as it adds to foundational knowledge.

After two or three hearings of the opening thirty seconds, most students have generated a "script" that allows them to identify the beginning of the A section when they hear it:

Brass:

Strings:

Brass:

Strings:

In addition to hearing the alternation of instrument families, they are now also able to see *visually* that the pattern of phrases depends on such musical values as contrast and repetition to delineate its structural components. More importantly, this new knowledge is acquired through a structural map that *students themselves have created*.

Generating a similar "script" for the B section should now be an easier task, so students may also sketch the characters' "lines" as they are articulated. "Lines" in this listening task are exactly that—line drawings that capture the contours of the melody as the piece plays. This task builds on the prior learning of pitch and melody as it adds melodic contour to foundational knowledge. On the first hearing of the B section, students generate the order of characters in the "script," and on the second (and third, if necessary) they sketch the shape of the individual lines. After two or three hearings of this small section, most students will have drawn something that looks like this:

Woodwinds:

Strings:

Woodwinds:

Strings:

Figure 4.1 Student's drawing

From this drawing, students can now see *visually* that 1) the alternation of instruments is different in the B section, and 2) this section is defined melodically by lines that descend.

In the final structural listening task for *March*, students work with the "scripts" they have sketched so far to observe and diagram the piece as a whole. Students readily hear that a return to the "conversation" between brass and strings follows the section in which the woodwinds and strings alternate. Many also hear that there is something different about the instrumental texture here as well: another "character" (strings) is "talking" underneath the brass in the conversation. This change provides the opportunity to add variation as an essential element in the articulation musical structure, as well as a chance to reinforce previously learned concepts of melody and accompaniment.

At this point, the instructor need only explain the practice of representing large formal sections by letters (i.e., A, B, C, A', etc.) and most students, upon one more hearing of the dance, are able to generate the conventional A B A' diagram for ternary form *on their own*.

To be sure, this listening exercise takes considerably more class time than the two minutes and thirty seconds required simply to play Tchaikovsky's *March* while pointing to a diagram of ternary form on a white board. But as recent research and literature on university teaching has demonstrated, students learn more effectively and retain knowledge longer when the learning process is active. Moreover, students will be more able to perform this type of structural listening by themselves, allowing them to apply this newly acquired foundational knowledge to other listening experiences (*application*). They may even begin to make connections between formal structures found in other styles and genres of music (*integration*).

Listening for Formal Structure With and Without a Score

Notoriously difficult to teach, the highly intellectual idea of isorhythm in fourteenth-century music presents significant challenges for any instructor promoting active listening in the classroom, not least of which is the possibility that listeners of the time themselves may not have even heard isorhythmic structures. But whether or not isorhythmic patterns were audible (or intended to be audible) in the fourteenth century, music majors today *can* hear them (with help), and the process of learning to hear them actively both with and without the use of a score helps to solidify the concept in their minds. Moreover, when the listening exercises are designed carefully and executed well in the classroom, this tremendous feat can often be accomplished in one class meeting.

Rather than embarking on a lengthy and abstract explanation of repeating and interlocking patterns of rhythm and pitch (which in my experience has produced only confused, frustrated, and sleepy students), setting up the introduction to isorhythm with an active and fun but *simple* listening exercise piques students' curiosity. Equally important, a listening exercise that provides the opportunity for students to express their initial impressions of this music, whether wonder, shock, amusement, bewilderment, disorientation, or even dislike, serves to diffuse anxiety. When students are relaxed, their tendency to resist something that sounds so seemingly foreign (if not downright strange) to their ears is dramatically reduced.

I have found, for example, that asking music majors to follow the score while listening to Sequentia's blisteringly fast performance of Philippe de Vitry's isorhythmic motet *Garrit Gallus/In nova fert/Neuma* produces a hilarious five-minute discussion that relieves the stress of approaching something new and exceptionally challenging. Immediately after listening to this piece with the score, students jot down three adjectives to describe their score reading efforts, three to describe their initial reaction to the music, and three more to describe the music itself. Because most students struggle to follow this score during the first hearing, an honest and good-natured sharing of their surprise, incomprehension, and perhaps even panic proves therapeutic. Moreover, students' own individual listening experiences are immediately valued and validated by the instructor, generating an air of trust in the classroom—a crucial ingredient when tackling difficult material collectively.

With tensions lowered, camaraderie established, and trust gained, the serious business of learning isorhythm proceeds more smoothly. To internalize the rhythmic pattern of the *talea*, students need to actively produce the rhythm themselves, something easily accomplished by the instructor leading a simple clapping exercise. Once the pattern is stuck in their heads, students are generally quite successful at performing the second listening task—counting the repetitions of this pattern in the tenor voice while listening to the recording *without looking at the score*. In addition to explaining this listening task clearly *before* the music plays again, it is also helpful to remind students in this kind of exercise that the first repetition begins with the first beat, so once the music starts they should begin counting immediately. The beauty of this kind of active listening exercise is that students come to understand the concept of *talea* through the use of their own ears. In the end, the instructor then need only provide the name for the concept.

Because the *color* is lengthy in this particular motet, the next listening task is best performed with the score in hand. As students listen again to *Garrit Gallus*, they transcribe to staff paper the pitches (just note heads) of the tenor. The only special instructions are:

1. Write note heads equidistant from one another
2. Put the note heads close enough to fit thirty-six pitches on the first line
3. Move to the second line at measure seventy-six (as transcribed in *Polyphonic Music of the Fourteenth Century*, Volume XX)

While performing this exercise, students start to notice the repetition of the *color* early into the second line of their transcriptions. The beauty here, once again, is that the instructor need only provide the name "*color*" for such a sequence of pitches, for students have already grasped the concept of *color* repetition through their own listening and transcribing work.

In the final listening task, students turn their attention back to the rhythmic pattern. Following their own transcriptions of the pitches while listening attentively to the motet one final time, they are simply to draw a vertical line at the point that the rhythmic pattern repeats. The end result is a sketch of the isorhythmic structure of the tenor voice of *Garrit gallus* (two repetitions of the *color*, six repetitions of the *talea*) that *they themselves have produced.*

One way to bring this kind of class to a satisfying close is to return to the opening discussion of students' initial impressions of the piece. Most students are genuinely surprised that they now hear such a clear organizational structure in a piece of music that initially seemed entirely chaotic to their ears.

Listening for Structure and Interpretation in Texted Music

While hearing structure in a piece of music is an essential step for students in music-historical understanding, acquiring the ability to interpret musical structures during a listening experience is arguably the more important learning goal. In demonstrating the potential for musical structures to communicate through their architectural designs, texted music can provide an especially accessible entry point.

In setting up any in-class listening to music with a text, it is absolutely essential that the instructor provide both the text and a translation. If the words are English, students still need to see the text as the music plays, for it can be difficult to hear the individual words in sung English (even with impeccable diction!). Also, if the piece is from a larger work, especially a dramatic work like an opera or an oratorio, it is important for students to know the story—interpretive work so often depends on the narrative context.

As with any in-class listening, to facilitate active listening, *all* tasks students are to perform need to be articulated clearly and to remain visible throughout the listening exercise. And when the interpretive goals of the exercise depend on analytical work that is also to be performed while listening, *presenting the tasks in the specific order to be accomplished* during repeated listenings guides students through the multiple steps required in the interpretation of musical structure.

Before embarking on an interpretive listening of "Possente sprito," for example, the aria in which the title character of Monteverdi's *Orfeo* undergoes significant character development,[3] students need to know:

---

[3]   Marjorie Roth also discusses how a relatively simple structural analysis of "Possente spirto" can lead students to a rich interpretation of Orfeo's character development. Indeed, this piece lends itself exceptionally well to this kind of self-contained, in-class interpretive exercise. See Marjorie Roth, "The 'Why' of Music: Variations on a Cosmic Theme," in *Teaching Music History*, ed. Mary Natvig (Aldershot and Burlington, VT: Ashgate, 2002), 86-89.

1. The story of the opera
2. The significance of music within that story
3. The point in the story at which Orpheus sings this piece

While the third item on this list probably needs to be communicated directly by the instructor, with just a few leading questions the first two items can likely surface on their own in a brief class discussion of the Orpheus myth. In addition to promoting a more active learning experience, acquisition of this information through students' own thought processes and sharing of ideas provides good mental preparation for the active listening tasks that follow.

The structure of "Possente spirto" is quite simple: a strophic aria with ritornellos played by various obbligato instruments. Most students, music majors and non-majors alike, can diagram the structure of this piece quite easily, especially if the text is given to them on a handout, the strophes are already numbered 1 through 6, and the requirements of the first listening task are clearly articulated— simply to note on the handout:

1. Where the individual iterations of the ritornellos are heard
2. Which instruments are featured in a particular ritornello

After just one hearing, students can see clearly from their own diagrams that the ritornellos feature different instruments, that the "strophe-ritornello" pattern holds until the fourth strophe, and that there are no ritornellos from that point on. Having made this simple observation, students can begin pondering just why the pattern breaks off and what the significance of this structural change might be.

To aid them in the next step on this interpretive journey, the second listening task asks the students to make observations about melodic lines and singing style. A simple listening task like jotting down adjectives to describe Orpheus's style of singing strophe by strophe enables students to observe *on their own* that something changes quite dramatically in the fifth and sixth strophes: the elaborate, highly decorated, and even flamboyant performance style is gone, leaving Orpheus singing a simple and rather plain melodic line. When students add this observation to the diagrams sketched during the first listening task, they notice immediately that the change in singing style happens at the same place that the strophe-ritornello structure breaks off. There is surely meaning in this, and now discussion can proceed to just what that meaning might be.

At this point, the instructor can ask the questions for which all of this structural analysis has been preparing:

1. How does Orpheus change during this aria?
2. How does the music participate in communicating this change?

A closer examination of the text is helpful here, for there are, of course, clues in the poetry—for example, the fourth strophe begins with "Orfeo, son io"

["I am Orpheus"] and the sixth "Sol tu, nobile dio" ["Only you, noble god"]. But ultimately, since the goal of this in-class listening is to interpret *musical structure*, the students will need to hear that Orpheus realizes that he needs assistance at precisely the point that the ritornellos drop out, the obbligato instruments go silent, and Orpheus's singing style becomes strikingly simple. Once the step-by-step analysis is completed, the instructor need only ask a few leading questions for students to arrive at a satisfying interpretation of the structural details they themselves have noticed: just as the music grows humility, so too does the character who is singing it.

The instructor may wish to push the point further, though, for listening experiences such as this one make for compelling demonstrations of music's powerful ability to communicate not just feelings and emotions but *ideas*. In terms of significant learning goals, the analytical and critical thinking performed during this exercise (*foundational knowledge, application, integration*) leads students directly to the *human dimension* of music-historical study: students begin to consider the potential for music to stimulate *intellectual* activity—and not just classical music but *all* of the music experienced during the courses of their everyday lives.

Listening for Style with Score Excerpts

While listening for style in the classroom invites students to apply knowledge of style to a new listening experience, it also requires students to discern similarities, differences, and interactions among the various stylistic attributes of different styles. As with structural listening, then, listening for style engages with several categories of significant learning goals—*foundational knowledge, application,* and *integration*.

When presented with the basic features of the broad style-period categories of Western art music, students can match quite readily what they have been told with what they are hearing. For example, hearing contrapuntal textures, spun-out melodies, terraced dynamics, and basso continuo in a concerto gross leads them easily to "baroque" just about every time. Likewise, hearing such features as the aggressive start, abrupt mood swings, wispy and angular melodies, syncopations, rhythmic drive, and sudden harmonic shifts in Beethoven's String Quartet in E minor, Op. 59, No. 2, students recognize the hallmarks of early romanticism if not the particular composer as well. The importance of such identification ability and the ease in which listening-for-style exercises can be made active notwithstanding, how might stylistic listening in the classroom engage with other significant learning goals? Can the basic pedagogical expectation that students master style move beyond mere identification to invite more sophisticated types of critical thinking, to raise deeper philosophical questions, and to activate broader human dimensions of music historical study?

One in-class listening activity that is exceptionally successful at engaging sophisticated music-historical issues is the deceptively simple "single sheet" composer identification debate. To set up this kind of exercise, the instructor chooses stylistically similar pieces by two different composers, hands out a single-sheet unidentified score excerpt for each piece, and readies a single audio source so that the two excerpts can be played back-to-back several times. The students are told only the names of the two composers; they do not know which composer composed which piece. Their task is not just to try to match the composer with his or her composition, but to construct as convincing a case as possible for *why* they matched the composers and pieces the way they did. The strength of their case depends on how they interpret musically and historically the stylistic features they observe. Once each student has had time to make his or her case individually (either in small groups or collectively, if the class is small enough), the task is to convince classmates who have matched composer and composition the opposite way to reconsider their decision. If the pieces are chosen carefully and the instructor guides the discussion toward the more philosophical issues of style determination and assignment, students leave the classroom that day having engaged in some rather sophisticated musical-historical thinking inspired by an in-class active listening exercise.

To give only one example of this type of exercise (the possibilities here are truly endless), I have used the first movement of Beethoven's String Quartet in B-flat major, Op. 18, No. 6 and the first movement of Mozart's String Quintet in C major, K. 515 not just to demonstrate Beethoven's classical inheritance but ultimately to address the more subtle and problematic philosophical idea of "progress" in the arts. During this particular single-sheet exercise, students are often baffled at first because the two pieces are so similar stylistically, especially in terms of texture, phrasing, and form. But after a listening a few times in alternation to the first minute or so of each piece, each student must commit to one way or the other and set about making a compelling case for his or her choice. In the ensuing debate, most students are ultimately convinced that the quintet must have been composed later than the quartet because of several features they deem more "progressive": the asymmetrical five-measure phrase structure, the grand pause and unprepared drop into the minor mode, the comparatively more expansive harmonic palette, and so on. The argument then follows logically: if these features are a sign of a later composition, the quintet must be by Beethoven.

When the correct identifications are revealed, students are often truly surprised. This strong reaction provides the ideal launch pad for discussion of much deeper and more abstract philosophical issues—for instance, the pitfalls of assumptions of linearity in any historical study, considerations of how aesthetic judgment intersects with personal tastes and biases, and how Western cultures tend to equate "later" and "bigger" with "better." Ultimately, I use this particular listening game involving Mozart's string quintet and Beethoven's string quartet, both of which are musical products of the age of Enlightenment, to lead students to a consideration of how our current-day thinking clings to certain tenets of eighteenth-century thought and how those lines of reasoning can easily lead us astray. But, with appropriate musical examples, this kind of single-sheet identification game adapts readily to promote a deeper philosophical engagement with questions that spring from studying nearly any historical era or musical style period.

In terms of significant learning goals, such in-class active listening exercises apply foundational knowledge, integrate critical thinking into broader academic contexts, and ultimately involve the human dimensions of aesthetic value judgment, musical assumptions, personal prejudices, and intellectual self-reflection. In other words, we have actively engaged with at least five of the six categories of Fink's taxonomy of significant learning.

Historical Listening

One of the greatest challenges in any music-historical work is to remain mindful of our twenty-first-century ears while listening critically to music from an earlier time. It is impossible, of course, for us to shed a lifetime of musical experiences and conditioning so that we might hear Machaut's music as his fourteenth-century courtly audience would have heard it. And perhaps this is not even a desirable goal, its unattainability notwithstanding. But it is nevertheless important for students to come to understand that what *we* value aesthetically quite often does not align with the musical and aesthetic values of a piece's original historical context.

One in-class listening activity that can help students develop an awareness of our tendency to listen anachronistically is to use a piece that students likely do not know and that does not adhere to their musical expectations. Jupiter's descent and first words in Rameau's *Castor et Pollux*, for example, the *deus ex machina* near the end of the opera (Act V, Scene 5), would seem, according to our contemporary aesthetic expectations (conditioned as they are so overwhelmingly by romanticism), to require grand, majestic, and even imposing music to express the awesome power of the god of sky and thunder, ruler of all other gods. Students anticipating anything even remotely awesome or sublime are understandably quite surprised, disappointed even, when Jupiter finally opens his mouth to resolve at once the story's dramatic impasse. Jupiter announces that the Fates are satisfied, releases Castor and Pollux from their vow, and makes the brothers immortal—all in a mere thirty-six seconds of simple recitative.

In setting up any kind of listening exercise that depends for its pedagogical success on a thwarting of expectations, it is imperative that students have considered just what their expectations are before any listening begins. One way to make this personal reflection more active (as well as to ensure that they actually *do* think for a few moments about what they expect to hear) is for the instructor to ask students:

1. To write down in a sentence or two what Jupiter's music would sound like if they were composing this opera
2. To compare their music with the person sitting in the next seat

3. To share briefly with the whole class what was similar and different about their and their classmate's respective "Jupiter music"

During any discussion in which the students themselves generate much of the content, the instructor can jot down on the board a few of the overarching themes. It has been my experience that in this case a striking consensus among students emerges that Jupiter's music should be powerful and confident, if not somewhat overblown.

With their musical expectations of Jupiter's music now articulated and tangible, students can notice more readily the features that do not line up with what they had imagined Jupiter would sound like—in other words, the stylistic attributes now listed on the board. To encourage active listening here, it is important (as always with texted music) for the students to have the text and translation in front of them, and (again, as always) for the instructor to set a specific task to be performed while students listen to the scene. Asking students to list three aspects of the music that correspond to or differ from their expectations, for instance, is one easy and straightforward way to encourage students to consider not just how but *why* Jupiter's simple recitative surprised them.

It is the active engagement with this second question—*why* Jupiter does not "sing"—that leads students to the consideration of historical listening. Conditioned as we are by *bel canto* singing, *Heldentenors*, and even the belting voices of American musical theater, it is next to impossible to hear Jupiter's music as anything but underwhelming. And yet, to listen historically requires us, at the very least, to know and understand the aesthetic context of a given work. In this case, to listen historically to *Castor et Pollux* demands that we consider this opera within the aesthetics of French rationalism. Once in possession of pertinent historical and philosophical foundational knowledge, and then directed by an instructor's leading questions, students can conclude *through their own line of reason* that, were Jupiter to "sing" in this aesthetic and philosophical context, his rationality would be compromised. By extension, so would that of the ruling monarch (in this case, Louis XV), to whose wisdom and intervention such stage moments typically alluded.

To be sure, it may seem a more efficient use of class time for an instructor to simply explain why Rameau sets Jupiter's lines in simple recitative and then to play the example. And students will likely understand this information; they may even remember it, at least for a short while. But such a presentation presents students with a passive learning experience. To reiterate, as current research on college teaching is repeatedly revealing, *active learning*—students "doing things and actively thinking about the things they are doing"[4]—is the more effective teaching strategy for today's students. Indeed, this particular listening exercise involves

---

[4]　Charles C. Bonwell and James A. Eisen, *Active Learning: Creating Excitement in the Classroom*, ASHE-ERIC Higher Education Report 1 (Washington, D.C.: George Washington University, 1991), 2.

all three components (as identified by Fink) that form a holistic conception of active learning (Table 4.2).[5] Finally, this listening activity also engages with all six categories of significant learning goals (Table 4.3).

Table 4.2   Components of active learning: historical listening of Rameau's *Castor et Pollux*

Getting information and ideas
- Reading or hearing about French rationalist aesthetics
- Reading or hearing about the use of opera (and other entertainment) to flatter a ruling monarch

"Doing" experiences
- Listing musical features that do and do not line up with those expectations

Reflection
- Noting personal expectations for Jupiter's music
- Considering where such expectations come from

Table 4.3   Significant learning goals: historical listening of Rameau's *Castor et Pollux*

Foundational Knowledge
- French rationalist philosophy
- French political history
- French musical history
- Text-setting styles in French opera
- Mythology

Application
- Recognition of simple recitative

Integration
- Relating a fictional character to a specific historical figure
- Interpreting musical portrayal as political flattery

Human dimension
- Recognition of the different aesthetic values of other cultures and times

Caring
- More openness to different aesthetic values
- Increased curiosity about earlier music

Learning how to learn
- Greater understanding of how to integrate historical knowledge into musical experience
- Awareness of how this integration furthers musical understanding
- Facilitation of richer opportunities for musical understanding

---

[5]   Fink, *Creating Significant Learning Experiences*, 102-10.

Thinking about Listening

There are, of course, many types of writing projects that engage students in active listening—for example, listening journals in an intimate and casual style, analytical essays in a formal, academic style, and concert reviews in a journalistic style, to mention only three. But I will leave the discussion of writing issues to the next chapter, which is wholly devoted to writing about music. Rather, by way of conclusion, what follows here are parting thoughts on how thinking about musical listening invites students to consider broader critical and philosophical questions.

It goes without saying that a classroom is not a concert hall. But with the convenience and undeniable pedagogical advantages of using recorded music in our teaching, whether through playback in class or streaming audio listening assignments, what might we be giving up in exchange? As Joseph Kerman and Gary Tomlinson put it in *Listen*, "music is communication, and human presence is leached out of a recorded performance."[6] Requiring students to attend concerts of live music, and then to actively reflect on their listening experience by writing about it, is one common and highly effective way to combat this particular challenge in teaching music history. But learning about listening from various historical perspectives (either through course readings or in-class activities) can be quite effective as well. Moreover, such learning nicely complements concert activities, whether required for the course or not, for it puts the students' personal listening experiences in direct dialogue with historical and "other" listening modalities.

For example, students are often quite shocked to learn that public concert audiences in the eighteenth century did not subscribe to the concert etiquette we hold as absolutely essential behavior today. Many student questions arise from this knowledge, of course, but I have found one in particular to provide an exceptionally effective springboard to deeper philosophical questions about musical listening: "If the audience was talking, eating, or even playing games, then how could people hear all of these musical details that *you* are expecting *us* to hear?" The short answer, of course, is that they didn't—at least not the vast majority of concert attendees. But this historical truth satisfies neither student nor instructor, not least because, despite this historical reality, we still expect our students to learn to hear certain musical details whether listeners in the past heard them or not.

If handled carefully and thoughtfully, such a student challenge ultimately provides instructors with invaluable opportunities to consider more contextual matters, deep issues, and weighty questions:

- How people listened differently at different times in the history of Western music
- What musical features people heard and valued in a musical experience at different times in the history of Western music

---

[6] Joseph Kerman and Gary Tomlinson, *Listen*, 6th ed. (New York: Bedford/St. Martin's Press, 2008), xvi.

- Notions of "art" versus "entertainment" in Western music history
- How notions of "art" and "entertainment" are intertwined with listening modalities, audience behavior, and social status
- The impact of recording and playback technologies on the experience of musical listening
- How listening can be a political or ethical act

As with the specific in-class listening activities outlined in this chapter, these broader questions and issues about listening itself can engage with all of the significant learning goals categorized by Fink—from *foundational knowledge* to *learning how to learn*. But it has been my experience that they speak most directly to the *human dimension*. By listening actively, learning about listening from various historical, critical, philosophical, and ethical perspectives, and reflecting on personal listening experiences, students accomplish nothing short of enriching their understandings of themselves, the world around them, and their place within it.

Chapter 5
Assignments and Homework

Eleonora M. Beck

Creating Assignments

While musicologists have spent hours debating the value of teaching one composition over another, or the benefits of a seminar focused on Haydn's string quartets rather than Mahler's symphonies, the fact remains that more so than repertory, or even spirited lectures, imaginative and challenging assignments are the backbone of a successful music history class.[1] Creative music assignments that encourage freedom of thought have the potential to delight a student like no other college endeavor. Students can learn about music history in a nurturing group setting or by engaging directly with the music. Moreover, what an individual thinks about a work of music, whether one is Leonard Bernstein or Lady Gaga, is of the same value—these are honest reactions to an ephemeral work of art, a work of sublime complexity, and just one word about a piece can influence its entire meaning (take "Moonlight" or "Revolutionary," for instance). Once students understand that music's mysterious properties liberate its study to multifaceted, informed interpretations, a magical world is revealed to them, and it is the object of the teacher to allow students their opinions and teach them to have confidence in their ways of thinking and feeling. In this environment, a student will strive to learn about music and find new ways to investigate their ever-changing musical landscapes.

This chapter presents a cornucopia of exercises that develop critical thinking, writing skills, and musical understanding. The exercises are grouped under five headings: worksheets, short writing assignments, experiential learning, reflective writing, and service learning—connecting students to a broader audience outside the music department and into the off-campus community. Some tasks encourage students to implement new digital technologies, while others ask students to use traditional methodologies to investigate hard copy sources. Some exercises are tailored for individual students, while others are intended for groups of students.

These assignments have been implemented over the course of more than twenty years of teaching Music Appreciation and History of Western Music to majors and non-majors. The exercises also work for specific kinds of courses, such as Writing

---

[1]   Colleen Conway and Thomas Hodgman write briefly about music history assignments in *Teaching Music in Higher Education* (New York and Oxford: Oxford University Press, 2008), 97-98.

about Music, Opera Survey, and various seminars on particular subjects, including Philosophy of Music, Music and Politics, and Medieval Music and Art.

Designing effective music assignments requires teachers to take chances. It is riskier to give students work that requires them to do the bulk of the thinking, rather than asking them to regurgitate statements made in your lecture or a textbook. One should write assignments that ask students to digest dates, styles, biographies, and formal analyses by requiring them to learn *how* to find dates, styles, biographies, and formal analyses of the works in question. In addition, to ensure maximum learning, one should write prompts that require students to bring together historical facts and hands-on experience. For example, by directing students to compose a piece of music that imitates one they are studying, they give meaning to the style through their own voices and gain a deeper and more meaningful understanding of it. Asking students to perform in class as much as possible, so that they actually create and feel what they are learning, is more effective than passively listening. Group assignments that foster teamwork and discipline are also useful tools.

It is best to be brief and clear in your prompts and requirements. Giving questions with several answers allows students to reap multiple benefits from each assignment. One should learn to measure the amount of time it takes students to complete a task, so as not to overburden them and you with unnecessary work. In addition, provide different types of assignments during the course of a semester: research papers, response papers, and blogs. Consider spreading the assignments evenly over the course of the semester, so the course has an even workflow for you to evaluate. Balance assignments around quizzes, mid-term and final, so you are steadily receiving responses from students. Return graded assignments to students promptly—in no longer than a week's time. Most of all, communicate your knowledge of repertory with the joy that the music gives you. The crossroad between facts and delight is the source from which exciting and creative music assignments spring forth, as if from a splendid Italian fountain. Before asking students to soar to the firmament of musical metaphor, put in place a mechanism that requires students to read the textbook and supplementary texts, and engage in active listening. Worksheets work!

Worksheets

After your magical lecture about Beethoven's dedication and rededication of the *Eroica* Symphony, delivered with the correct balance of gravitas and charm, how deflating to ask student A to describe the symphony's primary theme and be met with John Cage's *4:33*. Hand out the worksheet on the class day before the day the music will be discussed in class. The prompts should be designed for students to complete tasks that require close reading of the textbook and pointed listening to musical excerpts. This information creates the building blocks for the day's class. Ask students to research complementary information to discover music outside the parameter of the textbook. Worksheets may also be used to teach students to write correct bibliographic citations (i.e., Chicago style). Finally, when appropriate, have them practice and perform pieces or excerpts of the pieces they studied for the class.

Like an overture to an opera, a well-designed worksheet should introduce the major themes of the class and create the desired intellectual atmosphere for a consideration of the issues. For instance in a class about early Renaissance music ask students to define the terms "contenance angloise" and non-imitative polyphony at first. The new terms are the building blocks for the class. Then ask students to find three examples on line by Dufay or Binchois that feature the terms highlighted above. In the same class, ask students to write down the names of three peer-reviewed sources, in correct bibliographic format, that focus on Dufay. Have students prepare to improvise *fauxbourdon* in class. In this class that features Dufay's *Nuper rosarum flores*, ask students to draw Brunelleschi's dome and Solomon's temple and consider proportions in architecture and in music. In conclusion, ask them to find another piece of music that is related to a building. By following the trajectory presented on the worksheets in class, students will find it easier to engage with the lectures and believe that their professor is well organized and on task (without relying on PowerPoint presentations).[2]

Worksheets have advantages for the professor as well. The assignments function both as a way to ensure that students have completed the reading and listening and as a preparatory outline for your lecture. You may wish to use this outline in subsequent teachings of the materials, which will cut down on the amount of times reading and rereading the textbook. Worksheets are a quick and easy way to take attendance. Marking them can be completed rather quickly and efficiently.[3] Three sample worksheets are shown in Figures 5.1-5.3.

---

[2]   Teaching evaluations come to mind here. Students are usually asked whether the professor is well organized and prepared, and worksheets might be helpful for professors in addressing this issue.

[3]   The check, check plus, and check minus system works well. It does not require too much of the instructor's time. Limit the assignments to one page per student and sometimes write questions on both sides of the page to save paper. A professor may also wish to send the worksheet electronically. The process works best on paper. Feel free to be creative in the presentation of the work: you may wish to include pictures and diagrams. This will encourage students to do the same.

Beethoven, *Eroica* Symphony

Name_____

Trace the history of the original dedication of Beethoven's *Eroica* Symphony. Please summarize the story below.

_____
_____
_____

_____

Please listen to the first movement of the *Eroica* Symphony and mark the first movement sonata form in the margins of your scorebook.

Please watch a video of a performance of Beethoven's *Eroica* Variations accompanied by the score in Beethoven's own hand: http://www.youtube. com/watch?v=VvuyYT03mtk. Part I. Try to follow the score. What does his handwriting tell us about the composer?

_____
_____

_____

Please compare the piano variations to the fourth movement of the *Eroica* Symphony.

Name three differences between the two works.

1._____

2._____

3._____

What is an autograph score?

_____

Figure 5.1   Worksheet in preparation for a lesson on Beethoven's *Eroica* Symphony

Berlioz, *Symphonie fantastique*

Name _____

Find a famous written description of Berlioz.

Author_____

Date_____

Draw below a picture of Berlioz from this description.

To whom did Berlioz dedicate his *Symphonie fantastique*?

_____

Berlioz wrote a famous treatise on orchestration. Please copy one paragraph from it below and explain its importance in history.

_____
_____
_____
_____
_____
_____
_____

_____
_____
_____
_____
_____
_____

Listen to the fifth movement of the *Symphonie fantastique*. In your score please mark the different sections of the movement.

Figure 5.2   Worksheet in preparation for Berlioz's *Symphonie fantastique*

Character Pieces, Chopin, Schumann, Liszt

Name_____

Chopin was sickly: What did he suffer from? _____

Who was Chopin's primary love interest?_____

Find a piece of her writing in which she describes Chopin:
Title_____

Please copy a couple of her sentences describing Chopin below:

_____
_____
_____
_____
_____
_____

Schumann ruined his hand with a mechanism that he thought would strengthen it.

What was it called?

_____

Find the names of two other nineteenth-century gizmos that were used to improve one's piano playing:

1._____

2._____

2011 marks the 200th anniversary of Franz Liszt's birthday. Name three celebrations planned and where they will take place.

1._____

2._____

3._____

Listen to Chopin's Mazurka in A Minor, Op. 17, no. 4. Mark important structural pillars in your scores.

Please listen to the Liszt's *Etude d'exécution transcendante*, no. 1 with the score. What are three differences between Liszt's and Chopin's music?

1._____

2._____

3._____

Listen to the excerpts from Schumann's *Carnaval*.

Name three differences between Schumann's and Chopin's music.

1._____

2._____

3._____

Figure 5.3   Worksheet in preparation for nineteenth-century piano music

Short Writing Assignments

Think of the following assignments as "études" for blossoming music historians. Each paper assigned is brief (500-750 words) and focuses on a particular skill.[4] The first group, which includes micro research papers and program notes, focuses on basic musicological research techniques, research strategies, and proficiency in citing sources and compiling a bibliography. Begin by introducing basic reference tools such as the *New Grove Dictionary of Music and Musicians*, *Oxford Dictionary of Music*, and RILM (Répertoire International de Littérature Musicale), and accompany your class to the "M" and "ML" sections in the library.[5] Ask a librarian to visit the class to demonstrate new tools at students' disposal that help with citations and bibliography.

The second group of papers engages the student's critical voice and includes concert reports, album reviews, and article reviews. These assignments are interdisciplinary in nature and foster a comprehensive approach to music history. The exercises may be implemented in music appreciation and music history classes. Included is a description of each assignment and a formal prompt that can be handed out to students.

1. Research-based Writing

Formal Micro Research Papers
The micro research papers are organized in chronological order and require between two and three weeks for the students to complete. Give the students plenty of time to find sources and order books on interlibrary loan. Micro research papers require that the student do a significant amount of research, and as a reward they will find that they do not spend as much time writing it up.[6] Be sure to require a bibliography and citations (in text or as footnotes). Obligate students to consult at least three printed sources. Your papers should be designed in such a way that students must go to the library to do their research, rather than relying entirely on the web. To do this choose

---

[4] For more about students writing music history, see Conway and Hodgman, *Teaching Music in Higher Education*, 119-22 and Carol Hess, "Score and Word: Writing about Music," in *Teaching Music History*, ed. Mary Natvig (Aldershot and Burlington, VT: Ashgate, 2002), 193-204.

[5] See Trevor Herbert, *Music in Words: A Guide to Researching and Writing about Music* (Oxford: Oxford University Press, 2009), 160-73, for information about these basic sources.

[6] For an excellent section on citing sources in music, see Herbert, *Music in Words*, 70-86. Students and professors might also find helpful D. Kern Holoman's *Writing about Music: A Style Sheet*, 2nd ed. (Berkeley: University of California Press, 2008), with its more detailed discussions of punctuation and style. The quick tempo of writing the paper will seem more satisfying to students than the adagio tempo of the research because students are trained to believe (by their media world) that the faster they complete an assignment, the better the assignment.

tasks that ask students to compare sources or find music in printed sources that can be pulled off the shelves. For instance: compare two manuscripts that contain the same piece of Renaissance music. Students will quickly find that they cannot complete this assignment by sitting at their computers. A hypothetical student might search for the sources of Josquin's *Missa Pange Lingua* and find little mention of original sources in Wikipedia, Google, or their textbooks. They might find Oxford online. In this case the student found one source and reproduction of the source in the textbook, but not a second because the Vatican sources are hard to trace online and the student could not find a reproduction of the work online. Dead end. Encourage the student to head to the M1 section of the library and find the collected Josquin edition and read the introduction which lays out the names of all the concordant sources and includes a bibliography of works about the Mass. Quickly students run back to the computer and find that many of the Vatican sources found in the book are not available online. They are stuck again. It turns out that the *Missa Pange Lingua* is a difficult piece to find two concordant versions of on the web. At this point they usually come back to the instructor again or speak to a fellow student and decide perhaps to go in a different direction: a chanson. In completing this assignment students also learn to choose the best repertory for the task at hand. Reproductions of Renaissance chansons are more readily available because published facsimiles of the chanson sources are available. Students will also be able to find the *chansonniers* online and print reproductions of the pieces. Once they find the materials needed, insist that the papers be short and concise and include a *correct* works cited list and in-text citations.

Below are a few suggested assignments:

Medieval Music (1000-1400)[7]
Prompt: Music and Illuminations: In 500 words discuss a piece of music that has a strong connection to a work of art.[8] Discuss the nature of the music (chant, organum, song, for instance) and the image that accompanies it. In what way are the two related? Please learn about the text that accompanies the music and about the artist (illuminator) who composed the work of art. Please include a bibliography and citations.

Renaissance Music (1400-1600)
Prompt: Comparing Manuscripts: In 500-750 words, compare two manuscripts that contain the same piece of Renaissance music. Describe the history of each manuscript, its content, and the relationship between the two manuscripts. Please listen to the piece and submit a hard copy of the piece in transcription (please Xerox or download a copy and print it). Describe any difference that you note between

---

[7]   The dates adopted in this essay might be fodder for a musicological war. They are used here for argument's sake.

[8]   For the virtues of teaching the two disciplines together, see Barbara Russano Hanning's "Teaching Music History through Art," in *Vitalizing Music History Teaching*, ed. James Briscoe (Hillsdale, NY: Pendragon Press, 2010), 139-60.

the manuscript versions that you have found. Please include a bibliography and citations.

Baroque Music (1600-1725)

Prompt: Program Music: After listening to Vivaldi's *Four Seasons*, find three selections of program music in the Baroque. In 500-750 words, describe each piece of music and its relationship to the words that accompany it. Look at the original score of each piece and investigate the history of its association to the words. Who do scholars believe wrote the words to each piece? In your final paragraph, hypothesize about the reasons composers connect words to their instrumental music. Please provide bibliography and citations and copies of the texts of each selection.

Classical Music (1725-1800)

Prompt: Sketches and Handwriting: Peruse different reproductions of Beethoven sketches and handwriting. Find a piece of music that was published during Beethoven's time and trace its fruition from earliest sketch to fair copy to publication. Find all mentions of the work during Beethoven's time. Please consult *Thayer's Life of Beethoven*. In 500 words describe the piece's timeline from earliest mention to reception. Include an actual timeline. You can find timeline templates online. Include thumbnail reproductions of the sketches in your paper and any other relevant images.

Romantic Music (1800-1900)

Prompt: Art of Transcription: Find three transcriptions or arrangements of the same piece of music. Please limit your piece to the nineteenth century. In 500 words discuss the history of each transcription. Who transcribed the work? Who published it? How do the transcriptions differ from the original? Please include a hard copy of the original work and one of the transcriptions. Please also include a bibliography and citations.

Modernism (1900-1980)

Prompt: Serialism: 12-tone serialism is a ubiquitous compositional technique in the twentieth century. Describe the technique as best you can and provide an example from the Second Viennese School. What are the antecedents of the serialist philosophy? Please find three examples of serialism in music from earlier style periods. Describe how the pieces work in 500 words.

Contemporary Music (1980-)

Prompt: Longevity: In 500-750 words, name three contemporary classical composers whose music you surmise will be remembered in 200 years. Include short biographical descriptions of each composer, short analyses of the selected works, and the reasons for your choices. Include links to the works so your professor can listen to the pieces. Include reproductions of incipits of scores when available or try to transcribe them.

Program Notes

Program notes is a crucial genre for any aspiring musicologist-writer to master.[9] Ask students to describe one piece of classical music (the piece may have many movements).[10] Ask each student to listen to the piece at least three times and to provide a bibliography (no citations) to ensure that students are not merely copying Wikipedia. Ask them to consult primary sources related to the composers and music they choose and suggest that they follow the tried-and-true formula of devoting two-thirds of the notes to historical and cultural background and one-third to a description of the piece. Students will find staying within the allotted word count challenging.

Prompt: In 750 words, write program notes for one piece of classical music. (The piece may have several movements.) Research your piece carefully, both its historical background and the composer's biography. Include the title and date of the piece at the beginning of the paper. Due in one week.

2. Critical Writing

Developing and writing reviews encourages students to develop their connoisseurship skills. In these writing etudes, students are required to investigate a piece of music and its history, and learn how to describe what they hear, while also assessing the quality of the music and its performance. Encourage students to read, as examples, music reviews by excellent writers, including George Bernard Shaw, Donald Tovey, and Virgil Thomson, to name a few.[11] Peter Kivy's "How to Emote over Music (Without Losing Your Respectability)" from his book the *Corded Shell* is helpful in categorizing different approaches to music criticism.[12] Kivy includes "criteria" for determining varying levels of subjectivity, from the

---

[9]   For more about writing program notes, see Jonathan Bellman, *A Short Guide to Writing about Music* (New York: Longman, 2000), 51-65 and Trevor Herbert, *Music in Words*, 26-27. Thousands of program notes can be found in archives. For example, see the Cleveland Orchestra archive hosted by the Cleveland Institute of Music at www.cim.edu/library/locate/programnotes.php (accessed May 9, 2012).

[10]   You may also wish to ask your students to write notes for a pop or jazz concert. This is good practice for students in rock and jazz ensembles.

[11]   George Bernard Shaw, *Shaw on Music*, ed. Eric Bentley (New York: Doubleday Anchor, 1955); Donald Tovey, *Chamber Music: Essays in Musical Analysis* (Oxford: Oxford University Press, 1989); *A Virgil Thomson Reader* (Boston: Houghton Mifflin, 1981). You may also wish to encourage students to find current reviews in their local papers and discuss these reviews in class.

[12]   Peter Kivy, *The Corded Shell: Reflections on Musical Expression* (Princeton: Princeton University Press, 1980), 132-49.

"moderate skeptic" to the "extreme skeptic." The more moderate skeptic writes about selected emotions heard in the music, while the extreme skeptic writes only about formalist (not referential) qualities heard in the music, including structure, tempo, and rhythm, to name a few. These assignments work well in music appreciation and music history classes and can be used as a refreshing supplement to the micro research papers.

Concert Report
This group of assignments begins with the tried-and-true, and sometimes perplexing, concert report.[13] Tried and true because students hear live music and love to write about it, and perplexing because of the nature of the final product. What is a concert report anyway? We know what it shouldn't be more than what it should be. It is not quite a review. It is not a blow-by-blow description of the music. As professors, we often find ourselves dreading the thought of having to grades stacks of these essays. Think how the students must feel writing them! Here, then, are a few preparatory ideas to help ensure that students write about the music they heard. Successful concert report assignments are all about preparation. **Preparation**: Hand out a list of words that the student must use in the report. These include, but need not be limited to, melody, harmony, theme, rhythm, meter, tempo, dynamics, texture, form, and line.[14] Insist that students attend a live concert of Western classical music. (Many will plead with the professor to please, please not make them "have to do this." It's one thing to have to take a class on classical music, it's a whole other waste of time to have to spend part of their weekend going to hear it.) Warn students to avoid spending precious words discussing what their dates wore to the concert or what the audience was wearing. A student once received an "F" for spending circa 300 words on his pre-concert dinner. His rewritten paper began, "I materialized at the concert." Assign this paper one week before its due date.
Prompt: In 500-750 words, please describe the concert you attended. Discuss each piece and movement using the list of music terms below. Attach ticket stub and program notes. Please stay for the entire concert.

Album Review
This assignment used to be a much more straightforward endeavor. It is more difficult in the new millennium to ascertain the nature of an album, or perhaps more generically, a "new release." Ask students to choose two compilations to review, whether on CD or distributed on the web. In preparation, provide students with examples of reviewers you like. John Pareles from the *New York Times* might

---

[13] Jonathan Bellman writes about the concert report in his *A Short Guide to Writing about Music*, 28-32.
[14] I ask students to highlight these words with a marker to make them easier for me to find in the reports.

be a good start, though students might find the *Times* reviews somewhat turgid. The *Times*, however, is copyedited, which you will discover is a rather rare occurrence.

Bring sample albums to class and discuss ways to approach the project. Students might ask the following questions: "How do you begin?" "Do I discuss all the tracks?" "Do we discuss some history?" Ask students to share sample reviews that they enjoy reading, in print or on the web. Allow one week for the students to prepare this "étude."

Prompt: In 500 words write a review of an album. At the beginning of your review, include the album's title, a complete bibliographic citation for the album, and an image of the album's cover.

Article Review

Assign a musicological article for the class to critique and write about. Maynard Solomon's essays work well because undergraduates easily grasp his arguments and he tends to be polemical—which angers and ignites readers to want to respond.[15] He also writes about Mozart and Beethoven, in the view of most students, the titans of classical music. Allow students to select a different author, as long as the article is published in a book or a refereed journal, but be sure to sign off on the article yourself. The refereed journal requirement gives the professor the opportunity to teach the class about the relative merit of articles. Never allow students to quote an anonymous source, such as Wikipedia. Read excerpts of musicological articles in class and provide sample reviews of the articles.[16]

Prompt: In 500-700 words, write a review of an article published in a refereed journal or book. Please include a brief introduction that includes a description of the article's thesis, and research its author. Check the quality of the author's research by gauging the sources the author has selected to incorporate. Read at least two other articles on a similar subject. Assess the research's value or contribution to the field. Due in one week.

Experiential Learning

The assignments in this section require students to create a musical event (live or recorded) and write a paper commenting on or translating that event into cogent language. These assignments were inspired by the poet named Kenneth Koch, a close friend of Ned Rorem. In class he had students read a poem by a particular French poet, say Baudelaire, and then asked students to imitate the poem. He then read the "best" selections in class. The following prompts have been fashioned with the idea that writing effectively about music is a kind of poetry. You may also

---

[15]   You may wish to assign "Beethoven and His Nephew" from Solomon's *Beethoven: Revised Edition* (New York: Schirmer, 2001), 297-330.

[16]   Lewis Lockwood wrote an excellent early review of Solomon's work. See "*Beethoven* by Maynard Solomon," *19th-Century Music* 3, no. 1 (July 1979): 76-82.

wish to ask students to write a blog that captures their ideas as they navigate the waters of music history.[17] In addition to exhorting students to share experiences by performing for the class, the following assignments create a close-knit classroom community, one of the most important goals of teaching.

1. Music Video

Students have the technology that allows them to easily shoot and edit videos. Save two days of class time at the end of the semester for students to elucidate their work. Students can post their videos on YouTube and show them on the classroom's screen, or students can link their computers to the classroom's computer. Ask students to play the video before coming to class to ensure that there are no glitches during class time. Glitches take a lot of time to sort out and are a source of frustration for everyone. Ask students to adjudicate the videos with the goal of choosing the "best class video" at the end of the second day of screenings. Tell students that the winning video will be placed on the Music Department website.

Students may ask you if they can collaborate with one another. If two students work together, the video must be seven to eight minutes in length and each student must still write 500-750 words about the project from his or her perspective. Please warn students not to wait until the last minute to begin their projects, because the editing process will take much more time than they can imagine. No late papers or late videos should be accepted.

Students really enjoy completing the videos and the papers, and the best students work diligently to produce beautiful music videos that they are proud of—enough to show their families and friends.

Prompt: Prepare a music video to accompany any piece or pieces that we have studied in class. Your video must be three to four minutes in length. Show your video in class. Please write a paper describing your creative process in 500-750 words. In the paper discuss why you selected those piece(s). Also discuss the theme of your video and how you chose to film it. Include an explanation of the choices you made and the people who helped you. Please discuss what you wanted people to learn from your project.

2. Concept Music

This étude focuses on music as conceptual art and asks students to compose and perform a piece of "concept music" and write about it.[18] In completing the task, students inquire about the nature of music and learn about composers who stretched the boundaries of music.

---

[17] Blogging will be discussed in more detail later in this chapter.

[18] For more about "concept music" and John Cage, see Hartmut Obendorf, *Minimalism: Designing Simplicity* (Dordrecht: Springer, 2009), 41.

One suggestion is to assign readings from Harry Partch's wonderful memoir *Bitter Music* and have the students watch a video of his work.[19] John Cage is a natural fit, too, and they could watch a clip from his January performance on "I've Got a Secret" (January 1960).[20] Luciano Berio's *Sinfonia*, Philip Glass's *Einstein on Beach*, and Meredith Monk's *Dolmen Music* may be of interest.

The length of the students' performances may vary wildly. Ask each to present at least three minutes of his or her piece in class.

Prompt: Compose a piece of conceptual music and perform at least three minutes of it in class. In 500 words write about your "concept music." How does it relate to the music that you listen to? What other contemporary composers (pop, jazz, classical) delve into other untraditional musical worlds? Is there a future for your music?

3. Lip-synching

Lip-synching is a great exercise to engage students in performing—with a short amount of preparation time. Show several clips of celebrated lip-synching scenes, including Dana Carvey performing Jimi Hendrix's "Foxy Lady" in the film *Wayne's World* (Penelope Spheeris, Paramount Pictures, 1992), and probably the most famous cinematic example, Tom Cruise performing "Old Time Rock & Roll" in the film *Risky Business* (dir. Paul Brickman, Warner Bros., 1983). You could argue that Leporello is lip-synching "Deh, vieni alla finestra" in the second act of *Don Giovanni*. Encourage students to use props. You may want to show some lip-synching spin-offs, such as air guitar.[21] Students will need one week to complete this étude.

Prompt: In class, perform three minutes of lip-synching. You may use any type of music you like. Write a 500-word paper describing the process of creating your lip-synching performance. Research at least three other lip-synching performances and critique them. Due in one week.

4. The Opera

Students often look back at the "opera" as one of the most meaningful experiences of their entire college careers![22] The opera is a group project, appropriate for music

---

[19]   Harry Partch, *Bitter Music: Collected Journals, Essays, Introductions and Librettos*, ed. Thomas McGeary (Urbana: University of Illinois Press, 1991) and a Partch documentary, *The Dreamer that Remains* (1989).

[20]   John Cage, perf., *What's My Line?*, May 4, 2007 (originally aired January 1960), YouTube, http://www.youtube.com/watch?v=SSulycpZH-U (accessed May 9, 2012).

[21]   Students may wish to follow the US Air Guitar Championships at usairguitar.com (accessed May 9, 2012).

[22]   "Opera" is in quotation marks because the term is used loosely to mean a work that includes soloists and a chorus. In an interesting assignment, Melanie Lowe asks students

appreciation and music history students. It has been my experience that in any group of twenty or so college students, there will exist one diva, one male star, two supporting actors, three composers, three writers, one director, one choreographer, one producer (the most organized member of the class), two costume designers, some singers and musicians, and few who will not contribute no matter how much you threaten them with poor grades. This natural selection makes for an invaluable experience. If you have a class of forty, you might try dividing the group into two. It has been my experience that the project works less well with fewer than twenty people in the group.

Instructions for implementing this assignment: Assign the opera project, and everyone's role in the project, the first class session after the mid-term. Require students to produce thirty to forty minutes of music. If you have not already done so, explain the nature of opera and the basics of a traditional opera, in order to give students a framework in which to work. Describe the overture, chorus, aria, recitative, dance number, and libretto.

Explain traditional operatic themes: love, death, cross-dressing, duels, revenge, and spells, to name a few. Verdi's *Rigoletto* is an excellent example because it is relatively uncomplicated and short: explain the plot and the division of the piece into acts and scenes. In addition, show some legendary numbers from other operas, such as "Libiamo" from Verdi's *La Traviata*, "O mio babbino caro" from Puccini's *Gianni Schicchi*, and the first ten minutes of Philip Glass's *Einstein on the Beach*.

Students will be really excited and nervous at the prospect of completing the assignment. Leave ten minutes of class time for students to get together and meet about possible plot scenarios, and ask the "writers" to present ideas to the class the following period.[23]

Be sure to have the director or producer take attendance at rehearsals. She or he can ask students for help with this. It will become clear quickly who the slackers are. Allow ten minutes at the end of [each?] class for the students to go over their work and assign weekly tasks. Students will look forward to the diversion from the grind of the syllabus. The goal here is not perfection, but rather cooperation and hard work.

- Week One: Ask for the libretto from the writers. The writers present the libretto to the class and work with the director and producer and composers. Divide composition duties between the three or four students who wish to compose.

---

to develop their own productions of the *Marriage of Figaro*. See her "Teaching Music History Today: Making Tangible Connections to the Here and Now," *Journal of Music History Pedagogy* 1, no. 1 (2010): 45-59, , http://www.ams-net.org/ojs/index.php/jmhp/article/viewArticle/17/25 (accessed May 9, 2012).

[23]   Do not get particularly involved with the plot; simply advise students to be tasteful and respectful of others.

- Week Two: Ask composers to begin to share the compositional ideas with the class.
- Week Three: Composers give singers and musicians their parts. Director and producer meet with the class to check in and see how things are proceeding.
- Week Four: Lead singers begin to learn their parts. Ask students to sing one number for the class, with musicians.
- Week Five: Choreographer works with class on big dance number. Costume and sets designers begin their work.
- Week Six: Rehearsals begin with the entire group.
- Week Seven: Rehearsals continue.
- Costumes and make-up: Ask students to go to the theatre department to borrow a few things. Also, take students to the local Goodwill in town. This is always fun. Students are incredibly resourceful. Give them $30 to spend.
- Lights: Be sure to assign a student to do the lights for the event. One student will want to do this job.
- Week Eight: Performance during class time. Ask students to invite friends. Be sure to reserve the use of your concert hall. Also ask students to create a brief program magazine to be handed out to the audience that includes a paragraph about the plot and explains each person's role in the production.
- The performance: Ask students to set up video cameras or ask your instructional technology staff to record the performance. The performance can be loaded on a website, open only to the class—house it on your library's server with other projects, such as senior theses or composition recitals.
- Clean up: Ask students to clean up everything off the stage at the end of the performance.
- End of term—cast party!
- Grade: Students will be graded on attendance and participation. Each professor will need to work with the class to develop a grade scale based on a fair set of criteria. The more work a student does on the project, the better the grade.

Reflective Writing

The assignments in this section, a blog, a compilation of funeral music, and a rap, are more informal in nature. This type of writing is autobiographical, giving students the opportunity to be unreservedly subjective and critical about the music they listen to. The blog can be used in both music appreciation and music history classes. All three assignments have been successful and require a certain amount of oversight from the teacher.

1. Blog

Each student in the class, whether it is for music history, music appreciation, or a seminar, is required to establish his or her own blog and contribute to it throughout the term. The blog should begin with a name followed by a "philosophy" or reason for the blog's existence. Blogs are free and require no special training to establish. (Tumblr.com allows the user to quickly post and repost video and audio.) You could require students to post all their formal written assignments on the blog. The blog then can also serve as a portfolio. Students are not required, however, to go live with their blog if they do not wish to.

The following is an assignment that can be used as an introduction to blogging. Include a more formal writing assignment in conjunction with the blog to ensure that students take the work seriously and don't write on their site as if they are composing text messages.

Prompt: In 500 words write an introduction to your blog. Include a brief critique of the blogs of at least three other people. Please read Alex Ross's article entitled "The Well-Tempered Web" in the October 22, 2007 (78-85) issue of the *New Yorker* magazine. Discuss the pros and cons of blogging about music. Due in one week.

At the end of the semester, ask students to post a 500-word piece about the semester. What was your favorite piece of writing that you read? What was your favorite piece of writing that you wrote? Which assignments were challenging, which were easy? What do you see yourself doing next with your writing? What is your dream writing job? Students may discuss these ideas with others in class too.

A special note about grading blogs: Grade blogs according to the number of posts students have written during a semester. Each instructor can set his or her bar. Students should post on average about two a week, totaling around thirty. Thus you can make thirty equal an "A," twenty-five a "B," and so on down the grade scale.

2. Funeral Music

Ask students to read Billie Holiday's *Lady Sings the Blues*, and discuss writing their musical autobiography. Ask them about the funerals they have attended and the kind of music they heard at those events. Discuss the history of Mozart's *Requiem* and preparations many composers have made for music at their own funerals. Mozart's *Requiem*, for instance, was performed at Chopin's funeral.[24]

Prompt: Imagine your own (that is, the individual student's) funeral and write about it in 500 words. Please include details about where you imagine the funeral

---

[24]   For more details see Benita Eisler, *Chopin's Funeral* (New York: Knopf, 2003). Students feel honored that a professor is interested in the music that they hold dear, and students are eager to imagine how they might like to be remembered by friends. The assignment gives them a chance to step outside of daily college ruminations.

taking place, write words that you would like read at your funeral, and compile a list of at least five songs or pieces that you would like played at the funeral. Please explain why you chose those pieces and what they say about you. Please submit the pieces to your professor as an attachment to an email.

3. Poetry-Rap

Ask students to write and perform a three-minute rap song that they have composed. Have students read W. H. Auden's "On Music and Opera," found in the *Dyer's Hand*, a collection of essays.[25] Students will need to compose a "beat" and the words. They may work in pairs. They may read their rap from a paper or improvise and submit the words at a later time.

Students are particularly frightened by this assignment, but most if not all are grateful for the experience once they have completed it. Some students will have had experience rapping: you might wish to ask them to assist less experienced comrades. Ask students to submit the lyrics of their raps to you.
Prompt: Please compose and perform a piece of rap music. The piece should be at least three minutes long and include an original beat. You will perform the piece in class.

Service Learning

The final type of exercise presented in this chapter falls under the rubric of service learning. These assignments push students outside the classroom and the music department, a place that at times seems isolated from the rest of the college. These assignments do not have a formal writing component. Students may wish to write about the experiences on their blogs.

1. Arrange a Tune

Ask students to find a person who has a tune and would like the class to arrange it for him or her. This person may, for example, be someone a student loves or admires, or someone who is going through a difficult time. Once students find a few people with musical ideas, ask the students to arrange the tunes. Divide the class into groups and ask each group of students to arrange one tune that they can perform. Ask each group to perform the tune in class, and record the tune to give to the composer.

---

[25]   W. H. Auden, *Dyer's Hand* (New York: Random House, 1962), 465-74.

2. Interview

Ask students to interview a street musician. Students might wish to do this in pairs. Provide students with a couple of dollars each, so they can buy the musician a cup of coffee or tea. (They can give their interviewee the money if they wish.) Ask students to provide you, prior to the interview, a list of questions that they intend to ask the musician. Go over the questions together as a group in class.

Have each student test a recording device prior to the interview. Have the student place the device in the proper place for clear reception. The interview should take about fifteen minutes. (Otherwise the students will have too much material.) Ask the students to record where and when the interview took place and write down some details regarding the general appearance and personality of their subject. Share the experiences in the class and on the blogs.

3. The People's Music History Class

Students, working in groups of three, should bring a boom box or other type of player into a public space. Have them design a sign that reads "Music History Class" and specifies a topic for discussion and the time at which the class will be begin, say 12:30 p.m. Class should run a maximum of thirty minutes. Topics could include, for example, Mozart's *Eine Kleine Nachtmusik* or "What is a fugue?" or the "x" theme in Beethoven's Fifth Symphony, or "Was Schubert Gay?" or "Is Radiohead Relevant?" or "Who was Marian Anderson?" or "What is a Symphony?"

Have students prepare a handout with an outline of their teaching agenda and important names, dates, and titles. Have students report back to class. Practical places for the People's Music History class might include a town square, a college plaza, a dorm room, or a high school, middle school, or elementary school classroom. Encourage students to videotape their classes for further critique.

4. Preconcert Lecture

Ask students to listen to or watch a preconcert talk online or live.[26] Ask each student to find a concert on campus to attend and to prepare a ten-minute concert introduction to be delivered either live before the audience (if agreed upon by the concert performer) or as a broadcast to the college community. (If you do not have this capability already, ask institution technology to stream concerts from your auditorium to the college community. It is easy for them to set this up and at little cost.) If amenable to the performers, ask students to interview the performers before and after the concert in the blue room, to be streamed or captured on video. The interviews should be archived on the class or music department website. Ask

---

[26]   For instance, one can hear excellent talks for the Pacific Symphony at http://www. pacificsymphony.org/res/multimedia/audio/PreviewTalk_10-11_02.mp3 (accessed May 9, 2012).

students to dress professionally for the interviews and live concert introductions. This exercise gives students priceless experience and creates community between the players, students, and college-wide staff.

Conclusions

Many students enroll in music history and music appreciation classes with some trepidation. Some know little about the classical repertory and have the impression that Western music was written primarily for the pleasure of deep-pocketed adults their parents' age and older. Imaginative, demanding, and provocative assignments can ease their fears by requiring them to take ownership of this "new" musical world, which for the first time might include Landini and Landowska. The assignments introduced in this chapter, under the subheadings worksheets, short writing assignments, experiential learning, reflective writing and service learning, encourage students to make connections between their worlds and the history illuminated in their textbooks and lectures. Instead of resenting the study of Western music, students will joyously appreciate the benefits of learning the repertory and add it to their ever-expanding and mutating music libraries.

Indeed because of music's multifaceted nature, the objects of musicological inquiry are always changing. One could argue that musicology began in the eighteenth century as a series of travelogues in the work of Charles Burney.[27] The discipline has slowly broken its chains to literary history in Europe and the conservatory in the United States to emerge as a staple of study in liberal arts institutions, guided by the wisdom of peer-reviewed presses.[28] However, we are at a crossroads: primary source material is drying up. Musicologists have, in the last twenty years, reached out to the fertile ground of interdisciplinary study, and are becoming well versed in speaking about art and philosophy as well as music. We will soon exhaust this path as well.

Fortunately, we are at the edge of a new a frontier of study—the digital musical cosmos—in which we will be able to undertake magnificent comparative studies of manuscripts and performances by inputting and investigating data-derived digitization of visual and audio materials. This new arena of study requires fluidity with technologies and a willingness to traverse new frontiers. The explorative nature of Burney's seminal studies still resonates in musicology today, and the assignments presented above seek to capture the joy of discovering and rediscovering music history.

---

[27]   Charles Burney, *A General History of Music, from the Earliest Ages to the Present (1789)* (New York: Dover, 1957).

[28]   Joseph Kerman's *Contemplating Music* (Cambridge, MA: Harvard University Press, 1985) provides a cogent overview of the field of musicology.

Chapter 6
Technology In and Out of the Classroom

José Antonio Bowen

Musicians have always been at the leading edge of technology. Beethoven, for example, was in many ways the Bill Gates of the nineteenth century. As the most sophisticated musical hardware of the day (the piano) evolved, consumers needed software (compositions) to complete the package. Piano manufacturers realized that when they created new capabilities in the hardware, Beethoven and other composers would want to exploit them: creating a demand for their new pianos. Much as happened during the early days of the PC, consumers were caught in a constant complication of formats—as Beethoven would write for the latest technological improvements on the most recent piano, consumers with the old five-octave piano (think Windows 95) simply had to upgrade their hardware if they wanted to play the new six-octave piece.[1]

Technology in both art and teaching, however, is only a means to an end. Beethoven saw the increased expressive possibilities in improvements to the piano, and most teachers (certainly most students) can see additional opportunities for learning using new technologies. The end, however, remains good teaching and more learning. The most important point about technology is that it will force us to redesign our courses. New technology provides many more options for delivering content and feedback, for engaging students outside of the classroom, for ongoing and creative assessment, and for how and when we do discussion, writing, and listening: all of this increases our choices and demonstrates only more clearly the importance of course design.

An understanding of new technology is also critical for future faculty as an essential demonstration of relevance and our willingness to be lifelong learners: students will forgive you for not knowing about the most current contemporary popular music, but they will be suspicious of your desire for them to try new things if you won't use an iPod and want them to listen to CDs in the library. At the very least, students will expect that you know enough about their listing habits to give them access to music in the ways they expect (iTunes and Spotify). In a recent survey 92 percent of current high school students said that technology is an important consideration in their college selection process, and when surveyed about

---

[1]   José Bowen, "Beethoven the Businessman," *Ted*, accessed May 15, 2012, http://www.ted.com/talks/jose_bowen_beethoven_the_businessman.html.

why the use of technology is poor, the number one reason (from administrators, faculty, staff, and students) was that faculty do not know how to use it.[2]

Technology has changed the way we play, hear, and study music. It is also changing the availability of resources for college teaching, but it has also brought fundamental changes to the human condition in three ways. First, technology has changed the access and value of knowledge, which in turn has only increased the importance of critical thinking. The internet has greatly increased competition for ideas and intellectual property. By lowering the barriers to self-publication, it has allowed more competition. Before the internet, old exams were stored in frat houses and study guides were published by professors with Ph.D.s. Now anyone with a computer can publish a listening guide and a mountain of rubbish obscuring every good idea. Students and employers now crave two skills that music history has taught well for centuries: (1) how to find true and accurate information (what used to be called bibliography and is now digital literacy) and (2) how to analyze that information for quality and relevance (what used to be called a liberal arts education).

Second, technology has changed the nature of social proximity. Facebook has not actually given you any more friends, but it does allow you to stay in contact with old friends who are now physically distant and it greatly increases your awareness of friends in a more distant social circle. In our students, the need for contact has increased enormously, but its nature has also dramatically changed. Older faculty may remember college as a time of finding friends in the library and calling home once a week. Where now, students constantly text, Facebook, Skype, tweet, ping, or call friends and family both near and far away physically.

A third major change in our lives is the expectation of customization. Thank Starbucks or Burger King if you want, but most of us now routinely personalize everything from from our credit cards to the way we read or listen. For students now entering college, learning has always been personalized and online: students have been able to check grades or assignments before they get out of bed and if they did not understand a teacher's explanation, they simply looked for a different or better one at home. While not designed as a learning tool, video games changed expectations and molded a generation of learners.

Higher education has been suspicious that new technology will really bring radical change, but automakers in Detroit did not think much of the threat from small Japanese cars in 1970. That was before a gas crisis and before Nissan, Honda, and Toyota introduced Infinity, Acura, and Lexus. While young faculty may first encounter a classroom not much different from what they experienced in graduate school, it seems highly unlikely that they will end their careers giving PowerPoint lectures in classes with fixed seating. For a senior professor with

---

[2]   "2011 CDW-G 21st-Century Classroom Report" (industry online survey of 1209, students, faculty and IT staff conducted by O'Keffe & Company for CDW-G [26 July 2011]), accessed 28 April 2012, http://webobjects.cdw.com/webobjects/media/pdf/newsroom/CDWG-21st-Century-Campus-Report-0711.pdf.

decades of prepared lectures and courses, the sunk costs of change may seem overwhelming, but for new faculty, investing time in technology upfront will pay dividends both in reusable materials and in better teaching. New faculty will also surely be required to demonstrate that their teaching methods work in a way that old faculty never had to do; here again, the investment in technology, course design, and assessment will bring long-term rewards.

Course Design in the Digital Age

Teaching involves two parts: course delivery and course design. Most faculty are (or will become) at least competent at course delivery: there are plenty of opportunities for student interaction on any college campus. Course design is equally critical, but less intuitive, especially for faculty; we become faculty in part because we thrive in the traditional classroom structures. Most students are not as happy in a classroom as faculty are, and as technology changes and students experience success in other realms of learning, faculty using only traditional methods will be increasingly unsuccessful. We should not assume that just because we have taken college courses that we know how to design them, or that what worked for us will work for future students. There is also compelling new literature on how adolescent brains function in the classroom, how students learn, and what sort of situations and course design best fosters change and long-term impact on students.[3] There is equally important information on how to deal with multiple learning styles, and technology can be of great service here, but understanding the principles and goals of the learning is critical. Start with learning goals for your course before you determine which technology you may need. New faculty, or faculty in a new institution, should also seek out the university and departmental curriculum goals.

Learning goals need to be more than just content. What will students be able to *do* with this new knowledge? How will they apply and integrate? What do you want students to remember about your class in two or twenty years? Chapter 1's summary of Dee Fink's work demonstrates that students learn more when they care about the subject or can see the application, and motivation is part of what the best college teachers create. Finding the intersection of your goals and their goals is an important part of teaching; the best teachers combine high standards with a supportive and nurturing environment that supports risk and failure. Technology and the increased opportunities for access and feedback can play a huge part in providing motivation and multiple paths to success.

Once you have learning goals, then ask what sorts of technologies and activities will foster those goals. While your teaching activities and your feedback

---

[3]   James E. Zull, "The Art of Changing the Brain," *Educational Leadership* 62, no. 1 (September 2004): 68-72; Ken Bain, *What the Best College Teachers Do* (Cambridge, MA: Harvard University Press, 2004).

and assessment strategies should align with your learning goals, you do not want to limit your learning to what you can measure or assess easily. Since technology enormously increases what you can measure and how easily you can measure it, it is even more important not to compromise on your learning goals.

One of the most important changes that technology is bringing to higher education is the ability to time shift: content can be delivered at any time to any device and there are many more options for communication. So reserve class time for the most important or difficult learning objectives. If you want students to do better analysis or to be able to relate works to social contexts, then plan to have them do this in class. Face-to-face contact is still the most important (and expensive) so consider carefully if you should use it for first exposure, lectures, discussion, active learning, or exams.

Class size is clearly a factor in your course design, but again, start with the most ambitious learning goals and only then ask if you will need to make accommodations. If you are a mesmerizing live performer and your introductions to material will motivate students to learn on their own, then lectures may be an appropriate in-class activity. There are also a number of technologies that allow students in large classrooms to give you instant feedback. Allowing students to text or chat a question to you during the lecture lowers the barrier of embarrassment. You can immediately know if there is a problem and then choose how to proceed. If you have a TA, your TA can either sort through texts or be on chat during the lecture and can then flag you with questions. Clickers (also called "Student Response Systems") can serve some of the same function. These systems allow students to answer multiple-choice questions in class and you or everyone can see results instantly in a chart, but they only allow students to answer and not ask questions. There are many different systems of clickers and beware that if you use a textbook-based system, with its own clicker, then students may bring the wrong clicker to class. If your campus has a single solution and it is available for your classroom then it can be a useful way to keep students engaged and gather more feedback.

Frankly, my favorite large class technology is the index card. They are cheap and reliable. Instead of getting just one question at the end of class, ask every student to write a question on an index card and hand it in as they leave. If you do not want to be bothered with clickers, then ask a question and ask students to hold up a colored index card. This could be as easy as green for true and red for false or multiple colors for multiple answers: the beauty (and there is an aesthetic dimension to this) is that a sea of green cards tells you instantly that you are on the right track.[4]

Large classes, however, do not require lectures. Most classes are already hybrids of online and live materials and contact; the idea of three physical contact hours for three "credits" is fading. Large classes can meet once a week or never

---

[4]   My thanks to Anna Dollar at Miami University for sharing her use of the colored index card.

as a large group and instead only meet in smaller sections. If you are going to the expense of bringing 60 or 600 students into a large room, then you will eventually need to offer them more than just a live version of what they could watch online (see Chapter 2).

Digital Content

Part of your course design will include some delivery of foundational knowledge, but do not assume you have to write, create, or deliver this content yourself. First, assess what material for your class is already available online. Your students will do this for you: if you lecture and announce the subject of your talk, students will immediately begin looking for shortcuts. Your competition now includes videos of Leonard Bernstein demonstrating with the New York Philharmonic, or Harvard's Robert Levin demonstrating with period instruments. Your students can watch or listen to Craig Wright at Yale University introduce them to the vocal music of J. S. Bach in their dorm room or at home. (Wright is the author of six books, including *Music in Western Civilization* (2005) and the textbook *Listening to Music* (6th edition, 2011) upon which his course is based.[5]) Why would they spend precious time or gas money to come to your lecture on the same subject? An empty lecture hall might mean there was a great party on campus last night, but it might also mean there is a better lecture online.

For most composers, pieces, instruments, or styles, the internet contains a wealth of information. If you have something new to say about a Chopin prelude, then write a book, create a podcast, make a video for YouTube, or (if it is a very short insight) tweet it to your students. Otherwise, you can probably find at least some content online. Start by searching for your list of topics in Google, merlot. org, iTunesU, YouTube.com, Wikipedia, Yale, MIT, and other university open course sites. There are lectures, demonstrations, historic tours, study guides, test banks, scores, recordings, assignments, online activities, and games. You may find great content—governments, instrument makers, students, retired professors, and amateurs have often dedicated themselves to creating great study sites. At the very least you want to know what is out there, so you can prepare for students shortcuts.

At the MIT Open Courseware site (http://ocw.mit.edu) there are a wide range of entire courses from jazz composition to women composers. Many of them include assignments and solutions, lecture notes, exams, readings, and examples of projects. Universities around the world, including Stanford University, are actively competing to get entire courses online. In the fall of 2011 Stanford offered "Introduction to Artificial Intelligence" free and online to students worldwide,

---

[5]   Craig Wright and Bryan Simms, *Music in Western Civilization* (Belmont, CA: Wadsworth, 2005); Craig Wright, *Listening to Music*, 6th ed. (Stamford, CT: Schirmer Cengage Learning, 2011); "MUSI 112: Listening to Music with Craig Wright", "Open Yale Courses", accessed 28 April 2012, http://oyc.yale.edu.

including "feedback on progress and a statement of accomplishment."[6] While the site crashed temporarily after the first 100,000 people signed up, there will continue to be more and more of the best courses and content available for free online. Why not take advantage of this material?

There is also a wide variety of other sorts of interactive sites. Michael Tilson Thomas and the San Francisco Symphony, for example, have created a magnificent resource for some standard repertoire (www.keepingscore.org). In addition to listening to pieces while watching a highlighted score or watching a performance, students can explore Mahler's musical textures, walk the streets of Vienna, or follow the creation of *The Rite of Spring*.[7]

The start of a faculty career used to mean creating lectures that could then be recycled throughout a lifetime of teaching. Today, even if no material exists for your course—yet—it may pay more dividends over a career to invest in creating materials—podcasts, assessments, websites, resource lists, and games—than in creating lectures. While lectures are good at transmitting enthusiasm and finding the entry point for material, they are comparatively poor conveyers of content. Unless you believe you are an especially promising lecturer, you may find that your time is better spent developing other pedagogical skills like leading discussions (even in large classes).

Podcasts, for example, can allow you to add many more examples than you can in a lecturer and include simultaneous alternative approaches. Unlike lectures, podcasts are organized to allow the user to customize the experience. Some students can go back to listen again to a difficult concept, while others can skip ahead and stay engaged. In a course for non-majors, for example, you might classify your explanations or analogies by type (and label them as such in podcast chapters): chapter x describes how an engineer might think about Bach's organ music, while chapter y looks at it from the perspective of an anthropology major. My lecture on the Blues (available free online from teachingnaked.com) provides dozens of examples of a 12-bar blues in different genres from R&B to Western Swing. Few of us would give twenty examples of the same thing in a live class, but for a few non-majors, this might be the repetition they need.

You do not need to create an entire course or even borrow materials only from a single source (although it is easier to curate a course that holds together easily that way), and there is no shame in borrowing with attribution. (And most lectures are full of ideas, organization, analogies, quips, and examples borrowed from other lectures.) If you can use someone else's textbook, why not their lectures? It might seem as if the lecture is where the professor adds value, but if free and great lectures exist, maybe you can use class time for other things. If the goal is

---

[6] "Introduction to Artificial Intelligence," accessed 28 April 2012, https://www.ai-class.com.

[7] For another approach to Mahler, listen to how different conductors played the klezmer sections of the first symphony on David Pickett's site: "David A. Pickett Ph.D.—Musician and Scholar," accessed 28 April 2012, http://www.fugato.com/pickett.

learning, we should consider that leading a great discussion section or creating a learning activity that applies what students learned in an online lecture is perhaps even more difficult and more effective than delivering content for fifty minutes.

Musical Resources

Getting students to listen to music is both harder and easier today. It is easier because there is more access to more recordings than ever before. Most music libraries now provide access to one or more music streaming services where students can listen to a vast library of music anywhere. There is also plenty of free music on the internet, and you should at least check to see what your students will find on popular sites. Spotify is a service that pays royalties from ads (with an ad-free premium service) and it is widely used by students; there is plenty of jazz and popular music here and quite a lot of mainstream eighteenth- and nineteenth-century classical music. www.classiccat.net has a similar common-practice collection, while Wikipedia:Sound/list has most of the music references in its articles. YouTube is full of older sound and film performances and there are also terrific archives of historic recordings. The University of California at Santa Barbara, for example, has put more than 8,000 digitized recordings from early cylinders online. It is free to download or stream and students can also hear a completely way of playing, something that might create an additional reason for closer listening from music majors.[8]

For an opera course, consider that the Library of Congress (as part of its National Jukebox project[9]) has created a digital facsimile of the entire Victrola Book of Opera from 1919[10]: the plots and production histories of 110 operas along with recordings of almost every number, not only by the great vocalists of the day (including Enrico Caruso, John McCormack, and Geraldine Farrar) but additional recordings by bands and soloists featured on Victor's lower priced labels. There are, for example, four recordings of "Questo o quella" from *Rigoletto* featuring Caruso and McCormack in addition to Giovanni Martelli and Leon Campagnola (who sings in French). This is the sort of resource that is so fun to use that it is easy to spend more time than you planned; exactly the sort of student motivation we want to encourage. And, it is free.

Despite all these advantages, getting today's students really to listen to music is also harder than before; we have all become accustomed to hearing music without

---

[8] "Cylinder Preservation and Digitization Project," accessed 28 April 2012, http://cylinders.library.ucsb.edu.

[9] "National Jukebox: Historical Recordings from the Library of Congress," accessed 28 April 2012, http://www.loc.gov/jukebox. The Library of Congress notes that "historical recordings may contain offensive or inappropriate language."

[10] "The Victrola Book of Opera," accessed 28 April 2012, http://www.loc.gov/jukebox/victor-book-of-the-opera/interactive.

musicians, in some cases while we are doing other things. Streaming services are convenient, but since they work on computers, they encourage students to do other things while the music plays in the background. The "listening rooms" in the library are mostly deserted, and students will largely listen to class assignments as they would the latest pop album: while communicating on Facebook. At least on the treadmill they are listening, so getting the music off the computer and into the phone or iPod is probably worth the effort. Students do not like to buy CDs and will mostly just share, but even if they listen to them as CDs, the only CD player they have today is in their laptop.

It may be useful to do some extended group listening in class. While film departments still insist on screening times (where everyone watches a movie together on a big screen instead of individually on their computers) music faculty have mostly not insisted on "listening sessions." Students will need to be taught how you want them to listen to music and, ironically, class time may now be the best way to have them practice focused listening. Consider giving your lectures as podcasts and doing more listening in class.

Using listening guides with visuals may help as well. iAnalyse, for example, is a music software program that can synchronize the pages of a score with audio or video files and makes it easy to add annotations on the score.[11] Scott Lipscomb at the University of Minnesota has also done an excellent guide on how to create your own listening guides.[12] If you want to create your own materials, there are plenty of tools, but starting at Merlot.org or with a Google search could save you time: someone else may already have created the assignment, tool, or software that you need.

There are over 125,000 public domain scores in the Petrucci Music Library as part of the collaborative International Music Score Library Project (IMSLP): the scores are largely pdfs contributed by users. It is much larger than most music libraries and contains everything you need for most music courses covering music before 1923. It is a massive archive with everything from facsimiles of manuscripts by minor composers to all forty-six volumes of the *Bach-Gesellschaft Ausgabe*.

Engaging the Web with Online Tools and Assignments

Your assessments should match your goals. It is important to understand that assessment is different from measurement or grades. Teaching and art are both full of evaluation, and you should use your judgment to assess student progress. Students remain very grade conscious, but giving students more control over grades and assignments is a strategy that improves learning and motivation.

---

[11]   "Pierre Couprie: logiciels," accessed 28 April 2012, http://logiciels.pierrecouprie. fr.

[12]   "Interactive Listening Guide Templates," accessed 28 April 2012, http://www. lipscomb.umn.edu/form_templates.htm.

Technology allows for much more feedback, many more assignments, and can help you rethink what is possible and useful in assessment.

The paradox is that since there is so much content online, student will begin most assignments by looking for the answers online. One way to use that impulse is to build it into the assignment. Have students describe the differences between two online biographies of Chopin, compare an authored site about Bach organ music with a wiki fan site, discover four errors in this analysis or find three listening guides for a Mozart sonata and evaluate which is best.

There are a tremendous variety of tools, guides, and apps for music and music analysis. You might ask students to identify some of these and compare their usefulness. Shmoop.com has detailed guides (also available as phone apps) for popular songs and Passagio is a phone app that provides visual feedback to improve intonation. Thankfully, the iPhone app Shazam does not work for classical music, but be aware that students can use this app to identify most jazz and pop music in a few seconds. Since your students will look for these tools, start with a quick search of the iTunes app store and merlot.org for online tools. The most important point is that there are now many more types of assignments you can give and more options for when you give them. Two of my favorites are using online source material for guided undergraduate research and online writing.

Source Material

In addition to basic information and teaching materials, the internet has radically changed faculty and student access to source material. Now that the Beethoven sketchbooks and manuscripts are online (at the Digital Beethoven House in English, German and Japanese, www.beethoven-haus-bonn.de) is there some new way you can teach Beethoven? UCLA hosts a large online collection of sheet music and popular music scores including the digital sheet music consortium from five major libraries.[13] The European Library website allows searches of the major libraries across Europe and includes scores and manuscripts.[14] The Library of Congress, the British Library, and the Smithsonian all have large projects to digitize holdings of source materials for scholars.

We know that another characteristic of great teachers is that they invite students into the scholarship of the discipline immediately.[15] Demonstrating that music history changes, and that scholars disagree, motivates students to disagree with other students and even faculty. Asking students to debate different approaches and interpretations can be a critical way to teach how to approach all information.

---

[13] "Music Scores and Sheet Music Online," accessed 28 April 2012, http://www.library.ucla.edu/libraries/music/12291.cfm.

[14] "The European Library," accessed 28 April 2012, http://www.theeuropeanlibrary.org/musicscore_en.html.

[15] Bain, *What the Best College Teachers Do*, 101.

The new availability of source material makes it that much easier for students to investigate a controversy or do an error regression. One of the great problems of the web (and also of scholarship) is the repetition of errors. If an encyclopedia misprints a date of birth, most later sources will simply replicate the mistake; it takes some serious cynicism to request a birth certificate for a well-known historical figure. If you can find an error about your field on a popular website, the chances are this error is repeated on hundreds of other sites. See if students can discover the source of this error and correct it. You can hardly stop students from using the web, but teaching them how to use the web critically is a good learning goal.

It is work for students to transcribe from a manuscript facsimile, but there is also much to be gained. Comparing differences in drafts leads to substantial questions and creates a sense of urgency. Music performance majors often think music history is simply an irrelevant distraction from the practice room. They need an entry point that relates to performance and a problem that will force them to negotiate some practical history. For example, provide students with two different manuscript versions of a flute part from a Bach cantata and ask them if the differences represent mistakes or have some other explanation.[16] By providing information on the performance conditions, locations, dates, and the pitch of the organs (the standardization of the note "A" as 440 hz did not occur until the twentieth century), students themselves have to figure out which information is important and which questions to ask.[17] Creating assignments that end with "how will you play the piece now?" are more motivating for performance majors.

Online Writing

As musicologists, we want our students to write. Technology can provide ways for your students to write more without requiring you to grade more. Students will spend even more time on their writing if they know it is going to be read by their peers and not just by faculty. Technology offers several ways to accomplish this. First, it is now very easy to share student writing either by email or with Dropbox, or another cloud depository. (Most Learning Management Systems (LMSs) have this feature as well.) Simply assign a few students to write an introduction or response to a class topic and circulate it before class. Second, while blogging and other online writing may seem like a different type of writing, it is still useful, and more and more writing will occur this way in the future. A monitored discussion board (on an LMS or on Facebook) provides both more writing practice and a way to get students to think more deeply about material. Third, Calibrated Peer Review (CPR) is a website that allows students to enter essays, grade sample essays (where

---

[16]   You can find manuscripts, parts and prints used in Bach performances at "Bach Digital," accessed 28 April 2012, www.bach-digital.de.

[17]   I am grateful to Joshua Rifkin who created the original version of this assignment.

they are "calibrated" as graders), and then grade each other's writing.[18] You can simultaneously improve students writing and reduce your grading. The popular LMS Blackboard also includes a Self and Peer Assignment tool. Students submit essays, videos, compositions, or any sort of work, and other students are randomly assigned to critique.

A good rubric will improve learning as students can see before they complete an assignment what will make it better. Telling students they need a thesis and that it is worth twenty points will not help your students, but showing them the criteria and examples for a poor, fair, good, and great thesis will give them goals.[19] iRubric provides an easy way to create and use rubrics in grading.[20] They can be saved online or printed and used by your TAs. With a few clicks, iRubric will add up the total score and either display it or drop it into a gradebook: it will improve the speed, fairness, and usefulness of your grading. Combining a rubric with peer-assessment allows you to create a unique cloud-sourced grading assignment, where students can, for example, examine the other essays in class and determine the standard of thesis in each. A good rubric involves work to set up, but combining these new technologies with best practice pedagogies will save you vast amounts of time and improve students' feedback in the long run.[21]

Online Exams

We know that more feedback and lower stakes assessment improve students' learning. One way to accomplish both and also ensure that you have prepared students is to give them an exam before every class. Most LMSs have an exam function, often with multiple types of questions and automatic entry into the gradebook. This can accomplish several things at once.

First, it tells you what students understood and what needs further clarification. If you make the exams due online an hour or two before class, your LMS will give you an instant snapshot of how well your class did on each question. Knowing what percentage of students got every question correct before class tells you which concepts were easier or harder for students, and class can now be adapted to cover what is most difficult for students.

---

[18] "CPR – Calibrated Peer Review," accessed 28 April 2012, http://cpr.molsci.ucla.edu.

[19] You can find some basic forms and a rubric that can used to guide peer review feedback at the Writing Center at the University of Washington ("Peer Review," accessed 28 April 2012, http://depts.washington.edu/pswrite/peerrev.html). Using peer review will reduce your workload and both the process of evaluating and being evaluated improves student writing.

[20] "RCampus," accessed 28 April 2012, www.rcampus.com.

[21] See www.teachingnaked.com for more discussion of internet assignments.

Second, even multiple-choice questions allow you to support more critical thinking. Try questions in the form: "all of the statements below are true, but which would you use to support (or rebut) argument X?" This helps students think like historians. Blackboard and most LMSs support this ability to ask complicated multiple-choice questions with multiple answers and instant professor feedback.

Third, so much additional testing provides more structure and actually reduces the emphasis on grades. Five questions before every class will provide over 200 opportunities for students to practice critical thinking that can then be analyzed in class. At 20 percent of the final grade (and with partial credit allowed and five statements for each question) that makes every wrong answer worth 0.02 percent of the final grade. Try a policy that every question can be argued in class, but that no grades will be changed this year. (You can consider refinements next year.) This is less work for you, and creates an environment where the nuances and details of historical inquiry matter for the debate but not for the grades.

Fourth, this is a totally scalable teaching solution. Blackboard automatically puts all of the grades into the gradebook and students can monitor their progress easily. Once the questions are written, you can test thousands of students with a few mouse clicks and reuse everything the following year.

Set your expectations before the first class by giving students an online syllabus quiz. Email your students the course syllabus or the website link in advance. By requiring a short syllabus quiz just before class, you send a message about standards, you know if students have read the syllabus, and you acclimatize them to the feel of online testing before class.[22] If you really want to scare them, also administer a short closed-book quiz on the syllabus in the first minute of class.

The most important reason for these quizzes, however, is that students are now prepared for class.

Games for Grades

Video and online games are another way to lower the stakes and give students more control. James Gee has demonstrated how games, while not intentionally designed as educational tools, in fact do everything we want a good learning environment to do. Good games are easy to learn, but not easy to play. They are challenging, complicated, and engaging. Games are a constant stream of problem solving, assessment, and feedback; they are basically sequences of increasingly harder tests. But the good games have also managed to be intrinsically motivating. They promote mastery and exploration before moving to the next level and they allow for performance before competence. In other words, you do not have to read

---

[22]   For the first quiz only, I allow eight hours of grace after class to finish the quiz. For the rest, it is important to take the quiz offline an hour or more before class. This gives you time to analyze the results and creates clear expectations.

the textbook before you get to play. Like the best learning, Gee says the best games are "pleasantly frustrating."[23]

Walvoord and Anderson have argued that teachers can use assessment to turn grade-oriented students into learning-oriented students.[24] Like many musicologists, I used to give "drop the needle" exams in class. Then I created practice "click on the file" exams (using Blackboard) that students could take online. Eventually, I decided that once students had mastered the practice exams with over 100 randomized music clips, in-class tests were redundant. Students preferred the repetition of the online format, but there was little motivation beyond the grade. A gaming format, which replaced the grades with levels, greatly increased student time on task.

For example, one music game is basically a multiple-choice exam with a game interface, with the game "level" converting to a grade in the LMS. It is worth 10 percent of the final grade and students get a conversation of levels and grades as the semester progresses: in the fourth week of the semester, you should be on level three; to get an "A" on this assignment, you need to get to level nine by the end of the semester, and so forth. As a game it encourages mastery, although students can return to a lower level if they need the practice, so it gives students control.[25]

Most campuses have some sort of technical support for teaching, and that often includes courses designers and technical folks who can build simple games. Do a Google or Merlot search first to see if someone has already created the game you imagine. But if you have a new idea, start with a grading rubric: a table of both what students will learn and the standards of achievement that will convert to levels or grades. Take this idea to your campus teaching center where there are often designers with experience turning creative ideas into games.[26]

Engaging Students with Social Media

The plethora of communication streams and the constant need for contact provide music faculty with both opportunities and headaches. You will need to manage expectations carefully.

To start, your syllabus will need a communication strategy. Students are more likely to email you and less likely to come to office hours. Instead of physical office hours, students want to know (a) when you are available, (b) what channels of

---

[23]   James P. Gee, *What Video Games Have to Teach Us About Learning and Literacy* (New York: Palgrave Macmillan, 2003), 217.

[24]   Barbara Walvoord and Virginia Johnson Anderson, *Effective Grading*, 2nd ed. (San Francisco: Jossey-Bass, 1998).

[25]   *Jazz-By Ear* and *Jazz Bandstand* are both available for free at merlot.org and teachingnaked.com. Both can be freely adapted to other types of music.

[26]   For more on how to create educational games or online assignments, see José Antonio Bowen, *Teaching Naked* (Jossey-Bass, San Francisco, 2012).

communication work best, and (c) how long it will take you to respond. Use more channels if you want to reach more students, but even if you only do email and Skype, set clear expectations.[27] Here are some sample communication strategies to put on your syllabus:

- Email: I will respond to all email within 24 hours. If you email me before 9 p.m. at night, I will probably reply the same day. Do not expect a response between 9 p.m. and 9 a.m.
- I am not technical support for Blackboard (or whatever LMS). Contact our help desk at XXX.
- I am available for learning support from 1-2, MWF. During these times I will be on Skype (username) and on Facebook chat. If my Skype line is busy or your question is simple, send me a chat and I will let you know if there is a queue to Skype me.
- On MW, I will also be physically in my office.

Multiple communication styles will be especially helpful for students who live off campus or are intimidated by the halls of power. Skype allows user to share screens or files, so it is a terrific and easy way to edit a paper. Giving students multiple channels will most help the least experienced and supported students.

Note that poor students are less likely to have broadband or even a computer at home, so their phone is often the device they use for internet access. Clarity about communication strategies early will also allow students time to find you in cyberspace. Facebook, Twitter, and Skype are all free and work on phones, so most students will have access.

Another advantage of new communication technology is that it is immediate. Since teaching is about connections, this is an opportunity to connect. Sending tweets or texts or posting on Facebook is generally a way to communicate more quickly with your students. These posts have to be short, but these channels are a good way to send time-sensitive announcements or to demonstrate relevance. If you want students to analyze the Harry Potter theme music or notice how Super Bowl commercials use music, tweet or text them on Saturday night as they wait in line, or on Sunday before the game starts. If there is a story in the newspaper that relates to your class, send them a link with a brief comment. If they are struggling with the reading, send them encouragement and a new idea about how to approach the material. Demonstrating relevance improves motivation and learning, and instant messages are a great way to accomplish this.

Be clear that different channels are used for different things. Announcements in class are a waste of precious and expensive time: post all announcements on a website or LMS, and send them as email. Email is also a great way to introduce readings: the point of the reading is usually much clearer to faculty then to students. Sending your introduction to the topic, or reading ahead of time and providing

---

[27]   Skype is a free video conferencing program available at www.skype.com.

study questions, will have an immediate and dramatic effect on the quality of student learning and preparation for your class. (If you would rather talk, then make a podcast or send a voice message.) Do not send too much email, especially if you like long and complicated emails! If you send an email twice a week it will get read.

You do not need a Facebook account or to "friend" your students. Be aware that 80 percent of freshmen in 2011 sent a friend request to your admissions officer, but creating a Facebook group for your class may be a little creepy if you do not keep your personal information hidden.[28] When you create a profile in Facebook, it is useful to restrict most of your personal life to those you want to see it; then you can simply accept student Facebook requests and not worry. If you are new to Facebook or do not have an account, start instead in Google+ and ask students to join your class group there.[29]

Naked Classrooms: Getting Students to Class

With all this content online, why would students come to class? The only answer I can see is because you will offer something they cannot get online. While this might be inspirational lectures, in the future it is more likely to be activities and interactive learning. Providing content online, posting announcements on your course website, LMS, or Facebook, introducing the reading through email, creating shared writing assignments between classes, and doing online exams before every class will improve learning, but it will also free class time for naked face-to-face un-technological interaction. This might be discussions, debates, in-class writing, or any number of other ideas discussed in Chapter 2. Setting up technology for your course is a lot of work, but it does create time for faculty and student interaction. You can still do active learning in a large class, but consider the physical space and ask if you can break up the class into smaller rooms.

Technology can radically alter your students' access to source material, and their ability to practice and take risks, but it is not going to replace the need or importance of class time with students. It does, however, drastically change their and your ability to prepare for class. As class time grows proportionally more expensive than other forms of learning environments, it will be critical that faculty understand how to use this increased preparation and precious face time.

Consider how your expectations for an efficient meeting have changed. This may be hard for younger faculty to realize, but in the days before email and

---

[28] Rebecca Ruiz, "Twitter: The New Rules of Engagement," *New York Times* (Jan. 9, 2011), Lifestyle, 4. For extended introduction to Facebook privacy and student ecommunication strategy, see Bowen, *Teaching Naked*.

[29] It is impossible to predict how popular Google+ will become, but it is likely to be around for a while and it is free. Google+ will automatically sort your contacts into "circles."

even copy machines, meetings (and classrooms) were largely about the transfer of information. Meetings, classrooms, and even religious services were full of "announcements" about new policies, future events, and changes of schedules. Today, all of this information can be shared electronically in advance and we are increasingly frustrated by situations that do not give us the chance to participate. The point of a meeting is to discuss. Our students feel this even more acutely.

Asking students to prepare for class will meet with some resistance: we often lecture because students are unprepared and we at least want them to know something. Music schools are full of performers and there is often a premium placed on practice time. For a student who never reads and only does the minimum work needed to get by, raising standards will increase their work load. Giving them mobile options, for example, will increase their ability to access material, but they will actually listen more on their phone then if you leave CDs in the library. Most students will (with practice and time) accept that your use of existing video lectures or brief tweets, combined with rigorous debates, discussion, or activities in class is a more effective and efficient way to learn. Instead of spending hours and hours being hopelessly lost trying to do an analysis, they can watch the twenty-minute video while they eat and then do the analysis in class with you. It will not always be that simple, but if you are scrupulously efficient with students' time out of class, and stimulating in class, they will spend more time on task and learn more.

Managing Technology

First, don't try all of this at once. It takes time to develop new ways of teaching and new units of content. Rather than try to create the ultimate podcast about Josquin, just make something and see what happens. The technology makes it easy to edit and improve next year. Making podcasts for an entire course is a huge task: try replacing one lecture per unit or per week. (Also note that there are grants at most universities and states for creating new online materials.)

Second, do not overhaul everything every semester. It is easy to assume that a new pedagogy is failing when it is really user error. (Think about all of those times you were sure your computer was broken only to have a small child fix the problem with a single click.) User error is a common problem in teaching and since it is hard to do a controlled study (teaching the same course to the same students using two different methods) it is hard to know if it was the idea of the podcast that failed or if it was just a bad podcast. This is true for pedagogy, technology, or jokes too; if they don't laugh, maybe rework the delivery and try again next year. If they don't laugh after three years, it is time for new jokes.

The corollary to both of these is that lots of small trials reduce the pressure. Do not start by giving your final exam online—first make sure that you, your students, and your LMS can handle some quizzes. Next year you can add the final exam. If you are going to do a peer-writing project, make it two smaller projects in the same semester so that if it fails the first time, you can eliminate the grade and just count the second one.

Students will love having new technology to use, but they will hate being forced to prepare for class. When they say "I don't like podcasts," consider multiple possibilities. Many students like lectures because they are easy: students can show up unprepared and hungover and still feel like they are accomplishing something. Being accountable to do something before every class will be a shock for many students. Implementing required preparation for class is often best done as an entire department or for an entire series of classes. Student evaluations may still fall initially, but they will recover as both you and the students become more comfortable.

Students are increasingly bringing their cell phones, laptops, and tablets into the classroom and faculty need a policy. First recognize that there is little difference among these devices: students can look up data or send messages on any of them. Some universities have invested in switches to turn off the WiFi for exams, but unless you also have a cellular jammer, this is useless.

There are ways to try to minimize the use of Facebook in class. Some schools simply block Facebook, but again, students just use their phones instead. If it is a large class, you can place a TA in the back of the room to monitor what student screens are doing or place students in alternate rows so that you can walk in between them and look at what they are doing periodically. These all seem punitive and ineffective.

Instead, try the phrase "please close your laptops." Students will, of course, complain that they want to take notes. The easiest way to avoid this problem is to give them the content out of the classroom and activities to do inside the classroom. Another strategy is to provide hard copy lecture notes in advance and ban the laptops. I find it most useful also to use the laptops for interactive web activities: "Open your laptops (or use your phone) and find out how many symphonies Bruckner wrote." Students will be more engaged, but they are also learning multiple skills. Students will inevitably use different search strategies and find different information: demonstrating to students that you understand that the internet is full of information will also open the door for you to teach how to search, how to analyze what you have found, and most importantly, that the most significant part comes when you find the information and then say "please close your laptops" again.

Note also that everything you say in class can instantly be checked against the knowledge of the internet. Speakers in many industries are now quite nervous about the facts they deliver, as audiences can now Google and tweet your mistakes or corrections in real time. Wouldn't it be great if our students cared that much? So maybe you can harness this habit and also this power and ask your students to keep you honest: at least this way they will be tweeting about your class.

Sequence

The part of course design that most faculty understand is sequence; when we create a syllabus, we create a series of topics or units. Technology not only allows for new types of assignments, it also allows for the time-shifting of almost any learning activity. Students can access material, do assignments, or take exams at any time. Faculty too can now monitor what students are reading, doing, or understanding without having to see them. All of this expands possibilities and increases the importance of sequence.

Once you have assembled your new digital resources, content, learning activities, and assessments, you need to integrate your course structure with a strategy. For each unit, think about what students will do both in class and in between classes. Are there activities we used to be able to do only in class (debates or games, for example) that can now be done at home? Perhaps some of the mundane things that we do out of habit (like announcements and passing out handouts) can now be done online to create more time in class for more important things.

Think, for example, about when you want questions. For centuries, lectures have concluded with a call for oral questions and verbal jousting that has been a staple of the academic experience. Technology provides opportunities, however, to increase participation, and while it is most often used to speed up responses (as in the discussion of clickers above), it can also allow for slower contemplation and even the integration of units. Ask students to post a question between classes or units. Or you might ask them to respond to your question: What might you expect composers after Beethoven to do? Did our Stravinsky activity make you reconsider anything we learned about Mozart? Like a good game, your course should also increase in complexity and difficulty as the semester progresses. How do early theories get applied to later content? How are theoretical skills integrated with performance? Use technology to help students integrate and think more slowly.

Technology has created many more options for what students can do first. Is a class session the best introduction or is there a reading, video, or exercise that might better prepare students for significant learning? The traditional classroom is often a place of unprepared students having first contact with the material. Students then go home to "learn" the material and then return for assessment. Technology allows for an "inverted classroom" where students can first encounter the material at home and even be tested on that encounter before they come to class for deeper learning.[30] Students, for example, could do the reading or watch a video of your lecture at home and then do the listening, score analysis, or even the writing in class with the professor circulating to help as needed.

Think finally about variety and the importance of experimenting. Students need time to get used to new technology and new assignments, and they will often

---

[30]   Maureen J. Lage and Glenn Platt, "The Internet and the Inverted Classroom," *Journal of Economic Education* 31, no. 11 (Winter 2000): 11.

be more comfortable and do better the second time they try a peer-assessment, in-class discussion or online exam. But you also want to vary the types of learning activities, which will also give learners with different styles the chance to shine. For each unit, perhaps, try just one inversion and send out a podcast and then do either the writing or listening in class. They won't all like any one experiment, but someone new may blossom.

Since technology is likely to be the most obvious place where you know less than your students, your attitude about technology matters. Much of teaching will always be about personal modeling. If you want your students to be lifelong learners, but you claim you cannot deal with new technology, they will see your other proscriptions as hollow, or at worst, hypocritical. If you want to encourage your students to try new types of music, to experience new ways of thinking, and to struggle, stretch, and sometimes fail with new material, then you too need to experiment and struggle. Demonstrate to your students that the frustration and embarrassment of learning new things is still worth it. Watching how you deal with failure may be the most powerful life lesson you can deliver as a teacher.

Chapter 7
Evaluation and Assessment

Elizabeth A. Wells

Whether we like it or not, evaluation is a regular and relentless part of academic life. Although most instructors would probably list "grading" as one of their least favorite professional activities, the timely and effective assessment of students' work is one of the most potent ways we have of guiding our students' research and learning. It is also the area in which we spend a good deal of our teaching time, and in a context of increasing class sizes and pressure to provide accountability in undergraduate education, this is not likely to change. Since degrees are considered certification of expertise in the areas in which they are conferred, universities understandably need to ensure that students have learned something before graduation. Although exams and tests are a standard and traditional method of evaluation, they are being challenged by more inclusive and diverse methods.[1] This chapter will address different kinds of course assignments and testing, how to approach evaluation as a formative tool, and how to communicate to students how and why they are evaluated in both conventional and non-conventional ways.

Although evaluation presents difficulties to all graders, music history involves special challenges. What makes grading so difficult in this and other humanities is the degree to which subjectivity intersects with objectivity. Unlike mathematics

---

[1]   Within educational research and discourse, the difference between assessment and evaluation is an important one. Indeed, an entire scholarly journal entitled *Assessment & Evaluation in Higher Education* is devoted to just this topic and the distinctions made between these terms. Assessment focuses on process, using feedback to help students learn better and to provide the instructor with important information on his or her teaching methods and instruments. Alternatively, it describes measurements to help university administrators and curricular designers make policy decisions. Evaluation refers to the assigning of a grade or other marker that indicates to the instructor and the student the success with which the student has mastered course material or carried out an assignment (and evaluation is product of methods of assessment for higher education practitioners and administrators). Therefore, assessment is more formative and evaluation is more summative. As an instructor, particularly at the post-secondary level, the majority of preparatory assignments, including those that ask students to submit early drafts of outlines of a paper, are more clearly linked to assessment than to evaluation, the final grade that is given to the paper. For a summary of how evaluation and assessment methods are perceived by and affect student learning, see Katrien Struyven, Filip Dochy, and Steven Janssons, "Students' Perceptions about Evaluation and Assessment in Higher Education: A Review," *Assessment & Evaluation in Higher Education* 30, no. 4 (2005): 331-47.

or even music theory, the one "right answer" is often elusive in a field where so many interesting and valid perspectives are embraced and discussed in an endlessly varied discourse on a wide variety of musics. Although the multiple-choice test or identification question on an exam might provide the most simple grading experience for the music historian, those methods of assessment are probably the least employed in our field. Instead, essays, papers, and presentations often form the basis for evaluation in music history coursework, and as such many factors play into the evaluative scheme: evidence of effective research, originality of ideas, thesis and topic development, essay structure and writing, or presentation style. Even if hard and fast rules are in place to assess each of these components, the discipline of music history and musicology is still a much broader and more inclusive one than many others, making evaluation and assessment even more challenging. What works or composers are most appropriate or viable as research topics? What is a strong idea about music? Do we want students to argue a thesis, or do we want them to discuss a variety of perspectives and ideas? What are the best ways to present musical material and what are the best modes of musical analysis? What do we want students to take away from an essay assignment or a presentation?

In setting assignments, instructors should always think about what it is that students are expected to learn—not just about music history, but about writing, research, recall, and critical thinking. Frequent testing of factual information (through quizzes, pop quizzes, or listening tests) keeps students abreast of important information, but needs to be supplemented by activities that promote deeper thinking and learning. A mid-term or final should combine both factual content and recall, but also application of factual information and an opportunity for students to formulate answers to larger questions posed by music history. Also, the level at which the course is offered should determine kinds of assessment activities. First-year students may fare better with more straightforward and factual testing (and indeed, many instructors may feel that a foundation of factual knowledge is a solid start to further music history study). A senior seminar on music history would seem to dictate that a large research paper would be an appropriate major assignment, with perhaps ancillary assignments that prepare the student for that paper (such as an annotated bibliography, outline, or draft version of the paper). Clearly, as students progress through music history coursework (whether as musicology majors who are interested in higher level research or as students who may take one music history course in addition to a basic survey) there should be a move from straight factual recall to true application of knowledge and skills.

The Syllabus: the Scaffold of Assessment and Evaluation

Although it may seem obvious, showing the grade breakdown of a course on an official syllabus is important enough that it is often mandated by university policy. Students report that they consult the syllabus most frequently not for the often voluminous information we provide, but simply to check the breakdown of the grade. As students often determine the amount of time they will spend on a task according to the number of points it may earn, then it is important that specific assessment activities and how they are weighted reflect the gravitas the instructor wishes to assign such activities. In general, the more points the assignment is worth, the more time and energy students will devote to it. Therefore, in a senior seminar class in which a large paper may be one of the most important products, it would behoove the instructor to make that paper worth anywhere from 25 percent to 50 percent of the grade. In a large survey course in which multiple-choice testing is the main method of assessment, with a few short papers, then possibly 30-40 percent of the course should be devoted to testing whereas short papers may be worth 10-15 percent each of the final grade. If a mid-term written in a fifty-minute course slot is worth 15 percent, then a final exam that is written in three hours should be worth more points. Many novice instructors assign too many assignments that are individually not worth many points, thereby tiring students with constant work that seems, to them, not commensurate with the number of points earned. In general, for an assignment to be meaningful, it should be worth at least 5 percent of the grade. Here is a typical breakdown for three different styles of course (there could be an infinite number of possibilities—these are guidelines only):

Introductory Survey, large class size, 70-100 students

Multiple-choice quizzes, biweekly	30% (6 at 5 points each)
Two short papers testing different skills	30% (2 at 15 points each)
Mid-term, in class	15%
Final in examination period	20%
Attendance, participation	5%

Special Topics Course, 2nd or 3rd year level, 20-30 students

Short analysis paper (5 pages)	15%
Mid-term, in class	15%
Final, in examination period	20%
Topic and Bibliography	15%
Research Paper (10 pages)	25%
Attendance, Participation	10%

Senior Research Seminar, 8-12 students

Shorter Paper	15%
Presentation	25%
Topic and Bibliography/Outline	20%
Major Paper	30%
Attendance and Participation	10%

In each case, the weighting of the assignments reflects the style of the class. An introductory survey will probably involve little in-class participation, but the emphasis here is on keeping up with weekly work in a routine and rigorous manner. The special topics course emphasizes writing and preparation for a larger paper, but includes a somewhat higher expectation in terms of class participation and the structure of having a mid-term and final. The senior seminar focuses on the larger research paper and steps leading toward it; the shorter paper is more of a warm-up exercise, or takes another direction than the large research paper. Here a major presentation (either on the work in progress or another, substantial topic) asks the student to prepare and present at a higher level, and participation in the seminar is also weighed heavily. Here the instructor is preparing students for graduate work, which largely takes the form of seminars with little or no formal testing (although even doctoral courses may include take-home tests).

Frequency and Timing of Tests or Assignments

Class size, focus, or intent of the course, and type of course will all determine the methods and frequency of assessment activities. As well, an instructor's workload needs to be carefully considered when designing evaluation methods across that individual's courses. A research institution with a two-plus-two teaching load which includes graduate courses is very different from an undergraduate college with a four-plus-four course load, no teaching assistants, and large course enrollments. A course of eight students may seem luxurious if one's other class numbers fifteen. Not so if one's other class numbers 200 and is in addition to two other concurrent courses. For large survey courses or courses for non-majors, instructors are often faced with a large number of relative newcomers to music history and a dearth of resources in the form of teaching assistants or student graders. In this case, assessment may be reduced to a series of multiple-choice tests that can be scanned easily and quickly by machine or through online quizzes, and one or two short papers (three to four pages). The multiple-choice testing will usually focus on the facts of music history: names, dates, places, titles of pieces, and so forth, and may include a listening identification. The short paper is usually focused on a very specific and narrow topic that all students address, or is cast widely and asks for a more discursive discussion of one of the larger questions raised by the course. Indeed, some instructors are reduced to this kind of evaluation when facing classes numbering in the hundreds of students, and they should not feel guilty about the number or length of assignments. Getting graded student work back to students in a reasonable time frame should dictate the assessment methods and frequency. Students cannot learn unless they receive feedback.

For class sizes numbering 30-100, a combination of a mid-term or final and a series of writing activities (a short paper, and perhaps a longer research paper) is common, and if the instructor can access grading support, is certainly viable. The advent of educational technology has helped in this regard, whereby weekly or fortnightly online quizzes can reinforce factual learning and leave the instructor's time to devote to commenting on writing assignments and essays on tests. For classes between a handful and thirty students, most instructors have the greatest amount of leeway. Here, a series of online quizzes (weekly if desired, or less frequently) can be supplemented by one or two mid-term tests, a final examination, and writing assignments (either several small or fewer large).

The Examination or Written Test

Written testing provides among the fastest, most intense, and detailed evidence that students have understood, internalized, and mastered course material. A well-designed exam tests both absorption of factual information and a student's ability to synthesize and express ideas on what he or she has learned. If students are well prepared, an exam can be exciting, challenging, and rewarding, like a demanding game. One often learns something while writing the exam because the process forces the student to recall and reflect on what he or she knows in a concentrated and creative way. A student should leave the exam room feeling relieved, but also validated. Of course, for many students, exams engender more negative feelings, but with careful preparation and support, students can approach exams with a positive mindset.

Examinations in the humanities are structured carefully to allow students to demonstrate their knowledge in a logical sequence. Almost every exam follows this general format (some types may have seven or more sections):

1. Identification/Definition/Matching/Multiple Choice
2. Short essay
3. Longer essay

Section 1 gets the student "warmed up" for the rest of the exam. It elicits facts, names, dates, terminology, and concepts that students may call upon in their essays. This "nuts and bolts" section ascertains whether or not students have read the assignments, understood terminology, and remembered pertinent details of the course. In music, Section 1 usually includes score identifications or audio identifications, which determine how carefully students have studied scores or listened to assigned pieces. Section 2 expands the testing scope, asking students to combine some of the facts they may have provided in Section 1 or to discuss aspects of the reading or lecture material in a succinct and descriptive fashion. Section 3 tests the ability, after spending some time disclosing facts, to provide a synthesis or analysis of the course content. Essay questions are often broad and allow students to focus on selected aspects of a topic for a thoughtful discussion. The long essay is invariably the heaviest weighted part of the exam, the hardest graded, and the most challenging for the student. It determines if the examinee knows what the course is about, and how well that understanding can be communicated in writing.

Graders naturally want students to provide information, but to do so in specific ways which are suggested by the exam format. In the same way that the overall structure of the course and the grade breakdown should reflect the amount of time and energy that students should apply to various course components, so the breakdown of the grades in an examination should focus the students' attention on time management within the exam itself. The multiple-choice or short answer questions should probably take up no more than 25-30 percent of the exam, listening may well take up another 25 percent, and the longer essay should be worth at least 25 but up to 50 percent of the exam. Make sure that the breakdown of grade within each section is made clear, that is, 25 x 1 point = 25 points. It is also helpful to the student to have a breakdown of the essay grade (i.e. 25 points factual information, 15 points concepts and ideas, 10 points style and structure = 50 points). Some examiners will even suggest the amount of time the examinee should spend on each section of the exam.

Section 1: Testing of Factual Information

This is the easiest place for students to pick up points fast.

A. Multiple Choice and Matching

The first instinct in testing is usually correct. Students should be aware that going back to change an answer may be the result of second-guessing rather than the result of mature reflection. The factual information (correctly spelled names, dates, and titles) provided in multiple-choice questions can be used to fuel the other parts of the exam—the short answer and longer essay. Multiple-choice questions are usually worth only one or two points in an overall exam structure. Although many instructors in the humanities abhor the multiple-choice question as too trivial and not conducive to deep, critical thought, there are ways in which multiple-choice questions can be designed that allow them to move up from simple knowledge or comprehension to application and analysis.[2] Take this typical multiple-choice question:

> In what year(s) did Beethoven compose his *Eroica* Symphony?
> 1. 1800-1801
> 2. 1804-1805
> 3. 1810-11
> 4. 1816-17

---

[2]   For more on multiple choice testing, see David Battista, "Making the Most of Multiple Choice Testing: Getting Beyond Remembering," *Collected Essays on Learning and Teaching* 1 (2008): 119-122, and "The Immediate Feedback Assessment Technique: A learner-centred multiple choice response form," *Canadian Journal of Higher Education* 35 (2005): 111-131.

In this, most basic form, the question seems to test pure memorization, asking students to recall a date that was perhaps taught in class or assigned in reading. This question would fit into the lowest level of Bloom's taxonomy, *knowledge*. Although many instructors might argue that a serious student of music history should "just know" the dates of important or major works in the repertoire, others would shudder at what seems to be a baldly simple question that has no value outside the factual knowledge itself. The clever reader might notice that the dates chosen are not arbitrary; indeed, they ask the student to place the work into one of Beethoven's style periods, but this is not made clear in the question. To improve the pedagogical value of the question and bring it up to Bloom's *comprehension* level, one might make that underlying assumption more obvious, and ask it this way:

> In what year(s) did Beethoven compose his *Eroica* Symphony?
> 1. During the early years of his first style period
> 2. In his second style period
> 3. In his third style period
> 4. 1800-1801

Here, the answer 1800-1801 is a bit of a "distractor," asking the student to determine in what style period the dates 1800-1801 occur. However, the question is set on a higher level, asking students to place the (perhaps) memorized date into the larger context of a style period. The student has in effect applied the knowledge of the date of the piece to another context, the style periods. Although one might argue that it is "easier" to remember what style period produced the *Eroica*, one would probably at the same time argue that this is more important than knowing simply the date itself. However, the question and the possible answers can be improved further by asking the student to apply more comprehension and application to the information:

> What is significant about Beethoven's *Eroica* Symphony?
> 1. It was written in his first style period
> 2. It was written in 1810-11
> 3. It combines elements of Classical and Romantic style periods
> 4. It was his second symphony

Here the question is made more complex by asking students to determine which answers are wrong. They need to know the years of the first style period, they need to know that 1810-11 is neither the date of the piece nor in the first or third style periods, and they need to know that the *Eroica* was Beethoven's third symphony, and they need to know what characteristics define "Classical" as opposed to "Romantic" style. There is only one right answer here, but the other answers force the student to consider many other things he or she may know (or not know) about the piece.

Although this series of questions and answers shows how to ramp up or improve a multiple-choice question, the question could be redesigned completely to truly test application of knowledge.

> Which is the most significant aspect of the first movement of the *Eroica* Symphony?[3]
> 1. The seemingly premature entry of the French horn at the recapitulation
> 2. The C♯ in the opening melody
> 3. How it exemplifies the first style period of the composer
> 4. That it is in sonata form

In this question, the student already needs to know that the work is by Beethoven. The student also needs to know that first movements in sonata form are standard, and so this in itself is not overly significant or unusual for a symphony by this composer in this period. The third answer is clearly wrong, but does require the student to know something about the style periods and that the *Eroica* does not exemplify the first. A good knowledge of the analysis of the movement would dictate that although the horn entry is somewhat mysterious, interesting, and perhaps "Romantic," the C♯ is the most significant feature and leads to the most interesting events in the movement. A student who is trying to remember if it was Beethoven who wrote the *Eroica* would not stand a chance at answering this question correctly, and yet the answers given are not just distractors nor are they unimportant; they simply ask for the student to apply knowledge. Music historians may argue as to whether 1) or 2) is correct, but presumably they may already have indicated this in class discussion or lecture. If either would be considered valid, the instructor has the choice of allowing both answers to be counted as correct.

B. Short Answer and Definition

The purpose of most short answer or definition sections is to draw out basic information on a topic that can be treated in a succinct way. The student should be able to answer the "W5" questions:

> When? Time, date, year, era, point in someone's career
> Where? Country, city, milieu, intellectual circle
> What? Piece of music, literary work, theory, person, treatise, term, etc.
> Why? Use, influence, importance (to us or in its own context)
> Who? Writer, composer, artist, performer, inventor, audience

---

[3]   Do not let the seeming narrowness of the question and answers prevent you from asking a question like this. Presumably the instructor has already lectured upon or assigned readings that perhaps evaluate the significance of the C♯ in the opening measures as a means of effecting structural changes in the movement. Therefore, the student is asked to remember that discussion as well as discussions of other aspects. One can also allow two correct answers.

These questions can be applied to almost any definition in any field of study, and students can hardly go wrong if (in a 5 or 10 point definition) they have covered these questions. Suggest that students use point form (bullets) in this section unless there is a compelling reason to ask for full sentences. It makes the section easier to grade, and easier to see if the material has been covered. The instructions to these questions should clearly state that an example should be given, and that the student must always indicate what the importance of the term or definition is to music history. If they do not do this, take off marks. If they don't understand the importance of the topic, then they have not learned the material. Accordingly, design these identifications in such a way that there is something significant to say about them. In a survey of twentieth-century music, short definitions might be less well-known composers, easily definable trends, or important people. "Dadaism," "Harry Partch," and "Ballets Russes" might be good examples, depending on the scope and depth of the course.

C. Score I.D. or Sight Passage

Identification of musical or textual passages fall into two categories: recognition of something the student has studied or a "mystery" excerpt which has never been seen before. The former is easier if the student has studied, but often involves recalling secondary readings or lecture material related to the passage in question. The latter asks that students, based on knowledge of similar or related works, analyze, comment on, and usually make an attribution to an author, composer, or time period. The second category, of course, raises the question within Bloom's taxonomy. Both entail similar strategies. Here, the student can modify the "W5" to fit the situation. For instance, for a piece of literature or music, the following are helpful point of reference:

> When? Date of composition, publication or performance, perhaps including era in composer's or author's career
> Where? At what point in the work (i.e., which movement or part of movement), including what comes before or after, if relevant (i.e., "just after the false recapitulation")
> What? Genre, description of technical features, key, formal structure, harmonic language, cadences, voice leading, phrasing, articulation, instrumentation, orchestration, text setting, dynamics, extra-musical references (either musical "quotations" from other works or, in the case of programme music, to literature or other arts)
> Why? Significance, importance, or function of the passage
> Who? Composer, author, performer, including reception history and cultural context, if applicable. In an "instrumental literature" class, perhaps the performer(s) as well

To this one might add a "W6":

How? For music, this might include editorial issues, *musica ficta*, sources and manuscripts, performance practice questions, and perhaps interpretation.

When designing a listening or score identification, make sure that the excerpt allows the student to address all of these factors, to show what he or she knows about the piece. A good strategy for a sight passage is to give the students something quite similar to a genre or piece they have studied: instead of showing an excerpt from nineteenth-century Lieder, give the students an entirely new Lied by Schumann, Schubert, or Brahms, for instance, with a text translation. Ask the students to briefly analyze the style and structure of the poetry, then ask them to discuss how the composer has set the text. In this case, both a score and a recording (played twice, to get the best results) work together to help students to address the work. An attribution to a composer might be the ultimate question in the identification, and tests *application* of knowledge and *analysis*, the highest levels of Bloom's taxonomy.

For score identification of pieces studied (more exactly "score recognition") less time should be spent musing on the attribution and more on details specific to that piece and composer. More weight needs to be given here to the "reception history and cultural context" portion of "Why?" If you are asking students to identify a specific passage, make sure that there is plenty to say about it beyond simple recognition. Presenting to the examinee the opening measures of Berg's Violin Concerto, for instance, asks the students to focus on pitch content, the row, and the violinistic qualities of the row construction. Providing the section where the chorale melody appears tests different types of knowledge about the piece that might be more conceptual than factual. Both excerpts give the student something to write, whereas simply choosing any other part of the movement might test only the students' recall.

Section 2: Testing of Concepts and Ideas

Often called "Identification" or "Short Essay," these questions should more accurately be termed "Medium Answer." They usually involve either broad exploration of topics that you did not cover in depth or focused discussion on narrower topics. Here, the examiner asks the student to describe and explain theories, historical periods, processes, or generally "survey" a segment of information. Topics often include synthesis of different categories of study, so there is an emphasis on making connections. This is often the first "choice" opportunity in the examination process, and so students need to have enough options to demonstrate ability and knowledge in a variety of areas.

The focus here is still on clear presentation, not the nuance that should be employed in the longer essay. The danger of these questions lies in their generality; most could be answered in anywhere from two succinct paragraphs to several pages, depending on the depth desired. Many ask "what is a 10-point answer?" This is impossible to gauge, since grade distribution and allotment are different for each examiner. But five good points and five examples or details should be a minimum. Most questions involve combining different strands of the course: "Mozart's innovations in opera" or "Influence of social and political forces on nineteenth-century French secular music," or perhaps "Development of keyboard instruments, 1750-1850" might be good options. Alternatively, short essays test knowledge of material which was secondary to the core of the lectures and readings: "Hindemith" or "Zelenka" or perhaps "Women Musicians." These questions ask students to tease out more of the "middle ground" of the course, instead of the detailed factual information of the multiple-choice section or the broader strokes that are involved in the long essay.

Section 3: Testing of Synthesis and Coverage

The "long essay" is the most important section of any exam, and the opportunity for the examinee to shine. It would not be surprising to add one of the short essay questions here, as many things that can be dealt with in a shorter, more succinct fashion can also be elaborated upon in a long essay. Think about setting up questions that allow the student to think both deep and broad. Students should ideally be given a choice here, although occasionally one imposed essay question can help to focus students on what the instructor really wants them to learn. For instance, in the sight example discussed above, the student may be required to analyze the Lied text, and analyze the score. But, the essay question that follows might well continue this theme: "Discuss how the features of the Lied exemplify Romantic style characteristics, aesthetics, and culture." Such a linkage between sections makes the exam more organic, and asks the student to show everything they know about Lieder in a larger sense. Generally, when there is choice among essay questions, the instructor should provide questions that test different aspects of the course. "Describe changes in modes of production in the musical from 1950 to 1980" asks students to bring in a large number of possible works and issues, while an alternative choice of "Discuss the use of pastiche and parody in two works of Stephen Sondheim" covers the same time period but in a much more focused way.

At the graduate level, examinations are more rare, but a comprehensive exam in a Master's level or even at the end of the doctoral course can be useful in bringing together large amounts of information. Here the examiner might assign a large series of essay topics, of which the student chooses a certain number. Indeed, in doctoral comprehensives one is often given choice within each era of music history, as well as a field-style exam that focuses on the area in which the student intends to do their dissertation research.

Grading Examinations and Essays

Grading is never an exact science, and even with a breakdown of points within an essay question, there is plenty of room for subjectivity and flexibility. Although many instructors may grade in a more gestalt fashion, it is often helpful to show the students where points are lost and gained within an essay through the use of color coding. For example, three passes through an essay with different colored pens can mark the following: blue for quotidian issues such as spelling, grammar, sentence structure, and general prose and formatting issues; green for essay structure; and red for ideas and concepts. Quickly looking through the paper, the student can see which aspects have been commented upon the most, and a great number of questions or comments on conceptual content and ideas may indicate that either the instructor had a great deal of positive feedback or that this area was one that needed improvement. Color-coding also allows the instructor to make sure that he or she has commented on all aspects of the paper, not just getting bogged down in grammatical details or focusing entirely on the ideas and not the writing style. Although this method might prove a little more time-consuming, the result demonstrates more clearly to the student where improvement is necessary.

Alternative Methods of Assessment: Oral Examinations, Group Exams, Learning Portfolios

Although the written exam will probably be with us for some time, alternative ways of testing are gaining currency in an era in which universities are more responsive to students with different learning styles. An oral exam is an excellent way to prepare students for graduate coursework and comprehensive exams, and is quite viable for smaller class sizes. Typically, an instructor can assign a particular topic that the student comes to the examination having already prepared; the instructor can then ask questions of the student after the presentation of the answer. Then, the instructor can pose a series of shorter questions, and can play musical examples, asking the student to either identify an assigned piece or listen to a new piece and make an attribution of composer, genre, or period. One of the advantages for both student and teacher in this kind of examination is that the grading is done as the exam is in progress, so that one student could typically finish the exam in twenty minutes and be asked more probing questions than might be possible on a written exam. The instructor, through careful questioning, can also determine much better the depth of knowledge the examinee possesses. In a course of eight to fifteen students, then, the testing could be done in two to five hours. Given the proctoring of a written exam and the length of time it traditionally takes to grade, the oral exam does not have to require a great deal more time than a traditional written test. Also, the contact between student and teacher enhances the learning experience enormously.

In recent years, group examinations have started to gain some ground.[4] In this method, students are divided into groups to discuss the questions provided on the exam, then split apart to answer the questions individually in writing. Here, stronger students may help weaker students to think through answers, and the exam becomes more of a study session and discussion of course content than one of pure assessment. Although some students and instructors balk at this kind of open system, group examinations seem to cement knowledge more deeply in all the students through the preliminary discussion and (often) debate among them.

Another interesting development in assessment has been the use of the learning portfolio. In addition to or sometimes instead of completing the traditional essay or test assignments, the student gathers, over the course of the semester, reflections on and evidence of learning. This evidence can be anything from completed assignments that have been graded (with further reflection or feedback by the student), reflective journal entries, listening journals, essays on topics covered in the course, and peer and instructor feedback. The portfolio then becomes a further reflective work by the student on what he or she has learned, as well as providing evidence of that learning itself.

Preparing the Students: Using Rubrics and Providing Feedback

Instructors in a number of disciplines are seeing the benefit of making their marking schemes and criteria transparent and fair for students. Not only does this forestall perennial questions as to where students have lost or earned marks, it allows students to see what kind of work and how much work needs to go into particular assignments and how students can best succeed. The use of rubrics or marking guidelines, distributed to students well before assignments are due, is a proactive way in which instructors can communicate their expectations. Table 7.1 is a very detailed description of what is expected in a first-year intensive introductory course in music history for weekly listening log entries. In this case, each week students are given three to four works of different genres and style periods, collected under larger umbrellas such as "power and politics" or "ritual and myth." The rubric clearly shows what depth and breadth of information (as well as the quality of the source of such information) is required for each component of the grade, and that students need to comment on how all pieces in that week relate to the theme. Although creating a rubric at this level of detail is a time-consuming process, it certainly saves the instructor time in the evaluation of the work submitted. Typically, this kind of rubric should be distributed in the syllabus at the beginning of term, so that students know exactly what to expect from the instructor's perspective.

---

[4]   See D. R. Keyworth, "The Group Exam," *The Teaching Professor* 3, no. 8 (1989): 5, and A.D. Toppins, "Teaching by Testing: A Group Concensus Approach," *College Teaching* 37, no. 3 (1989): 96-99.

Table 7.1   Listening log rubric

When your listening logs are marked, check them against the listening journal rubric. If you have questions, feel free to contact the instructor.

There is no shame in aiming for a B or a C. Notice that the rubric is not geared as much toward what is *not* done for those marks as toward what *is*. A 'B' is a good mark, so if your focus is not musicology and you don't wish to devote the time to the course to obtain an 'A', there is no shame in that.

	A	B	C	D
Basic piece information	Includes basic information about dates, composer, scoring, performance listened to.	There is no good reason not to have an A in this section.		
Research	Demonstrates *concise* research *relevant to the piece.* At least two credible sources regarding composer history, social setting of piece, earliest performances, musical trends of the period. Research is perfectly intertwined into the explanations of the piece.	Demonstrates research from at least one *credible* source about the piece. Research is fairly clear and concise. Most research connects to the surrounding observations and information, however some appears stand-alone. Discussion of composer history, social setting of piece, earliest performances.	Demonstrates research, although not necessarily from an entirely credible source with known writers (i.e., Wikipedia, random websites). Research lacks some clarity and each morsel of research takes its own sentence or section without connecting to the surrounding information. Discusses composer history, social setting of piece, and early performances somewhat, however with ambiguity, error, or irrelevance.	Demonstrates vague research, perhaps 'off the cuff' or from skimming a bad source. Half or more of the research does not connect well to the piece or the rest of the paper. Research is cluttered and unnecessarily drawn-out. Discussion missing of several of the topics of composer, social setting, earliest performance, and musical trends of the period.

	A	B	C	D
Original Observations	The journal demonstrates at least three listenings and repeated listening to important sections of the work. The author comments on overall structure, musical timbres, harmonies, rhythms, potential programmatic aspects, words, and interpretation, while tying in these aspects to the research concerning the piece. The writer observes and discusses how the piece relates to others works of its period and genre.	Demonstrates at least two listenings, commenting on overall structure, musical timbres, harmonies, rhythms, potential programmatic aspects, words if present, interpretation of specific recording.	Demonstrates a good listening to the piece, where some notes have obviously been taken. Comments on some musical and extra-musical observations regarding the piece, although mostly obvious and apparent ones.	Demonstrates perhaps only one listening to the piece where the student did not pay close attention or take notes on the piece. The observations are vague and relate only to surface musical features. The observations offer little in terms of inference or critical thought and act as stand-alone observations with little relevance.
Relation to Week's Theme	In a small paragraph, the writer goes in depth into the week's theme and how it relates to the piece, touching also on how the composer's approach varies in comparison to other composers' approaches in the same week. The paragraph should also discuss subtleties in the music that relate to subtleties in the theme, if possible.	With approximately two sentences, the writer ties in the relevance of the particular piece to the theme for the week.	In one sentence, the writer makes a general connection between the piece and the theme.	In one sentence or part of a sentence, the writer vaguely connects the piece to the theme, relying heavily on the obvious and displaying no research or in-depth thought about the work.

	A	B	C	D
Language (proper musical)	Demonstrates musical and extra-musical language at an advanced university level. The log is introduced in a readable manner and flows well between sections. Paragraphs are in proper structure. There are no typos.	This is not a test of grammar or essay writing, however a good introduction with the basic piece information (see above) is best. It is most important to demonstrate musical language used in this and other university courses, used properly. The writing shows a balance of good vocabulary in all areas of the music (i.e., not just harmony, but also rhythm, timbre, acoustics, etc.).	There is a vague introduction preceding the bulk of the log. The language demonstrates high-school level music knowledge or only demonstrates university level knowledge in certain fields (i.e., a percussionist may have strong vocabulary pertaining to rhythm and tone, but not harmony or melody).	There is no clear structure to the log (i.e., a 'sewn-up point form'). The writing shows little or improper use of musical vocabulary, relying instead on the explanation of concepts through extra-musical terms or the outright avoidance of relevant observations.

Table 7.2 shows a simpler rubric as to how an essay is graded. The rubric serves not just as a justification for the grade awarded, but also reveals frequent errors or stumbling blocks for students: depth of musical analysis, the correct spelling of names, dates, and places—as well as the professional expectations of a formal written paper and its presentation. The essay rubric can easily be adapted to presentations. The rubric can often point students to idiosyncrasies of particular instructors, and this can also help to ensure student success and reduce instructor frustration. On a more global level, a description of what earns an "A" or a "D" in a course helps students from the very beginning to understand what instructors are looking for. Table 7.3 provides such a general guideline as to what constitutes excellent, good, or fair work in music history coursework. Talking through this material at the beginning of the course keeps instructor and students on the same page and allows students to consider aspects of the course that they have not considered before.

Table 7.2   Sample music history grading rubric

Grading Scheme: 1/3 of the grade for the paper will be allotted to factual detail, evidence of effective research, or analysis. 1/3 will be allotted to the ideas presented. 1/3 will be allotted to "presentation" which is primarily writing style, but also includes correct citation and bibliography styles, typos, and professionalism of presentation. A check mark below indicates that this element is adequate; a *lack* of check mark means this area is *missing or inadequate.*

Factual and Historical Content
1. Evidence of effective research
2. Correct spellings of names, places and pieces
3. Effective and correct analysis, poetic or musical
4. Adequate historical details
5. Adequate number of sources cited
6. Fulfills specifications of assignment

Ideas Presented
1. Ability to address existing scholarship
2. Originality of ideas presented
3. Maturity and nuance of ideas
4. Clearness of writing and expression of ideas

Presentation
1. Adequate citation of material
2. Correct citation style
3. Correct bibliographic format
4. Typos
5. Grammatical, sentence structure, paragraph structure, etc.
6. Professional formatting, printing, binding, etc.

Overall Grade
Commentary

Table 7.3   Guidelines for grades in music history courses

A-/A/A+

[A-, A, A+] This range indicates varying degrees of excellence.

[A+] is awarded to a student whose written work and class contributions are of an outstanding nature, well beyond expectations for an undergraduate. Written papers and other assignments are free of any typographical, grammatical, or factual errors, with proper bibliographic format and presentation. In-depth and extensive research supports mature critical thinking expressed in elegant prose with impeccable structure and argumentation. Exams and tests display mastery of the subject matter and show evidence of knowledge well beyond course requirements. All work is submitted in a timely manner and professionalism is always of the highest order. Major graduate programs in musicology will be trying to outbid each other to recruit this student.

[A] indicates outstanding course work and class contributions. Thoughtful, informed and appropriate contributions to class discussion display mastery of assigned reading and listening and an ability to synthesize larger concepts with historical and musical details. Written papers and other assignments are free of typographical, grammatical, and factual errors, with proper bibliographic format and presentation. Research both in quantity and quality are above average for this level, and essays demonstrate exceptional prose, structure, and thesis development. Research projects and assignments show substantial independent thought, planning, and creativity. Exams and tests display complete mastery of all assigned course material, and the student displays outstanding professionalism in the course. This student could feel confident writing a placement test in music history for a graduate program in music performance, education, and such like at a major institution.

[A-] indicates excellent work. Thoughtful, informed, and appropriate contributions to class discussions suggest excellent grasp of assigned reading and listening and a desire to learn and share knowledge. Written papers and other assignments have very few typographical, grammatical, and factual errors, with proper bibliographic format and presentation. Research quality, quantity, and the ability to develop and argue a strong thesis are excellent. Research projects and assignments show independent thought, planning, and creativity, and exams and tests show a broad and deep understanding of assigned course material and an ability to synthesize. The student's professionalism in the course is unquestionable. This student would feel confident taking courses in music history at a graduate level.

B-/B/B+

[B-, B, B+] This range indicates good performance in music history classes.

[B+] indicates a very well-prepared student. Contributions to class discussion are thoughtful, informed, and appropriate, focusing on important issues and questions drawn from assigned reading and listening. Written papers and other assignments are essentially free of typographical, grammatical, and factual errors, with proper bibliographic format and presentation. Research quality and quantity is consistent with expectations for this level, demonstrating the student's ability to undertake solid, independent research and presenting it in an engaging and clear manner. Tests and exams show very strong knowledge of assigned reading and listening and adequate preparation. Professionalism in class and individual work is unassailable.

[B] indicates that, in addition to mastery of assigned listening and reading, this student contributes to the class through engaged and informed class discussion. Written papers and other assignments are relatively free of typographical, grammatical, and factual errors, with proper bibliographic format and presentation. Research quality and quantity are appropriate for this level, and the student expresses sound and thoughtful ideas effectively in written prose. Tests and exams show mastery of course material and adequate preparation.

[B-] The student's work is above the minimum acceptable standard for this level. Class contributions may show some ill-preparedness or be too infrequent, but the student demonstrates completion of all assigned reading and listening. Research quality and quantity might be sparse, and essays and other written assignments might contain typographical, grammatical, or factual errors, but still show the ability to undertake independent work and present it effectively. Tests and exams show a good grasp of course material, and professionalism is appropriate for this level.

C-/C/C+

[C-, C, C+] Marks in this range are an indication that the work is of a minimum acceptable standard for a music student at this level. Any or all of the following areas need to be addressed: lapses in professionalism and class conduct, infrequent or unprepared contributions to class discussion; research quality and quantity inadequate for this level; written assignments contain typographical, grammatical, or factual errors, or are weakly structured or argued. Thesis development and the ability to conduct independent and responsible research at the university level needs work; exams and tests show adequate understanding of course material, but suggest that the course may be more challenging to this student and thus requires more study time; submitted work lacking in appropriate presentation. Overall, marks in this range indicate a minimum standard of performance.

D-/D/D+

[D-, D, D+] This range indicates that the work is below the minimum standard expected of a music student at this level, and does not allow the student to use the course as a prerequisite. A grade in this range might indicate a first-year student who entered with a weak background who is not "catching up," or a student at any level with sufficient background and ability, but unsatisfactory work habits. This grade reflects one or all of the following: lapses in professionalism and class conduct; unexcused absences from class or frequent tardiness; unprepared or inappropriate contributions to class discussion, insufficient research quality and quantity for this level; weak thesis development and argumentation; tests and exams show inadequate mastery of course material and/or ill-preparedness. A mark within the "D" range should be interpreted as a strong indication that a student is in serious danger of not completing the program successfully without major improvement.

Educational technology can be used profitably in music history assessment, especially to provide feedback to students. In most quiz modes of online course management systems (Blackboard, Moodle, and so forth) a multiple-choice question can provide feedback either immediately or after the quiz has closed to all students. For the multiple-choice question on Beethoven discussed above, each student can be given an individual feedback answer to correct or incorrect answers, as well as a general feedback to the entire question and answer set. For instance:

> Which is the most significant aspect of the first movement of the *Eroica* Symphony?
> 1. The seemingly premature entry of the French horn in the recapitulation
> 2. (Feedback if this question is chosen: This is not the most correct answer, but it is a good answer to this question. The horn entry is an important moment in the movement, to be sure, and raises questions as to how Beethoven conceives of the form of the piece and its narrative elements ...)
> 3. The C#
> 4. (Feedback: Correct! Indeed, the different directions that the movement takes harmonically begin with this unexpected note ...)
> 5. How it exemplifies the first style period of the composer
> 6. (Feedback: This answer is not correct. This symphony, written in 1804-1805, represents Beethoven's second style period, which is exemplified by these characteristics ...)
> 7. That it is in sonata form
> 8. (Feedback: Indeed, this movement is in sonata form, but remember that sonata form was the most common form for a symphony first movement during this historical era. However, it is important to remember that Beethoven stretched formal boundaries quite a bit in his work ...)

A general feedback that would go to all students might read: "This movement of the *Eroica* is being included on this test because it exemplifies many of the characteristics of Beethoven's style at this point in his composition career. Other important aspects of this movement and of Beethoven's symphonies in general include ..."

In this way, the teacher teaches the student, either by expanding on the correct answer or by contextualizing the wrong answer. These feedback answers can be quite lengthy and provide more opportunities for the student to learn. The beauty of this system is that once these feedback answers are entered into the quiz, they go to all students automatically and do not have to be repeated by the instructor. Essentially, a very good review or additional lecture on the *Eroica* can be possible from this simple feedback system alone. Technology should never be used just for the sake of using it; to be effective, educational technology must be wed to specific learning objectives and educational goals, as is the case in this example. It should never be used as a "quick fix" or to free the instructor from interacting with students; instead it should allow the instructor to focus in different and more personal ways with students.

Participation or Professionalism Grades

Most courses, with the exception of very large survey courses, allot some points to participation and attendance. Although some instructors feel that taking attendance is unnecessary or perhaps insulting to the (now adult) student, all instructors see the value of having students attend classes. The participation mark often serves as a kind of buffer in the grading scheme that allows instructors to reward students who are fully engaged and penalize those who never attend class. However, this subjective mark often haunts the instructor as a grade component that is ill-defined and often not explained clearly to students. The substitution of a "professionalism" grade for a "participation" grade allows instructors to reward (or not reward) students for a variety of class activities and behaviors that enhance the learning experience for all students.[5] Showing up on time for class, giving one's attention entirely to the class (and not to technology or social media), asking proactive questions, respecting the ideas of others, and handing in assignments on time and in a professional manner of presentation are all ways in which students can earn points. Asking questions that have just been asked, showing a lack of respect for instructor or classmates, and walking in half way through a class are all ways in which a student can lose professionalism points. Given the competitive nature of professional musical life, teaching students these important life skills and rewarding them accordingly produces professional, accountable, and mature graduates who have better job prospects and chance of success in the "real world," as well as improving the class dynamic. It also helps students to outgrow some attitudes and behaviors that were more appropriate to a high school environment than to the university one. Making professionalism grades a substantial portion of

---

[5] See this author, "Professionalism Marks," *Collected Essays in Learning and Teaching* 1 (2008): 115-118.

the course (up to 15 percent) gives a clear signal to students that the way in which they do their work is as important as the content of the work itself.

Learning Styles, Peer Evaluation, Learning Disabilities

For some time, educators at the elementary and secondary level have been aware of different learning styles among students. This awareness has come a little more slowly to university educators, but with increased interest in pedagogy at the post-secondary level, instructors are changing their teaching to address different learning styles. Assigning work to be presented in a variety of learning modalities is one way to allow students with different kinds of abilities to shine. Therefore, in course sizes where assessment can be somewhat flexible, having a combination of oral presentations, musical performance, written essays or assignments, and traditional examinations allows students to excel in areas that may be more conducive to showcasing their talents. Some instructors even allow students to choose the weighting of particular course components according to their strengths. Although clearly there is much that can be learned by working hard in a student's weaker area, the element of choice is an important factor in allowing students to succeed over the length of an entire course. Also, universities are becoming increasingly responsive to students with various learning disabilities and limitations, often allowing those students extra time on examinations, note-takers, and peer or professional tutors. If your university has a learning disabilities service or center, make sure that students know that this aid is available to them, confidentially. We cannot account for every learning style or disability, but we can extend to students with demonstrable limitations some humane solutions to their individual challenges.

The methods of assessing music history work are wide and vary greatly from one instructor to another. Remember, however, that assessment should not be used just to test students' knowledge and recall, but to indicate how well other learning activities have succeeded. Teachers use assessment results as much to evaluate themselves as to evaluate students. Performance on exams and assignments tell instructors how engaging were their lectures, how helpful were reading assignments and recitation sessions, and how realistic were their expectations about the amount and difficulty of course material. Instructors often improve their courses based on what such results teach them, so the process of completing assignments and taking exams is an active role that students take in the development of pedagogy. Do not take poor performance across the board on an activity to be simply a symptom of general student unpreparedness or ambivalence; instead ask whether the learning activities engaged in before the assignment were truly effective in teaching the information. In designing all evaluative material, ask what the student is meant to learn from the activity, not just about music history, but about the act of learning itself.

Chapter 8

The Research Paper

Scott Warfield

The "term paper" has been one of the ubiquitous experiences for college students of all majors, and this has been even truer for students in the humanities.[1] Late nights in the library, often in the last days of the semester, and the "all-nighter" have been portrayed frequently as clichés of college life in motion pictures, literary fiction, and other media. One might assume from such (unsubstantiated) images and reports that college students everywhere are diligently engaged in the process of finding data and other information, reading and digesting those "facts," and then using those ideas to write reports, essays, and other papers that demonstrate their understanding of their chosen subjects' contents. Or are they?

Issues and Considerations (Some Background)

Not surprisingly, increasing class sizes and teaching loads have led many faculty members to reduce or even eliminate writing assignments from their courses.[2] For those who still require students to write, the serious decline in writing skills among American high school graduates, compounded by the easing of admission

---

[1] Wilbert J. McKeachie, *et al.*, *McKeachie's Teaching Tips: Strategies, Research, and Theory for College and University Teachers*, 11th ed. (Boston and New York: Houghton Mifflin, 2002). The author of this well-known guidebook for graduate teaching assistants and beginning college instructors notes that "When I began teaching, most courses in the social sciences and humanities required a term paper" (170). McKeachie earned his Ph.D. at the University of Michigan, where he taught in the Psychology Department from 1948 to 1992.

[2] Among numerous other reports on this issue, see the following articles and reader responses in the *Chronicle of Higher Education*: Audrey Williams June, "Some Papers are Uploaded to Bangalore to Be Graded," April 4, 2010, http://chronicle.com/article/Outsourced-Grading-With/64954/; Laurie Fendrich, "Ethics? Let's Outsource Them!," April 8, 2010, http://chronicle.com/blogs/brainstorm/ethics-lets-outsource-them/22408; Gene C. Fant, Jr., "Class Size vs. Teaching Load," May 19, 2010, http://chronicle.com/blogs/onhiring/class-size-vs-teaching-load/24112; and Thomas H. Benton [William Pannapacker], "A Perfect Storm in Undergraduate Education, Part I," February 20, 2011, http://chronicle.com/article/A-Perfect-Storm-in/126451/ and "A Perfect Storm in Undergraduate Education, Part II," April 3, 2011, http://chronicle.com/article/A-Perfect-Storm-in/126969/ (all accessed October 1, 2011).

standards at many institutions, has often meant dealing with student writing that verges on the incoherent. Thus, many faculty members—even those in English departments—have been loath to teach writing skills, especially given the time-consuming nature of this work.[3] Additionally, the low status accorded the teaching of composition—seen chiefly in the tendency to assign such courses to adjunct and non-tenure-track faculty—contributes to this attitude.[4] Outside of English departments, professors may have an overly optimistic impression of their students' writing abilities, and many instructors simply assume that "someone else" has taught their students at least the basics of grammar, punctuation, spelling, and composition. Finally, and perhaps somewhat surprisingly, even those professors who themselves regularly write for publication may not have complete confidence in their own abilities to teach writing.[5]

Given all of those reasons, one might ask why any music history teacher would want to include extended writing assignments in the standard music history sequence required of virtually all music majors in the United States. For most instructors, there are scarcely enough allotted credit hours in most music degree programs to cover the factual content in music history, which has grown exponentially in the last few decades, much less to add significant writing and other tasks to a syllabus. Nevertheless, there is ample longstanding evidence that students do most of their learning outside of the classroom and that writing is one of the best ways for students both to master content and to develop the ability to think independently and critically.[6] While writing does help students to learn the subject matter—often assumed to be the acquisition of the facts of music history, which many music history teachers see as the primary goal of their courses—in fact, writing assignments can do much more than simply improve a student's ability to recall dates, names, and other raw and sometimes seemingly random bits of data. Barbara Walvoord offers a dozen good pedagogical reasons for including writing in any course, ranging from the focusing of a student's reading and the clarification of concepts and consequent expression of ideas on tests and

---

[3]   Kim Brooks, "Death to High School English," Salon.com, accessed October 1, 2011, http://salon.com/mwt/feature/2011/05/10/death_to_high_school_english.

[4]   Roger Gilles, "The Departmental Perspective," in *Strategies for Teaching First-Year Composition*, ed. Duane Roen *et al.* (Urbana, IL: National Council of Teachers of English, 2002), 2.

[5]   Heather Dubrow, "Teaching Essay-Writing in a Liberal Arts Curriculum," in *The Art and Craft of Teaching*, ed. Margaret Morganroth Gullette (Cambridge, MA: Harvard University Press, 1984), 89-90.

[6]   Joseph Lowman, *Mastering the Techniques of Teaching* (San Francisco: Jossey-Bass, 1984), 170-71 and especially Chapter 8, "Integrating Learning In and Out of the Classroom."

elsewhere to such practical matters for the instructor as identifying students in need of remedial help and providing grading opportunities.[7]

Beyond the immediate goals required by a course's content—objectives that will naturally be paramount in any instructor's planning and execution of a course—contributing to the general improvement of any individual student's basic research and writing skills can and should be a part of as many courses in the curriculum as possible. There are many specific and practical reasons for assigning research papers. For example, in the era of "Google," with that company's avowed intention to make virtually any book and innumerable other sources of information available through only a few clicks of a computer mouse, few students are aware of the actual limits and reliability of what is available on the World Wide Web, and an ever-decreasing number understand the subtleties of searching a library catalog or even the value of consulting a book in hard copy. Still fewer know of—or how to use—such basic music resources as *The New Grove Dictionary of Music and Musicians* (and its spin-offs), RILM, and the like. Thus, the simple task of acquainting and familiarizing students with an institution's library and its many resources, both for music and other subjects—including the full range of print, electronic, and other media—should pay dividends well beyond the course(s) in which those resources are first introduced. Research assignments are also generally a student's first encounters with scholarly and professional writing beyond textbooks, and such reading often leads to the realization that the literature on a subject can be much more complex, open-ended, and changing than the more straightforward and simplified explanations of introductory textbooks.[8] Consequently, students engaged in research assignments should become more attentive and even skeptical readers of all texts, better able to evaluate and judge materials that they might use throughout their professional careers, rather than remaining passive and unquestioning recipients of whatever they read.

At the same time, students who find little of personal interest in a music history course's content may have their enthusiasm for the subject sparked by the additional readings they do for a research paper. Much of the history of Western

---

[7]   Barbara E. Fassler Walvoord, *Helping Students Write Well: A Guide for Teachers in All Disciplines* (New York: Modern Language Association of America, 1982), 9-10.

[8]   For example, even though Arthur Berger first described the use of octatonic scale formations (based on alternating whole and half steps) in Stravinsky's music as early as 1963 (Arthur Berger, "Problems of Pitch Organization in Stravinsky," *Perspectives of New Music* 2, no. 1 [Autumn-Winter 1963]: 11-42), it has taken several decades for this knowledge to be integrated into the standard music history texts. Donald Jay Grout and Claude V. Palisca's *A History of Western Music*, 4th ed. (New York: W. W. Norton, 1988) barely mentions the term "octatonic scale" as a possible corrective to the then usual explanation of a "juxtaposition of two tonalities" in the so-called *Petrushka* chord (845), but by 2006, the 7th edition, revised and updated by J. Peter Burkholder, shows examples of octatonicism in several of Stravinsky's works (822, 823-24, and 827), notes the historical roots of the scale in the music of Rimsky-Korsakov and others (708-709), and gives additional examples of octatonic usage in the music of Debussy, Messiaen, and Scriabin (782, 785, 911, and 793).

art music can seem irrelevant to students whose own performance areas are in repertoires often bypassed in traditional music history courses.[9] Connections made between the repertoires that students study and perform in lessons and ensembles and the fundamentals of a subject area can be one of the most powerful motivations to investigate a topic further, and so having students write papers on topics of personal interest can awaken their interest in music history. Finally, as a practical matter, a growing number of students will need writing samples for graduate school applications and often for state education certificate credentialing.

Issues and Considerations (Practical)

Whatever the reasons for assigning a research paper or other writing assignments in a music history class, it is incumbent on the instructor to determine exactly what those projects add beyond the course's textbook and why they are being given to the students. Reasons like "all college students write term papers" or even a vaguely noble objective to help one's students improve their writing are not sufficient for assigning a research project in an undergraduate music history course. Such well-meant intentions may descend from the instructor's own graduate training, where doctoral students repeatedly produce extended essays of twenty to thirty pages or even more—frequently of publishable quality, no less—from only a graduate professor's minimal instruction to "write a paper on something related to the seminar's topic." Indeed, writing in musicology graduate programs, which reflects one of the musicologist's primary professional activities, is so common that presumably only the strongest writers—those who required little or no instruction in the art of writing—earn their degrees and move into positions as teachers themselves. Thus, what might seem obvious to an instructor about an assignment will need to be stated explicitly, and often repeatedly, to undergraduate students, whose concepts of writing and associated skills may be limited primarily to the five-paragraph essay that is the commonplace of high-school instruction in writing.[10] In short, instructors should explain to their students exactly what the objectives of a writing assignment are and how they are to be accomplished.

---

[9]   At the 2007 National Meeting of the College Band Directors National Association in Ann Arbor, Michigan, during a session devoted to a discussion about bands and band music in music history courses, one college band director who had earned B.M., M.M., and D.M.A. degrees at Indiana University noted that in the seven different music history and literature courses that he had taken over his years at the university, he had never once seen or heard a reference either to the saxophone, his primary instrument, or to any kind of band music.

[10]   Benton, "A Perfect Storm in Undergraduate Education, Part I." For a less pessimistic view of the five-paragraph essay, see Rob Jenkins, "Accordions, Frogs and the 5-paragraph Theme," *Chronicle of Higher Education*, February 21, 2010, accessed October 1, 2011, http://chronicle.com/article/A-Return-to-the-5-Paragraph/64255/.

Such instructions might begin with a single, basic goal for a project that then determines other parameters of the assignment. For many instructors, the sine qua non assignment is the "research paper" or "term paper," generally understood as an extended essay of some minimum number of pages or words (a minimum of ten pages in double-space or about 2,500 words is a frequent choice), written in formal English, complete with a suitable number of footnotes drawn from a minimum number of sources, and submitted in a physical format (or more recently, the electronic equivalent) of strictly prescribed parameters (1" margins, 12-point typeface, double-spaced text, and using some preferred system of citation and bibliography), which is usually due in the last few days of an academic term.

Such an assignment is undoubtedly intended to demonstrate a student's mastery of a subject, including the ability to find, evaluate, and transmit information at the highest levels, and presumably reflects the notion of "research" as defined in the *Oxford English Dictionary*: the "systematic investigation or inquiry aimed at contributing to knowledge of a theory, topic, etc., by a careful consideration, observation, or study of a subject."[11] Facing such a daunting task, especially when a significant percentage of a course's grade may be determined by this assignment, some students may feel compelled to acquire a paper from a term paper mill, a fraternity or sorority file, or simply by searching the web. Others may attempt to complete the assignment by finding a few books on a topic and then copying or paraphrasing those contents into something approaching an essay. Neither of these solutions, of course, is genuine research, in the sense of reading widely and carefully in a field, sifting for relevant information, and then synthesizing that material into an essay that confirms a student's understanding of and even demonstrates original thinking about a musical subject.

While there may be a few well-prepared students in any music history class who are capable of the advanced sort of writing just described, the reality nowadays is that most students in the music history sequence will rarely have the advanced skills necessary to carry out true "research," as most musicologists might understand it. Among the limitations that an instructor needs to take into consideration are such basics as the level of the students' theory preparation. Many students, for instance, take music history while completing only the second year of music theory, and few will be skilled at analyzing chromatic harmony, describing any of the vast array of twentieth-century compositional techniques, or tackling modal theory in music before 1600. Even those students who might be able to handle the challenges of more complex pieces and larger scores generally lack the experience with enough repertoire to place particular works easily into a meaningful broader context.

---

[11]   *Oxford English Dictionary*, "research, n. 2a," accessed October 1, 2011, http://www.oed.com. The definition under "research, n[oun]," is Number 2 in the list of possible meanings and continues with "In later use also: original critical or scientific investigation carried out under the auspices of an academic or other institution."

Beyond the concerns with purely musical skills, moreover, instructors should also be aware that few undergraduates have the ability to read the foreign languages in which some primary resources or fundamental scholarly work necessary for a particular topic may have been written. Likewise, the individual students' general knowledge of history, culture, literature, and the other fine arts can vary widely. This is not to say that a music history instructor should assume that all students are incapable of advanced research, but rather should determine what the realistic limits are for any assignment given to students who are still acquiring rudimentary intellectual tools of all kinds. Left to their own devices, overly enthusiastic students may decide to tackle projects as musically daunting as the analysis of a major work by a late nineteenth-century symphonist or as linguistically tricky as sorting out the problems of nomenclature in seventeenth-century instrumental genres. While such eagerness to investigate complex and demanding topics is commendable, it is incumbent on the instructor to guide those students into more modest projects that challenge but do not overwhelm the abilities they bring to the task.

Getting Started: Learning to Read and Digest Scholarship

One might reduce the stakes for novice student writers by thinking of research as simply "gather[ing] information to answer a question that solves a problem," a definition put forth by Wayne C. Booth, Gregory G. Colomb, and Joseph M. Williams in their indispensable *The Craft of Research*.[12] With that premise, almost any sort of writing assignment, no matter how short or seemingly modest, can be a "research" paper—even when the materials investigated are actually well-established facts, for example, the biography of a major composer or the history and reception of a repertoire warhorse—so long as the question or problem is new and unknown to the novice scholar. The emphasis then shifts from the *result* of the student's "research," that is, the final paper, to the *process* through which the paper is fashioned. Moreover, with the emphasis on the method rather than the end product, all sorts of assignments, including multiple interrelated ones, become possible, the sum total of which can be more productive than a single large research paper. As McKeachie notes, "[a] ten-page paper is not necessarily twice as valuable as a five-page paper," and from a practical standpoint, "[s]hort papers can be evaluated in less time than long papers and may provide sufficient stimulus for student thinking and sufficient opportunity for feedback."[13]

These shorter assignments need not simply be smaller versions of the extended research paper. In fact, the variety of assignments is limited only by the instructor's imagination, although the most typical and useful can probably be found somewhere

[12]   Wayne C. Booth, Gregory G. Colomb, and Joseph M. Williams, *The Craft of Research*, 3rd ed. (Chicago and London: University of Chicago Press, 2008), 10.
[13]   McKeachie, *McKeachie's Teaching Tips*, 175-76.

on the list by Barbara Gross Davies in her *Tools for Teaching*.[14] Some of her suggestions which seem most adaptable for use in music history courses include reactions to readings, abstracts of articles, reviews of books, research proposals, letters, obituaries, contributing to or editing in an open-source database on the web like Wikipedia, and so on. Obviously the individual instructor will need to consider the particular teaching situation—beginning with such factors as the number of students and their general levels of experience in everything from music theory and English composition, and continuing through any previous courses in music history and the writing and research assignments from those earlier teachers—before crafting the instructions for specific assignments. In institutions where students must pass through a fixed sequence of music history courses, departments and their faculties can establish a series of interrelated assignments that develop writing and research skills over several semesters. Even when students are not required to take music history courses in a rigid sequence, various sorts of writing assignments can be spread throughout the history sequence, making sure that each semester's assignments are self-contained, with none depending directly on having mastered any previous skills elsewhere in another course.

Regardless of the learning situation, the process of teaching writing can begin with many different kinds of modest assignments, but one initial concern might be to reduce the emphasis on grades with what McKeachie calls "low-stakes writing," that is, assignments that either do not receive a grade or count for only a very modest portion of the grade.[15] Carol A. Hess has reported on success with a number of brief in-class assignments, such as a letter from Johannes Brahms to Clara Schumann describing the genesis of his First Symphony or a press release written for the premiere of *Les Huguenots*.[16] One can also forego those sorts of exercises, especially when class time is at a premium, in favor of circumscribed writing assignments outside the classroom. A short abstract of a published article might at first seem too much like a high school book report, but requiring students to read professional writing carefully and then to summarize the ideas of a scholar with correct music terminology is an important first step toward being able to gather and evaluate information for an extended research paper, whether those students ever write such papers or not.

Such an assignment also works well in a course devoted to the earliest portions of the music history survey, that is, Antiquity through the Renaissance. Rather than have students attempt to learn how to do research in unfamiliar territory, the instructor can carefully choose readings from a journal like *Early Music*. By avoiding articles that demand exceptional linguistic skills (frequent untranslated passages from primary sources), a strong background in theory (complex

---

[14] Barbara Gross Davies, *Tools for Teaching*, 2nd ed. (San Francisco: Jossey-Bass, 2009), 318-21.

[15] McKeachie, *McKeachie's Teaching Tips*, 171.

[16] Carol A. Hess, "Score and Word: Writing About Music," in *Teaching Music History*, ed. Mary Natvig (Aldershot and Burlington, VT: Ashgate, 2002), 195.

discussions of mode or rhythmic notation), or detailed knowledge of medieval history, in favor of articles that offer straightforward discussions of music-making and listening, biography and iconography, students may often be pleasantly surprised to learn about music cultures that might otherwise seem uninteresting in short textbook excerpts.[17]

Moreover, instructors can challenge students by making this sort of assignment a "response" paper. Rather than ask students merely to summarize an article, they might also be required to include limited observations or opinions about the reading, perhaps in relation to the course's textbook or even a specific piece of music. For example, does the article confirm, amplify, or even contradict some information presented in the course's textbook? As a second attempt at this exercise, one might even give students multiple related items and ask then for not only summaries of the readings, but also a possible "solution" to a problem that uses the items. The controversy over the size of J. S. Bach's choirs is an excellent example of what can be done with basic materials. The initial claims were laid out by Joshua Rifkin and Robert Marshall in three articles written specifically for general readers, and the central document in this argument is readily available in an English-language translation.[18] A score or two, a few recordings that utilize different-sized ensembles and either period or modern instruments, and even lists of additional related writings can be added to the mix. Depending upon the instructor's objectives and the students' collective abilities, the assignment can range from a simple sorting out of the competing claims of Rifkin and Marshall up to the requirement that the individual students each determine which side is "correct"—with the understanding that neither side is "wrong" and without the option of calling it a draw—and, more importantly, offer an explanation of why one conclusion is better than the other. If time allows, the debate can even be brought back into the classroom, with students arguing their individual conclusions or even assigned to one side of the dispute or the other. Instructors can certainly find other unsettled points in the history of music for similar assignments, so long

---

[17]   For only three examples of articles on music before 1600 that may be easily read by beginning music history students, see Richard Sherr, "Competence and Incompetence in the Papal Choir in the Age of Palestrina," *Early Music* 22 (1994): 606-29; Adrian Rose, "Angel Musicians in the Medieval Stained Glass of Norfolk Churches," *Early Music* 29 (2001): 186-217; and Andrew Ashbee, "Groomed for Service: Musicians in the Privy Chamber at the English Court, c. 1495-1558," *Early Music* 25 (1997): 185-97.

[18]   The basic argument is found in Joshua Rifkin, "Bach's 'Choruses' – Less Than They Seem?" *High Fidelity* 32, no. 9 (September 1982): 42-44; Robert L. Marshall, "Bach's 'Choruses' Reconstituted," *High Fidelity* 32, no. 10 (October 1982): 64-66, 94; and Joshua Rifkin, "Bach's 'Choruses': The Record Cleared," *High Fidelity* 32, no. 12 (December 1982): 58-59. The primary document, J. S. Bach, "Short but most necessary draft for a well-appointed church music; with certain modest reflections on the decline of the same," is Item no. 151 in Hans T. David and Arthur Mendel, eds., *The New Bach Reader: A Life of Johann Sebastian Bach in Letters and Documents*, revised and enlarged by Christoph Wolff (New York: W. W. Norton, 1998), 145-51.

as the issue has a small nexus of articles, which then relieves students of the task of gathering information to concentrate instead on understanding and interpreting that evidence.

Defining Topics, Finding Resources and Evaluating Them

In fact, gathering the best reliable information for a project can be one of the most daunting tasks for students, especially those enrolled at major universities with libraries that might hold millions of volumes of actual books. Even an independent music library within a campus-wide library system will probably dwarf the high school and community libraries used only a few years previously by most students. Finding books somewhat relevant to a topic is seldom a problem for most students, and adding in online resources like JSTOR for articles usually ensures that a paper can always include whatever arbitrary number of sources an instructor requires for any written assignment. Unless students know how to evaluate resources, however, papers written with a mix of good, bad, new, old, scholarly, popular, and any other random sources will simply reflect the indifferent skills of the novice scholar. For students who have not had much experience writing extended papers, a dedicated assignment or two in the formulation of a research topic, and the basic techniques for gathering, evaluating, and presenting a bibliography may be quite helpful.

Booth, Colomb, and Williams offer a number of excellent suggestions for leading a novice writer from a generalized interest in a subject to a more focused question that can serve as the topic of a research paper.[19] For music history students this process usually means limiting an initially vague interest in some broader repertoire by such means as focusing on a single composer or group, adding temporal or geographic boundaries, or identifying other logical limits. This process can often be facilitated in a brief conversation or perhaps an email exchange through a series of questions that uncover a student's real interests in a topic. Thus, the voice major who "likes Italian opera" may be guided to study a single opera by Verdi or Mozart, or even just a scene, an aria, or a character from an opera. Topics need not be so obviously tied to a student's major area of study, as singers can certainly investigate instrumental works. Jazz majors are similarly not restricted from looking at medieval music, and so on. Whatever the student's interests, the exercise should lead to a reasonably well-defined topic and a good idea of the kinds of materials and information needed for the paper. The proposal should be submitted to the instructor as a one-page (or less) description of the topic, complete with some explanation of the topic's boundaries, that is, what will be included and what will not.

Armed with an instructor-approved topic, students can then begin searching for relevant materials. Curiously, the literature on teaching college-level writing

---

[19]   Booth, Colomb, and Williams, *Craft of Research*, Chapters 3, "From Topics to Questions," and 4, "From Questions to Problems," 35-65.

says almost nothing about this stage of the research paper, as if the techniques for finding books, articles, and other resources were self-evident. The explosion of electronic resources and the sheer size of most research libraries, however, demand that students be given some sort of guidance in effective searching, so that they are not overwhelmed by the available resources. While the music history class is not a graduate course in bibliography, instructors can devote a modest few minutes at the beginnings of a few classes to introduce students to their university's library catalog, the Music Index and RILM, WorldCat, JSTOR, and perhaps indices for dissertations, newspapers, and a few other resources. Most of these electronic resources have similar search features, so that students who have mastered searching in one database can transfer those skills to the next. Additional features like the ability to save, print, and email search results, and even to format bibliographic entries with programs like EndNotes, are now common in many online library catalogs and other databases, and so students may be enticed into using the best tools when search results may be easily streamed or loaded onto any of the many electronic devices owned and used daily by most undergraduates. For the classroom instructor who may not be current on the latest such technological advances, most college and university libraries offer instruction in these and many other topics.

To encourage students to look critically upon any items they might want to use in their research, the next step should be a formal bibliography, preferably one with annotations or at least an essay on what has been found to date. Lacking much experience in any research topic, many students will fail initially to distinguish between good, less good, and unacceptable items, generally because they do not read much beyond an item's title, which always seems relevant (to them) to the topic. Asking students to annotate their bibliographies, that is, to provide a brief sentence or two for each item in the bibliography that both describes the content of the article or book and also says something about its significance to the research topic, forces a student to consider why one book rather than another, why this writer and not that one, and so on.

To facilitate annotations, students can be taught a few simple criteria to use in evaluating scholarship. Assuming that they have completed some sort of response paper (described above), students should be able to skim the opening and closing pages of a book, check its chapter titles, index and other features to determine if a book really fits the intended topic. The same skills can be applied to an article or essay within a collection. Beyond skimming parts of an item, students should also learn how to find outside authorities whose evaluations can be trusted. Reviews of individual books are easily located via directed searches in RILM, the Music Index, and JSTOR, and published bibliographies are available for innumerable topics in music.[20] Consulting the selective bibliographies for relevant items in

---

[20]   See, for example, Vincent H. Duckles and Ida Reed, *Music Reference and Research Materials: An Annotated Bibliography*, 5th ed. (New York: Schirmer Books, 1997), especially sections 4, "Bibliographies of Music Literature," and 5, "Bibliographies

the *New Grove Dictionary of Music and Musicians*, 2nd edition, is one way to verify at least the authority of scholarly work, although not necessarily an item's relevance to a student's topic, and a tool like the *Reader's Guide to Music: History, Theory, and Criticism* offers brief essays that describe the best English-language scholarship on many of the basic subjects in music scholarship.[21] Since mid-2011, *Oxford Bibliographies Online* has offered a growing list of reference articles in a style that "combines the best features of a high-level encyclopedia and a traditional bibliography," giving beginning researchers an authoritative overview of many basic music subjects.[22] Beyond searching secondary resources, students can be taught to consider such obvious factors as an author's professional status and other writings, the book's publisher and reputation, the date of publication, and even physical features of the book, such as its length, writing tone, and apparent audience.

In summarizing this information into a sentence or two that follows a properly formatted entry in a bibliography, the student must stand behind the choice, which the instructor may grade or simply use for commenting. As an end in itself, the annotated bibliography can be used just to teach techniques for using library catalogs and databases, while some instructors may want to stress (and grade) the formatting of the bibliographic entries as well. Regardless of whether a paper follows or not, exercises in bibliography are an important step in the development of genuine research skills.

Planning, Writing and Editing the Paper

With a well-defined topic and a good bibliography of relevant items, the student researcher is ready to read, to think, and to write. Given the solitary nature of writing, some instructors may assume it best simply to assign a paper at the beginning of a semester and then collect the finished product fifteen weeks later. Few undergraduates are able to organize and manage a semester-long research project without some supervision, and left to their own devices, many students procrastinate at one stage or another on the way to the final draft, with inevitably lesser results. Carol Hess notes that she devised her own three-stage method for assigning and grading term papers simply "to deter students from beginning their papers the night before the due date."[23] In fact, insisting that students complete preliminary tasks on a reasonable schedule is a step toward instilling good research and writing habits, and also saves the instructor from the time-consuming task of

---

of Music," 163-335. These two sections alone contain a *selective* list of nearly 1,000 such resources.

[21] Murray Steib, ed., *Reader's Guide to Music: History, Theory, and Criticism* (Chicago and London: Fitzroy Dearborn, 1999).

[22] http://www.oxfordbibliographiesonline.com/ (accessed October 1, 2011).

[23] Hess, "Score and Word," 200.

grading too many inferior papers. The question becomes: at what points and to what degree should the instructor intervene in or at least check on a student's writing?

The process begins with good planning by and clear instructions from the teacher who creates a reasonable timeline for the project. These instructions should include such obvious information as the intermediate goals or deadlines for each stage in the assignment, minimum word counts, formatting, and so on. They should also include a statement of the paper's objective—is it a fact-gathering exercise, an analysis of a piece, persuasive writing, and so on—and how it will be graded—what percentages of the grade are devoted to the factual content, to grammar and spelling, to footnotes and bibliography, and to any other criteria— any of which might not seem immediately obvious to the students. At a minimum, the topic proposal should be due very early in the semester, with some sort of check on the (annotated) bibliography only a few weeks later. Such a fast start might seem counterproductive with students who have barely begun work in a course, but getting these essential tasks finished sooner rather than later ensures enough time for the demanding job of writing. False starts and adjustments in the topic, whether due to changing interests or problems with sources, can also be better accommodated earlier in the semester. Following that beginning, the instructor can then set as many additional checkpoints as seem necessary and reasonable, given all the circumstances. With less experienced writers, an instructor might wish to see outlines and drafts, and even speak individually with students before the final paper is submitted. In practice, the frequency and extent of the interaction between teacher and students will depend almost entirely on the available resources, course load, number of students in a class, and other work assigned to an instructor.

Whatever those limitations, there are ways to use time efficiently and still help students.[24] With the rise of email, text-messaging, and similar forms of electronic communication, students can now ask questions at any time and receive a swift answer, assuming the instructor is online and willing to act. Such availability can be detrimental, however, when a student uses the instructor as an instant resource to resolve problems that can be worked out without help. To encourage independent work, instructors should set clear limits on what help they will offer and when. Online office hours might be established for a writing project, with the assurance that acceptable brief questions will be answered quickly via an exchange of email messages. More complex issues can be reserved for face-to-face meetings, either during a drop-in period or at a formal appointment. As for requiring conferences with individual students, the sheer numbers in a course section may make it impossible to meet every student for more than a few minutes each. Faced with such large numbers, the wise instructor may make such conferences voluntary, limit the number of students per semester given such help, or even divide student

---

[24]   See Walvoord, Chapter 3, "Communicating with Students about Their Writing," 25-42, for general suggestions on how to advise, correct, and encourage students during the writing process.

conferences over a sequence of courses.[25] If the instructor's time is limited, students need not be left to fend for themselves, as there are several excellent published guides to writing about music, which can be added to a course's list of textbooks.[26] Similarly, a growing number of university libraries have online tutorials for topics such as how to conduct research, evaluate websites, format bibliographies, avoid plagiarism, and so on.[27]

Email and word-processors can also be used effectively for grading or simply monitoring any of the various preliminary stages of a paper. Students can submit work as attachments to email messages, which the instructor then downloads, grades, or simply corrects using the "comment" (or "review") function found in most word-processing programs, and returns electronically. The efficiency of email can be deceptive, however. Inexperienced teachers often see their job as fixing problems and eradicating errors, which can become an urge to mark virtually every mistake and less-than-perfect passage. It is important to recognize the limits of what one can do, and so as a practical matter not every problem need be noted and commented on, especially with students whose writing may require extensive help. Instead, the instructor can focus intently on a few brief passages, marking nearly everything that needs attention for only a page or two at most, with advice to the student about problems that recur elsewhere in the draft, but without marking them all.[28] Finally, one must resist the desire to rewrite student prose into something in a higher style. One may not care for a word or phrase, but unless it is seriously incorrect, it is better left alone.

Grading the Paper

If students have been conscientious about the preliminary stages of their writing, one might hope that the end of the semester will bring with it a group of

---

[25]   Wolvoord colorfully describes the best attitude toward this problem, "If your rowboat reaches the sinking *Titanic*, you can take on five victims, even though you can't save everyone" ("Communicating with Students about Their Writing," 35).

[26]   For brief reviews of several such guides, see Kendra Leonard, "Review Essay: Guides to Writing about Music," *Journal of Music History Pedagogy* 2, no. 1 (Fall 2011): 111-16, accessed October 1, 2011, http://www.ams-net.org/ojs/index.php/jmhp/article/view/45.

[27]   See, for example, the "Information Literacy Modules" at the University of Central Florida Library's website, which includes a dozen self-instruction units in various research topics. Faculty can even require students to complete specific modules and then receive electronic confirmation when students have completed the assigned work. "Information Literacy Modules," accessed October 1, 2011, http://infolit.ucf.edu/students/modules.

[28]   Walvoord suggests using a "never-again notebook," in which a student can record persistent personal writing errors, as a way to fix these sorts of problems ("Communicating with Students about Their Writing," 173-74).

well-written papers. Truthfully, what most students submit as their "finished" papers are more often preliminary drafts of varying quality, and so if possible, students should be given an opportunity to submit their papers a few weeks before the end of the semester for an initial reading. As Justice Brandeis (among many others) observed, there is no good writing, only good rewriting.[29] As time allows, papers can be marked, at least in a cursory fashion, and returned to the students for revision.[30] Some instructors like to give a preliminary grade—one that stands without further revision of the paper—to encourage students to revise their work seriously.

Whether marking preliminary drafts or the final version of a paper, the subjective nature of judging writing makes grading extended papers one of the most demanding and time-consuming tasks for a teacher. Without obvious correct/incorrect choices, and often seeing positive and negative traits mixed in vastly different combinations within student papers—for example excellent prose with poor sources, a good argument with little support, unacceptable grammar and style with a well-defended thesis, and so on—the instructor pressed for time may simply retreat into holistic grading, that is, "it looks like a B+ to me," without immediate evidence for the grade. Experienced teachers may well have a good feel for such an approach, but many students will want to know why they received a certain grade (actually, why they did not receive a *higher* grade), and so one needs to establish clear criteria for grading, which can be shared with the students in advance. Quite simply, the better informed the students are, the more likely their papers will conform to the instructor's expectations.

Such rubrics—also known as "Primary Trait Analysis" (PTA) among education researchers—simply describe the criteria or traits that will be considered in the grading of an assignment. Each trait is then assigned a scale of measures that may be as detailed as necessary. These can range from simple yes/no evaluations for basic elements like the required word count, proper margins, and so on, to five- or even ten-point scales for other aspects like the general organization of the paper, the quality of argumentation, use of proper music terminology, technical aspects of writing, and so on. The scale for each element then describes the sort of performance expected at each level. For basic elements like grammar and spelling, the scale might simply describe an average number of errors per page or the overall severity of such problems. "Measuring" such factors as the quality of an argument or the appropriateness of evidence cited to support a point is admittedly more difficult, but PTA does enable a teacher to make judgments in a more objective fashion. The use of rubrics with well-defined scales also ensures a greater degree

---

[29]   Cited by Dubrow, "Teaching Essay-Writing," 92.

[30]   As Lowman notes, it can take up to about forty-five minutes of concentrated reading to grade a typical ten- to fifteen-page paper, and poorly written papers will demand even more time. Additionally, the effort required to read and to grade will probably limit most instructors to only a handful of papers in a session (*Mastering the Techniques of Teaching*, 177-78).

of consistency in grading an entire class, across multiple sections, and even from year to year.[31]

In grading the final drafts of student papers, plagiarism may regrettably become an issue. Despite the best efforts of the instructor to teach students how to use sources, one or more papers may have passages, ranging from a sentence or two up to entire papers, which simply do not read like student work. Whether intentional or not, such problems must be checked, and given that the source of most plagiarized materials is the internet, so are the best tools for combating unacknowledged borrowings. Instructors can simply check questionable passages by hunting for them with any web search engine. More efficient and effective are commercial products, which many institutions use and even mandate.[32] Students submit their papers through a website, and the program then checks the entire paper against its database of writings and the entire web before issuing a percentage score that describes the paper's borrowed content. There are also a number of less sophisticated, but free "plagiarism checkers" on the web that identify matches between submitted work and possible sources on the web.[33] Regardless of how unacknowledged borrowings are identified, the instructor must consider the severity of the violation within any paper. Wholesale copying, with or without footnotes, is obviously a problem, but a single sentence—or even multiple occurrences—in an otherwise well-documented paper may simply be a student's oversight or a misunderstanding of the conventions for citing borrowed words.[34] Dealing with plagiarism can also be a complex matter, and the instructor needs to know the institution's policies, which are generally quite clear and legally binding, since they affect student grades, and follow them closely.

---

[31] For ideas on how to construct assignments and grading rubrics, see Barbara E. Walvoord and Virginia Johnson Anderson, *Effective Grading: A Tool for Learning and Assessment*, 2nd ed. (San Francisco: Jossey-Bass, 1998), especially Chapter 5, "Establishing Criteria and Standards for Grading," 65-92.

[32] Marc Parry, "Software Catches (and Also Helps) Young Plagiarists," *Chronicle of Higher Education*, November 6, 2011, accessed November 15, 2011, http://chronicle.com/article/Escalation-in-Digital/129652/.

[33] Turnitin (turnitin.com) is the commercial site most commonly used by high schools and institutions of higher education. Free plagiarism checkers on the web include "The Plagiarism Checker", http://www.dustball.com/cs/plagiarism.checker/; "Plagiarisma.Net", http://plagiarisma.net/; "Advanced Plagiarism Checker", http://searchenginereports.net/articlecheck.aspx; and many others (all accessed October 1, 2011).

[34] For an excellent discussion of the problems in determining what is and is not plagiarism, see Rebecca Moore Howard, "The Ethics of Plagiarism," in *The Ethics of Writing Instruction: Issues in Theory and Practice*, ed. Michael A. Pemberton. Perspectives on Writing: Theory, Research, Practice 5 (Stamford, CT: Ablex, 2000), 79-89.

Final Considerations

In his brief history of how the teaching of composition developed in the United States, Douglas D. Hesse begins with the statement that "We cannot promise a single, correct formula for writing, an algorithm guaranteed to produce success. There is none."[35] Thus, all that has come before this closing paragraph is merely suggestion. Certainly there are dozens and even hundreds of good ideas on how writing can be taught, some of which have been offered here, but in the end, each teacher must survey his or her own situation and determine what can reasonably be done. Whether one has the luxury of small classes and the opportunity to work closely with a handful of individuals or, more often, looks out on a sea of faces and wonders how to reach all of them, research and writing assignments can be designed that will help most students write better and learn more effectively than they did before they entered the music history classroom.

---

[35]   Douglas D. Hesse, "Writing and Learning to Write: A Modest Bit of History and Theory for Writing Students," in *Strategies for Teaching First-Year Composition*, ed. Duane Roen *et al.*, (Urbana, IL: National Council for Teachers of English, 2002), 38.

Chapter 9

Music as a Liberal Art: Teaching Music to Non-Majors

Marjorie Roth

Appreciate: To grasp the nature, worth, quality or significance of; to value or admire highly; to judge with heightened perception or awareness.[1]

Almost twenty-five years ago, when I first began teaching Music Appreciation[2] courses to non-music majors, I came across a Gary Larson "The Far Side" cartoon featuring a goggle-eyed elephant sitting at a grand piano on the stage of a packed concert hall. The text bubble over the panic-stricken performer revealed his thoughts, which were: "What am I doing here? I can't play this thing! I'm a flutist, for crying out loud!" That hapless elephant-flutist has stayed on my mind (and my office door) ever since, as a constant reminder of the Music Appreciation teacher's perpetual pedagogical predicament. His disorientation is common to all who face the challenge of teaching a "music" course to non-musicians. We understand his creeping, sinking, anxiety-dream sensations as he realizes something is *very* wrong. And, like the elephant-flutist, the Music Appreciation teacher eventually confronts the profound existential question: What am I doing here?

That question resonates at several important pedagogical levels, depending upon whether we address the "what," the "I," the "doing," or the "here." Satisfactory responses are required on all counts for success in any classroom, but the Music Appreciation classroom presents special challenges to instructors with respect to who they are (the professorial "I"), how they approach their task (the pedagogical "doing"), and what their understanding is regarding the role of the Music Appreciation course within the liberal arts/general education core curriculum requirement of their particular college or university (the institutional "what" and "here"). In this chapter we will explore each of these issues with an eye toward creating a classroom environment that is true to the integrity of the subject matter, comfortable and challenging for the students and the teacher,

---

[1] Merriam-Webster online dictionary (accessed November 4, 2011).

[2] "Music Appreciation" is the out-dated title for any number of more trendily titled general studies music courses found in college catalogues today. For the purposes of this essay, the old but still serviceable designation will stand as representative of any undergraduate course for non-music majors offered through a music department as part of an institution's liberal arts core curriculum. The term will refer to both general survey courses (e.g., Intro to World Music) and topics courses (e.g., Women & Music).

and supportive of the institution's educational mission. We will contemplate the nature and goals of the liberal arts/general studies music course by highlighting the philosophical and methodological differences between teaching music as a fine art and teaching music as a liberal art. Suggestions regarding course content, preparation, assignments, teaching materials, and teaching methods will be included along the way, but these are offered as generalized models intended to be adapted to suit courses of different types and sizes, functioning within a variety of institutional frameworks, taught by teachers with differing interests and skills.

First Things First: Know Thyself

Who are you? Think about it. What is your background as a musician, and how do you consider it adequate preparation for leading this kind of course? Before you select your textbook, plan your teaching methods, choose your repertoire, articulate your student learning outcomes, and create your assignments and tests—even before you consult your departmental chairperson and colleagues for advice—take careful stock of who you are. Because when all is said and done, you will be your own best resource as your class unfolds.[3]

If you've been hired to teach Music Appreciation at the college level, you no doubt possess the required academic credentials. You may even feel a bit over-qualified, given that your course is "only" a general education course for non-majors and not a "real" music history course for music students. You might be an applied vocal or instrumental instructor with years of studio experience. You might be a professor of music theory, a composer, or a musicology or theory graduate student. You might be a music educator or therapist, recruited to fill a gap in the teaching staff. You might even be a musicologist or ethnomusicologist with considerable classroom experience, unambiguously equipped to teach bright and gifted young music majors. You might be any combination of the above. Whatever your area of expertise, you were hired to teach this course because you are a professional in the field of music. You've made a commitment to your career, pursued advanced levels of academic and/or applied study, and your department chairman is safe in assuming that you will know a great deal more about "music" than your general education students will know.

With these impeccable credentials, you will approach your task secure in the knowledge that you can certainly teach a "simple" Music Appreciation class for non-majors. But despite your expertise and your entirely reasonable self-confidence, as the semester progresses the day will come when you gaze into the eyes of your smiling math or business or physical therapy majors and realize that they are not of your kind. Their minds are made of decidedly different stuff. They don't speak your language. Unlike you (and probably unlike everyone else

³   For literature on self-study, see Anastasia P. Samaras and Anne R. Freese, *Self-study of Teaching Practices Primer* (New York: Peter Lang, 2006).

of significance in your life) your Music Appreciation students have not lived and breathed classical music since childhood. They have not spent years contemplating structure and meaning in art music. The majority of them will not have experienced the satisfaction of unearthing the *Ursatz* of a Beethoven sonata, or the pure sonic thrill of playing the piccolo part in the *Dies Irae* of the Verdi *Requiem*. They are unlikely to have been moved to tears by a Schumann song. Most of them will not read music. And if music is part of their lives at all, they probably "appreciate" it in ways very different from yours. For them it is probably something to dance to, or create non-professionally with friends and family; something to serve as background to activities like studying, exercising, or scrubbing down the shower.

It is a chilling experience to look out over a sea of faces and realize that when it comes to the very topic you have convened to explore, you and your students are worlds apart. Even for the experienced Music Appreciation teacher this is a transcendent moment, one that never fails to inspire a curious mix of awe and humility. But for the first-time Music Appreciation teacher, it can be terrifying. It is the moment when you realize that all your hard-won tools for thinking, feeling, and speaking effectively about music are essentially useless. Your professional moorings are gone. You feel alone and exposed. The well-mapped territory of Planet Music Department is far away and you are captain of an alien crew, navigating the unfamiliar spaces and spheres of music as a liberal art. And you ask yourself, *what am I doing here?*

A Matter of Philosophy: Music as a Fine Art vs. Music as a Liberal Art

You might also find yourself wondering how you got "here." Where, exactly, *is* "here"? Is music as a liberal art so different from music as a fine art? If so, how so, and why should it be uncharted territory for most trained musicians? Even more important, how does this situation impact daily reality in the Music Appreciation classroom?

Part of the problem stems from the fact that higher education in America has lost a meaningful sensitivity to the important historical and practical differences between the traditional liberal arts and what we now refer to as the fine or performing arts. Although music is, technically, both a liberal art and a fine art, the conceptual definition of "music," as it exists in those two arts, differs significantly and this fact has important pedagogical ramifications.[4] Reinforcing the confusion is the fact that most people hired to teach Music Appreciation courses typically have had little

---

[4]   The seven liberal arts of Antiquity comprised the "qualitative" arts of the *trivium* (Grammar, Logic, and Rhetoric), and the "quantitative" arts of the *quadrivium* (Arithmetic, Geometry, Astronomy, and Music). The term "fine arts" came into general use in the eighteenth century as a way to distinguish the categories of artistic activity aimed primarily at aesthetic contemplation from the more humble, purely practical arts we describe today as crafts. The most recent curricular incarnation of the fine arts tends to emphasize the

experience with music as a liberal art. A professional musician is a fine artist; he or she thinks first and foremost in terms of "the music" itself, the "work of art" in all its technical, aesthetic, and stylistic glory. There's nothing intrinsically wrong with this relatively narrow definition of music; indeed, it represents the primary orientation necessary for any professional musician.

But while the fine art of music has a role to play in the liberal arts classroom, it is not the conception of music that can—or even *should*—serve as the foundation of a music course for non-majors. Undue emphasis on the technical and stylistic aspects of music as a fine art sets up an unwelcome tension in the Music Appreciation classroom, where "the music itself" must function not so much as *the end toward which all course content and activities will develop*, but instead as *the means by which students pursue and attain* a much larger and more unified end; that end being, specifically, the habits of mind necessary to build a free, satisfying, and balanced human life. Stated another way, this means that although you will certainly help your students appreciate the fine art of music as you know it and insofar as their limited skills allow, your first and most important task is to guide them toward a deeper appreciation of the nature, worth, quality, and significance of music as a liberal art—that is, as an important part of human intellectual, cultural, and spiritual history. You must help them to perceive music's inherent ability to translate the abstract concept of a truly "harmonic" universe into the sensible reality of human experience. And therein lies the heart of the Music Appreciation instructor's dilemma, the problem of the elephant at the grand piano. You are an impeccably trained fine artist; but in your Music Appreciation classroom you must perform as a liberal artist.

Practical Solutions I: Introducing Music as a Liberal Art

Fortunately, this problem is not insurmountable, although the solution requires flexibility, creativity, and a (potentially liberating) willingness to reinvent yourself and your ideas about what is most "appreciate-able" about music. You may also have to reassess your assumptions about your students' level of sophistication about music. Although they are not likely to know much about the fine art of classical music, your Music Appreciation students will display astonishingly diverse—and potentially useful—levels of experience with many different kinds of music. If your focus is purely classical and your pedagogical orientation based on the technical, generic, and historical aspects of the fine art, your students will probably come across to you as "the great unwashed" and you will see your task primarily as one of addressing a deficiency. But if you can reprioritize the fine art of classical music and contextualize it as *a part* of the over-arching liberal art of music, you might begin instead to see your task as one of enhancing your

---

performative aspect of the aesthetically based arts thus fusing the fine arts with the more modern and inclusive category of the performing arts.

students' competencies rather than addressing their deficiencies. In this case your job becomes a bit more challenging than simply familiarizing your students with art music. Instead, it will be your task to harmonize the classical repertoire you know so well with the popular or world music repertoire they will know equally well by examining them all within the context of human experience.

The biggest mistake to avoid when planning your class is the all-too-common assumption that Music Appreciation is—in terms of content, organization, method, and goals— simply "watered-down" music history. Be very careful about this, because any attempt merely to dilute the content and rigor of a music history course for music majors and offer it up as an adequate contemplation of music as a liberal art is a recipe for disaster in the classroom. You will find your own material weak and uninspiring, your students will perceive and adopt your apathy, and they will likely find even your simplified terms and concepts incomprehensible. This does not mean you must abandon a chronological/generic framework if that is the most comfortable approach for you.[5] It does not mean your students are exempt from acquiring a basic level of terminological, conceptual, and stylistic competence. But it does mean that your *point of departure* and your *primary focus* cannot rest upon those things; the very things that you, as a fine artist, naturally assume are the things most worthy of appreciating. As you gain more experience with teaching non-majors you will eventually find that it is indeed possible to bring them to an adequate (and even enthusiastic) understanding of genre, form, style, and performance practice. But you must set those particular priorities aside at first in favor of establishing a common ground with and among your students, through mutual exploration of "music" as an *idea* rather than as a sounding phenomenon.

Figure 9.1 provides a useful point of departure, and can serve as focus for discussion on the first day of class that will help articulate this important common ground. I have used this illustration in music classes for many years, and have found that it provides a holistic framework for exploring music as a liberal art in the broadest of terms, while also putting enlightening differences in the students' attitudes about music on the table for class discussion. The rectangles on the left of Figure 9.1 are adapted from Boethius, and illustrate his three-fold medieval articulation of the liberal art of music as it unfolds within the framework of an over-arching harmonic cosmos.[6] The key word for discussion here is "harmony" (a synonym for "music" in the *quadrivium*), in all its possible meanings. Before you start your discussion, you might ask your students to write down three of

---

[5]   Indeed, this may be the best starting place for Music Appreciation teachers with little classroom experience and no familiarity with their institution's liberal arts core goals and practices. As you gain experience with the expectations and abilities of the general education students, however, you will find yourself more able to depart from the safety of a chronological/generic approach and to experiment with ways of organizing your class according to topics or ideas (see Practical Solutions III, below).

[6]   Anicius Manlius Severinus Boethius, *Fundamentals of Music*, trans. Calvin M. Bower, ed. Claude V. Palisca (New Haven: Yale University Press, 1989).

their own definitions of the word harmony, to which they will return for further reflection after a group perusal of Figure 9.1 is completed.[7]

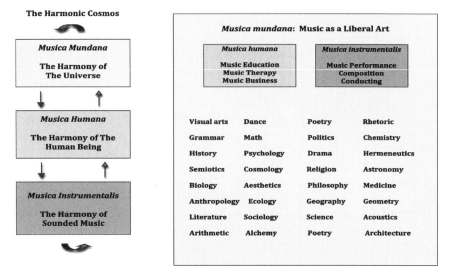

Figure 9.1   Cosmic harmony and music as a liberal art

Students will have little difficulty understanding Boethius's *musica instrumentalis*, which is a kind of music (or harmony) they are all familiar with at a conscious level. It is music they can perceive with their senses, "sounded" music produced by singing or playing instruments. The other two manifestations of Boethius's cosmic harmony, however, *musica mundana* (the harmony of the macrocosm, i.e., the universe) and *musica humana* (the harmony of the microcosm, i.e., the human being) may take a bit more time for students to grasp, because they require students to embrace the idea that there are "harmonies" they cannot perceive through the sense of hearing, but must instead perceive through less conscious means by the mind, the body, or the soul. To facilitate exploration of the idea in your class discussion, you can introduce two useful musical terms at this point: consonance and dissonance. Demonstration of the two terms on the sensory level of *musica instrumentalis* can be accomplished easily at the piano. You can then proceed to the levels of *musica mundana* and *musica humana* by asking your students to imagine other things in the universe that might be described as consonant or dissonant; things that pertain either to their own disciplines,

---

[7]   Post-discussion reflections on the topic of harmony can form the basis of a formal essay assignment, a journal entry, or a quick "exit" paragraph at the end of class. However you decide to frame the assignment, it serves as an excellent way for you to establish a baseline understanding of how your students think and communicate in general, and what they think about music, specifically.

future career areas, or personal experiences. To get the discussion rolling you might suggest that at the level of the macrocosm, political structures, religious and philosophical systems, or scientific theories can be consonant or dissonant. Similarly, at the level of the microcosm, a human being's health, mental or marital state, or economic condition can be either consonant or dissonant.

The large square on the right-hand side of Figure 9.1 brings Boethius's three-fold division of music up to date by connecting it directly to the typical liberal arts core curriculum. The two smaller boxes contain professional and performance careers in music most common today. These will indeed be part of your course material, but they will be framed by the larger box representing *musica mundana,* the broadest conception of music as a liberal art and the true focus of your course. Make the point that for Boethius—and for your Music Appreciation class, as well—appreciation of all three types of music is necessary. His goal, like yours, is not only to become familiar with sounded music, or to recognize the value of musical professions in modern society, but also to produce a human being capable of integrating the sensory delights of *musica instrumentalis* with the cosmic connectedness of *musica mundana,* in order to reap the physical and spiritual benefits of *musica humana*—that is, to become a truly "harmonic" human being. Spend your first class period and your first writing assignment exploring these ideas about music and harmony, and you will be well on your way to establishing the primary method of appreciating music as a liberal art.[8]

Practical Solutions II: Resources

Since your usual range of fine art resources are largely unavailable when teaching non-musicians, to what other resources can you turn? First, familiarize yourself with your music department's mission and vision statements regarding its contributions to a general studies curriculum. If you are not a full-time faculty member, or if you are new to your department, you may not be aware of specific requirements. Most general education classes in music will have been designed and proposed by the music department, but they will have passed through a fairly rigorous liberal studies core curriculum evaluation and approval process. As such, they will reflect two components: the specifically "musical" content of the class, and the over-arching goals of your institution's liberal arts requirement.

Speak to your department chairperson in order to clarify the music department's expectations. There is usually some flexibility in terms of method and materials, but most music departments will have given some thought to what a course for non-majors should cover. Some may require students to have at least one simple

---

[8] Figure 9.1 is only one way to introduce the idea of music as a liberal art in the humanities classroom and can be adapted to fit different needs. The specifics of the model are less important than getting students to think about the nature of music as a liberal art, and the relationship of music as a fine art to the larger idea of universal harmony.

experience with practical music-making. Some might require demonstrated competence in terms of a given repertoire. Others might expect the Music Appreciation courses to support departmentally sponsored concerts by requiring student attendance. There might be any number of expectations established long before you took over the Music Appreciation course, so be sure to find out what they are before you organize your syllabus. You should also consult faculty members who have taught the class in the past. They can provide invaluable information regarding the typical size of Music Appreciation classes at your institution, the kind of students who usually take it, and the classroom resources available to you (CD and video capability, internet connections, etc.). They may also be willing to share syllabi and assignments they have found to be effective with such classes.

Possibly even more important than what the music department has in mind for its liberal arts courses is what the institution has in mind for them. Again, check mission and vision statements with respect to the liberal arts core. Requirements might include anything from guaranteed exposure to primary sources to demonstration of advanced writing and critical thinking skills and/or an explicit commitment to an interdisciplinary orientation. A required element of service, community engagement, or global experience is also not uncommon these days. Any or all of these pre-established conditions can have a significant impact on the way you create your assignments and evaluation procedures, which will in turn affect your choices when it comes to how you organize and present your material. Such requirements may seem irrelevant and intimidating, since you may at first have trouble connecting the content of a music course to things like service, community engagement, or interdisciplinary study. But remember that your Music Appreciation course is part of a much larger institutional framework. Make an effort to learn about other courses, programs, and so forth that could overlap with the content of a Music Appreciation course. Take time to meet the faculty and explore the possibility of "guesting" in one another's classes, or creating collective experiences or assignments. For example, if the physical sciences at your institution offer a course covering acoustics, you might ask that professor to give a talk on the overtone series and Pythagorean ratios as an accompaniment to your own discussion of the perfect intervals that generate the harmonic and structural basis of medieval music. Efforts to connect one discipline to another within the liberal arts core curriculum are much appreciated these days at most institutions, by the administration and by the students.

If you are unfamiliar with the various resources available to support the liberal arts core, it is important to keep in mind as you approach the somewhat daunting task of creating a liberal arts course in music for the first time that you are indeed *not* alone. Although you cannot use the top layer of your own personal expertise when you teach non-majors, you do have access to the large and complex institutional support system that typically surrounds a general education curriculum. Find out if there is a Writing Center on campus. Find out if there is a pool of tutors or teaching assistants available to you. If your liberal arts curriculum has a service or global expectation built into it, there will probably be centers for international education and for service learning on your campus. Find out what those centers offer in terms of support for the general studies curriculum and work with the coordinators to design assignments or activities that can connect your course to those particular expectations. Your library and media center will also be invaluable to you in terms of electronic resources for research, inter-library loan, and audio-visual technologies. Consider those resources, too, as you envision ways of presenting your material and creating assignments.

On the subject of textbooks and repertoire I will say little, since these decisions should be your very last ones, made only after you have become thoroughly familiar with curricular expectations and resources. You may prefer to stick with the generally chronological/generic organization typical of the many excellent Music Appreciation texts available today.[9] If you choose instead to move further in the direction of music as a liberal art and experiment with an idea-based approach to your material, you might consider a textbook that is organized more along topical lines, and which includes repertoire that is somewhat less focused on Classical and/or Western music.[10] Or, once you have become a bit more experienced with thinking about and teaching music as a liberal art, you may find yourself willing to dispense entirely with any textbook, and explore music with your non-majors using your own intimate experience with selected works as a springboard for discussing the more universal aspects of cosmic harmony. In this case, in addition to specific works of your choice, you might want to use a textbook that is not specifically musical in content but instead takes a long view of human cultural history as expressed in the arts. If you choose this daring but rewarding approach, your task (and your pleasure) will be to connect music to all the other arts—both liberal and fine—as you contemplate their value in human history and culture.[11]

Ultimately, the textbook you choose to use and the repertoire you select for study are not all that important, since your goal is not to make sure students are well-schooled in the "chestnuts" of any given repertoire. At the outset of this chapter I suggested that, when all was said and done, you would be your own best resource when planning and teaching your Music Appreciation course. When you

---

[9] A few examples include Mark Evan Bonds, *Listen to This*, 2nd ed. (Upper Saddle River, NJ: Prentice Hall, 2011); Kristine Forney and Joseph Machlis, *The Enjoyment of Music*, 11th ed. (New York: W. W. Norton, 2011); and Roger Kamien, *Music: An Appreciation*, 10th ed. (New York: McGraw-Hill, 2010). If you are a full-time faculty member you can request review copies of these from the publisher. If you are adjunct faculty, your department chair can see to it that you receive these materials.

[10] Mary Natvig and Steven Cornelius, *Music: A Social Experience* (Upper Saddle River, NJ: Pearson, 2012).

[11] One example of this kind of textbook is Gloria K. Fiero's *Landmarks in the Humanities*, 2nd ed. (New York: McGraw-Hill, 2009). Helpful also to an instructor contemplating a truly interdisciplinary approach is Tanya Augsburg's *Becoming Interdisciplinary: An Introduction to Interdisciplinary Studies* (Dubuque, IA: Kendall Hunt, 2005).

have gathered all the necessary information regarding the goals and requirements of your course you will notice that the exercise of creating your syllabus has been an exercise in recreating yourself as a musician, as well. As you come to know your inner liberal artist, you will experience a new freedom with respect to your beloved fine art. All the things that attracted you to music in the first place, probably when you were very young and not yet formally trained in music, will come back to you and will form the foundation of your pedagogical approach. The indefinable sense of connectedness music inspires in you, the heightened perception if the world around you it affords—your reconnection with those most basic instincts about music will be your most valuable resource as you plan the first steps of the journey you and your students will take together. Choose the music you love most when you teach non-majors; you will be most convincing when you do so. Remember, the specific paths, signposts, and destinations are not important; in the liberal arts classroom, it's the journey that counts.

Practical Solutions III: Suggestions for the Classroom

The remainder of this chapter will outline a few practical examples of how an instructor can translate fine arts expertise into meaningful lectures, discussions, and exercises for the liberal arts classroom.

Terminology, Form, and Genre

All Music Appreciation courses must deal to some extent with terms, forms, and genres, and although your students' familiarity with these things need not be as rigorous as that of a music major, establishing a working vocabulary for speaking and writing intelligently about music is still critical. Most Music Appreciation textbooks open with a section on terminology, which you can adapt to your own needs. I usually make a list of the most important terms, and then define and demonstrate them by playing excerpts in class (using a mix of Western classical, popular, or non-western excerpts). This is not only a pleasant lecture/discussion to prepare, but is also a good way to make the point that the musical terminology required in our classroom is applicable to conversation about all kinds of music in "real life." A quick summary exercise at the end of class discussion, framed as a quiz or an "exit" exercise in informal writing, involves playing a piece of classical music and a piece of popular music, and asking students to describe both works using their newly acquired language.

Form and structure are often difficult to teach, even to music majors. But non-majors are often unaware that form even exists as an important element of music, and they will typically have given little thought to the structure of their own favorite musics. Since they are not trained musicians and cannot understand form in abstract terms, you must find other means of making them aware of the importance and meaning of form in music. I have found the idea of quotation to be a good way of introducing the formal and structural principles of all early music based on cantus firmus technique. For example, I introduce the genre of organum by playing a "doo-wop" recording from the 1950s of "I Only Have Eyes For You."[12] We listen to the whole song once and then focus on the four-bar instrumental introduction, because it is used by the Fugees as the basis for a new musical creation.[13] After describing the way the quotation works as the musical foundation of the new pop song, and speculating on the possible connections (or lack thereof) between the original song's meaning and the text of the new creation, non-majors are primed to appreciate the general structural principles of any composition based on borrowed material. They are also happy to acknowledge at least the purely intellectual fun of historical genres they may have trouble relating to on purely aesthetic grounds, like the thirteenth- and fourteenth-century polytextual motet.

Sonata form, another important structure in Western classical music, can be made more accessible to non-musicians by introducing it as a kind of narrative drama. If the musical themes of the exposition are presented as antagonists, students can practice using their newfound terminological expertise to support speculation on the personality, gender, nationality, and so on of each theme in the exposition. The development section can be explored by considering the impressions made by the way the composer chose to dissect and deploy the characteristics of each theme. Discussion of the recapitulation might include contemplation of both the musical and the non-musical significance of that section. "Capitulation" is certainly involved here: but who capitulates? How do the students respond to it? Clearly the eighteenth century saw sonata form as a satisfactory resolution of tension. But does it seem so to the students, or does the resolution also imply potentially unsatisfactory compromise? The potential for deep digression away from the purely musical details of sonata form in this discussion is obvious, but that need not present a problem. It is less important that your Music Appreciation students remember perfectly the specific musical terms and harmonic principles associated with sonata form than it is for them to come away from your class with a clear idea that the shape of a musical composition—*any* kind of composition—can mirror the structure of a dramatic human interaction, whether in life, in literature, or in the theatre.

Similarly, the genre of chamber music can be presented as a viable model for conflict management.[14] All chamber musicians know that the art of small ensemble performance requires careful negotiation at many levels—technical, artistic, interpretive, and egoistic. If you are a member of a chamber group, you might want to bring them to class and let your students observe the subtle communications that go on among the performers as they interact with one another and with the score.

---

[12]　The Flamingos, "I Only Have Eyes For You," on *The Best of Doo-Wop Ballads* (Rhino Records, 1989).

[13]　"Zealots" on *Fugees: The Score* (Sony Music Entertainment, 1996).

[14]　Many thanks to Professor Rena Sharon of the University of British Columbia in Vancouver for this interesting way of thinking about chamber music.

Or, you might require they attend a chamber music concert and then interview the ensemble members afterward, asking them to comment upon the kinds of verbal and non-verbal negotiations they make in order to produce a satisfactory and convincingly "harmonic" performance.

While history and political science majors often respond most creatively to the examples cited above, psychology, theatre, and literature majors are much inspired by the structural and musical aspects of the strophic variation aria *Possente spirto*, from Monteverdi's *L'Orfeo* (1607). They enjoy being led through the specific correspondences between formal, timbral, and stylistic elements in the music and the various psychological/emotional stages of recognition, denial, and acceptance Orpheus undergoes during his showdown with the underworld gods.[15] As they follow Orpheus through his redefinition of himself and his role in the cosmos, strophe by strophe, non-majors also discover how a first-rate musical dramatist captures and represents, in purely musical terms, fluctuating emotional and intellectual states.

Experiential Learning and Student Research

In terms of experiential learning, many creative opportunities present themselves for exploration in a liberal arts music course. Students with an interest in spirituality can contact resources within the institution related to spirituality, and create research projects in which they can observe and report on the way music is used in various spiritual contexts on campus and off campus. If an element of service is required in your liberal arts course, the campus center for service learning should be able to provide a list of on- and off-campus locations in which music might be combined with service or community engagement. My own students, for example, often volunteer at a local shelter, preparing and serving meals to homeless members of the community. The shelter has a piano at the far end of the dining room, and I encourage students to work with shelter supervisors to add an element of music-making to their meal-service duties.

If an element of performance is required in your institution's music courses for non-majors, any number of non-threatening contexts can be created for students with little or no musical background. In the classroom, simple clapping games allowing the students to experience multiple layers of rhythm are easy to invent. Similarly, leading students in the performance of Gregorian chant is not difficult, gives non-musicians contact with a repertoire they might not otherwise encounter, and usually prompts some interesting comments on the calming effects produced by the exercise. Chant singing also allows you to make some important points about the oral transmission of certain repertoires; points that will provide an interesting frame of reference as you later discuss the notation of music. Even rudimentary experience with composition is possible in a Music Appreciation

---

[15]   Marjorie Roth, "The 'Why' of Music: Variations on a Cosmic Theme," in *Teaching Music History*, ed. Mary Natvig (Aldershot and Burlington, VT: Ashgate, 2002), 77-94.

classroom. I once taught a class of mainly physical education majors to write simple two-part compositions by starting each class with a fifteen-minute vocal "warm-up" using the basic solfege syllables. A short description of which syllable combinations produced consonant intervals, which produced dissonant intervals, and which parallels were to be avoided (accompanied by a chart of note-names for those who did not read music) resulted in some admirable first attempts at adding a second line to a simple cantus firmus. Finally, if your school has a stock of small percussion instruments, borrowing them for a drum circle during finals week not only gives your students a viable experience with making music, but also provides a welcome opportunity for tension release.

Curricular expectations of interdisciplinary content and/or student research in the liberal arts classroom can be met by having your Music Appreciation students make use of library resources for music study. These can be as simple as the *Grove Dictionary or the Music* index or as sophisticated as RILM or Humanities abstracts. Allowing your students free rein to explore any musical topic that catches their interest is a bit risky and will certainly produce uneven results, especially in classes open to students at any level (i.e., freshmen to seniors). But again, extreme sophistication in terms of both the topic and the research ability of the student are not the primary goal. It is the experience simply of *doing* some kind of individual research on a musical topic, and learning how to articulate the ways in which the experience of research has transformed a student's way of thinking, that should be the main point of the assignment. In my classes, I require students to complete a "state of research" project that requires students to work with me in defining a musical topic they would like to know more about, and creating a series of questions they have about the topic. Eventually, this definition and series of questions will be the basis of the formal introduction to their research paper. Next, using the library resources available, students choose five to ten sources of information that they will read and annotate in considerable detail. These annotations comprise the main body of the research paper. Finally, the conclusion of the paper summarizes the student's reflections on the experience of digesting sophisticated source material pertaining to their topic. They must describe the way their ideas on their topic have changed; what they learned, what new questions and connections emerged as their research progressed. Although challenging, this assignment never fails to generate a great deal of excitement. Students gain experience learning about, thinking deeply about, and writing about some aspect of music that is close to their own hearts. I have found over the years that their enthusiasm for their projects often spills over into our lectures/discussions, and I routinely devote final class periods to verbal presentations of the projects.

Conclusion: Universal Harmony Beyond the Classroom

What does it mean for the non-musician to truly appreciate music? It means that your students will come away from your class with a heightened ability to understand the nature, worth, quality, and significance of the art of music as part of human culture. They will be able to evaluate, promote, and articulate the value of music, at all three of its Boethian levels, with respect to their own individual lives and the collective human culture it will become their responsibility to create and maintain in the future. As a fine artist you will occasionally miss those exquisite pedagogical moments when you can savor some truly heart-stopping, goose bump-rendering harmonic progression, or some astonishingly sophisticated formal innovation with like-minded music students. But what the fine artist in you must sacrifice in purely musical depth, the liberal artist in you will gain back many times over in breadth of human response and continued confirmation of the universal significance of music.

Chapter 10

On Being and Becoming: The First Year of Teaching on the Clock

Michael Markham

Being an Academic and Becoming a College Professor

The original topic suggested to me by this book's editor in conversation was "things you wish you knew that first year." I have taken "that first year" to mean "the first year of teaching on the clock" rather than simply the "first year in which you taught *something*." For most of us there will be a number of such firsts: the first time we ran a classroom as a TA for one of our professors during graduate school, the first full course we were put in charge of as lecturer in that same setting (for me, a summer-session Music Appreciation class), the first year teaching as part of a post-doctoral fellowship in another department, the first year teaching as an adjunct on/in the market, and the first year in which you find yourself in what you consider to be a permanent appointment. It is the last of these that is my focus.

Based on conversations with colleagues, unease that first year is common if not nearly universal. It is a profound transition when teaching is rather suddenly your central professional concern. It is also different from all previous steps forward in your academic life. It is, for instance, the first that places the responsibility for other people's development in your hands. In this way it marks the beginning of the central phase of your professional life, during which you are viewed as a figure of authority by everyone you encounter daily. This was not true during graduate school, and even during post-graduate work, be it as a post-doc., research fellow, or even as an adjunct lecturer. Those phases, which primarily mark your development as a scholar rather than a teacher, happen during a period that is institutionally set aside and recognized as preparatory, falling vaguely under the "becoming" phase of your professional life, when you are in one way or another still labeled as "becoming a professor."

Your development as a classroom teacher is not as sheltered and there is no similar period set aside for it. You will begin discovering many of the new skills unique to the classroom only *after* you have already been placed in a job for which you are presumed to be a fully formed professional. At some point, gone by too suddenly to properly react to it, "becoming" turns into "being." That moment of transition and the year of teaching that follows is the focus of this chapter. To the extent that it still represents a goal to which most in our field are aspiring, it also still represents one of the most important and bewildering moments in the professional life of the lecturer in Musicology.

As much as this presumed change from "becoming" to "being" may catch you off guard, equally daunting is the sudden shift in the meaning of the object, the thing into which you have been transformed ("Professor"). For the preceding ten years "becoming a professor" has meant any number of things: becoming a scholar, becoming a published author, becoming a critic, becoming a colleague, becoming a specialist, becoming a Ph.D. Presumably, somewhere in all of that was "becoming a teacher." That, however, which had been the most neglected aspect of your larval development, is suddenly the dominant feature by which the title Professor is defined by the vast majority of people with whom you interact: your students, the university administration, the School of Music studio faculty, and the academic faculty outside of the music department, to all of whom your scholarship, publications, dissertation, and conference papers are something of an exotic (and invisible) novelty.

Thus at a moment when the projection of an authoritative teaching voice suddenly becomes a daily concern, you may find yourself unsure of exactly what this particular authority is supposed to be based on. Unlike at the end of other stages of graduate work, there is no institutional moment by which authority is conferred. Unless you secure a permanent position directly upon finishing your doctoral exams, there will be no ceremony, no exam-committee handshake, no celebratory wine and cheese reception. In all likelihood, you will not be in the same place that you did most of your graduate work. You will be travelling to research or write your dissertation, or already teaching as an adjunct who-knows-where. There will be a phone call, and then a second for a brief, clumsy negotiation of terms with a department chair that you have met once. And that will be it. You will be a professor of Musicology with a full slate of courses upcoming and a personnel committee eagerly awaiting your first-semester's student evaluations to see if they made the correct hire.

There is much in the way that musicologists are trained, and in which they receive their early teaching experience, that fails to prepare one to do well immediately as a classroom teacher at the college level. During my own first year I had constantly to remind myself that this would not be my best year of teaching and, in fact, there was no logical reason that it should even go down as a particularly *good* year. There were simply too many aspects of the work that I either failed to anticipate or about which I had a distorted or unrealistic perspective. Of course, you have the job because you succeeded in convincing a search committee that you are *already* a great teacher, but don't you buy into it yourself. If your first year is anything like mine and like those of colleagues I have talked with, it will be marked primarily by a constant string of surprises, by small advances, and at times by large failures. The goal of this chapter is not to help you avoid any particular failing, but to help you interpret these failures correctly. They are less an indictment of your ability than of your experience and of the process by which academics are trained. Thus, the most important thing about your first year is that it will force you to admit to yourself that you are not really "complete," and that you are just beginning to learn a new and unfamiliar skill set.

If I were asked for just one advisory axiom on the first year, it would be: Don't rush to judgment on your teaching. It's not as late as you think and you are just getting started on a very long process of improvement. You can help the process along by anticipating some of the issues likely to arise and some of the preconceptions that might distract you from making needed adjustments as you move from graduate (or post-graduate) research and into full-time teaching. In outlining some of these, I offer some specific examples of how these obstacles revealed themselves to me during the daily grind of my own first year. Not everyone's experience will be the same, but certain elements are common to most who make this transition.

I am Become Professor, the Bringer of Quizzes

You will encounter unanticipated challenges almost daily during that first year and you will frequently find yourself questioning your instinctive reactions. Some of these challenges will soon become mundane new realities to which you will accustom yourself, like for instance the sheer amount of time it takes to grade written assignments. Somehow, in the previous six years of graduate school no one bothered to warn me about this. My first undergraduate class had 140 students in it, and I assigned writing each of the first two meetings. In my first weeks I was eager to analyze and improve my own classroom performance and instead I was swamped with grading. I pulled away considerably from written assignments for the rest of that semester and the following year, only beginning to reincorporate them as I became a more efficient planner. It is certainly not ideal to avoid written assignments in an undergraduate survey. Thus, my early versions of the course were inherently flawed. However, the first year is no time to dabble in ideals. It is necessary to come to terms with the difference between the perfect version of a course as you've envisioned it and what you are actually capable of handling at this moment.

It may be useful to conceive of those earliest classes not as demonstrations of your competence, but as lessons from which you yourself have much to learn. You will likely not have time to delve too far into issues of presentation technique or classroom methodology simply due to the extraordinary amount of mundane preparation during a year when almost every lecture you teach will be your first time through that topic: time required to prepare lecture notes or PowerPoint slides, choose scores and recordings, and rehearse analytical examples. Your first year you will measure this very basic level of preparation in tens of hours per class meeting and it will frustrate you. Each time you repeat a course or revisit a topic, you will be able to think further beyond such basics and devote more time to exploring new teaching techniques, or to other elements like written assignments or group discussions.

Not all of the problems you encounter, however, will have such obvious solutions as "don't do that, yet." Some will require you to come to terms with bigger issues surrounding your own transition from graduate-school "academic" to college professor. This can only begin, however, with an assessment of your new academic setting, your particular department, and the students you are now charged with helping.

Getting to Know Your Department

Not all graduate programs are the same, and some people will arrive in their first permanent teaching position feeling more prepared for this shift than others. Whatever the temperaments and tendencies of our particular graduate school, however, almost all new musicology hires will have one thing in common— we will have spent much (or most) of our adult lives in one type of academic environment. Your image of "university" will be somewhat narrowed by this as you emerge from the cocoon of graduate school. Thus one of your most important first-year tasks is coming to understand your new academic milieu. Along with this will come an unexpected irony: that while you will have already been a university academic in some capacity for most of (if not more than) a decade by the time you begin your first permanent teaching job, you may find yourself, in that first year, suddenly feeling rather new to "college."[1]

You may already begin to sense this when you are on the job market, attempting to adjust your identity as a scholar to match as many situations and schools as possible. The breadth of missions, expectations, and departmental profiles you will encounter may surprise you. This will only increase as you move further along the process. After having defined your own academic identity primarily through specialist research during your formative years, you may now find yourself interviewing only at schools with no graduate research program (or no graduate students at all) and with nothing resembling what you consider to be an academic library. After working within an almost exclusively academic environment, your first long-term teaching job may be at a school dominated by its performance program or populated primarily by music education students, with few, if any, sharing the interest in history that you had as an undergraduate.

Talking with my graduate-school colleagues, with whom I shared similar early teaching experiences (as TAs at the University of California, Berkeley), I now find that none of us are teaching students who have much in common in terms of their backgrounds, needs, and ambitions. Only one of us is teaching in a department similar to the one that spawned us and we each find ourselves in unique situations regarding the mission of our respective schools (ranging from conservatories of

---

[1]   A number of anecdotes about this shift in personal identity are collected in Colleen M. Conway and Thomas M. Hodgman, *Teaching Music in Higher Education* (New York and Oxford: Oxford University Press, 2008), 86-91.

music to small liberal arts colleges to large state schools, some with and some without any research or graduate degrees in musicology). One of my former colleagues is responsible for only graduate-level seminars in Musicology and dissertation advising, while another has no graduate students at all and is called upon to teach not only every music history course, but also courses in art history, world music, and so on, primarily for non music-majors.

We also have dissimilar expectations in terms of teaching load, publication, and service. At least one expressed his delight that he experienced almost no pressure at all in terms of publication. Others felt intensely the pressure to publish quickly and often. Teaching loads the first year ranged from two-plus-one to four-plus-four, meaning that one of my former classmates began by teaching five courses more than another in the same year. Some were in situations where a research sabbatical was expected in the first four years, others where the notion of time off to pursue research is absurd. Some work in departments with up to seven other musicologists on faculty and with Ph.D. candidates under their mentorship, others are alone in terms of disciplinary colleagues and have no students whose focus is Musicology.

You will need to adjust to the semester-rhythm of your new department. The college life of the undergraduate moves at a different pace than that of the research student. My experience of graduate school studies was that it was "end-weighted" with a slow build toward the crunch of seminar papers at the end of the term. In my new department, I have learned to adjust to just the opposite. My students tend to have much more time, energy, and enthusiasm for academic work in the early weeks. This is, in part, due to the overwhelming pressures of ensemble concerts, degree recitals, and juries that pile onto their plate in the final two months of each term. Each individual week is also much more fragmented for them than it was for me as a graduate student. They measure their week in increments of hours, with large segments of time set aside ambiguously for "practice" (orchestra, choir, lessons) and much smaller fragments allotted for "everything else" (including all of their academic and skills classes). Their academic classwork will likely be done in a few short bursts near the end of the week. There is little chance of forcing a change in this. Mine is a performance department, and if my students have to choose between disappointing their history professor in class or being scolded by the orchestra conductor in front of the entire orchestra, it is obvious what choice they will make.

Getting to Know Your Students

It may surprise you how much and how quickly this diversity of circumstances and the unique nature of your new department and students will shape your development as a teacher. In fact, much of your progress will depend on how quickly you open yourself up to what your students are revealing about themselves and about the program they are working through. You may begin the year assuming that your focus should be on yourself as teacher, refining specific techniques and engaging in a series of hit and miss attempts at putting them into practice. I did just that and was left frustrated over my lack of progress from week to week. My thoughts were no longer organized by the active dialog of seminar discussions and scholarly debate but were now a series of monologues planned in secret and delivered to large classrooms full of students who seemed unprepared to do anything but passively listen. This passivity can be particularly acute in music departments, and working to overcome it will eventually become an important part of your teaching technique.[2]

Early on, however, I kept my attention on myself, honing the content of my lectures. In conversations with colleagues, my biggest gripe became how much time I was spending on each class meeting. I never seemed to stop fussing with my notes, writing and rewriting, outlining and diagramming, rehearsing and revising. Content preparation took up every moment I had, leaving me little time to get to know my colleagues or my students. The process, however, did not seem to get easier no matter how much time I devoted to it and I never felt secure with what I had prepared. I was unsure where to begin each topic and how far to go. I had no sense of whether I was aiming too high or too low. It was the editor of this book who first suggested to me that "where to begin" and "how high to aim" is not really something for me to figure out. It was something I needed to find out from my students. I paraphrase: "Remember you are not dictating a history book, you are teaching people." In other words, I needed to stop worrying so much about doing justice to the *topic* and base my planning instead on what will most benefit the *people* sitting in front of me. Of course, in order to do that I needed to stop talking and start listening so that my students could reveal to me what they needed to know and how much they could absorb in one class. This does not mean simply to hold more discussions or to ask more questions, but to open yourself up to a general knowledge of your students' ambitions and experiences, where they are from, what language they have for talking about music, how they approach the classroom, what sort of ideas they harbor about art and expression, what they think they know about the business of classical music, what they assume a history class is meant to do.

Three years later the process of visualizing and planning a lecture on almost any topic is much easier. I have a rough template in mind for who will be in the room and where they are in terms of their development as musicians and as students. I can anticipate what sort of questions will generate immediate, confident, and free conversation, and what sort will cause the room to fall into a panicked silence. Both, of course, are useful and I am now able to sense when is the proper time to deploy one or the other. I am familiar with the backgrounds and cultural experiences that my students bring to class. I know where to start and I know how

    [2]   James A. Davis, "Classroom Discussion and the Community of Music Majors," *Journal of Music History Pedagogy* 1 (2010): 5-17, accessed November 18, 2011, http://www.ams-net.org/ojs/index.php/jmhp/article/view/8.

far I can expect them to follow me in one sitting. My assumptions will not be the same as yours, as my students are not the same as yours. Nevertheless, a quick summary of some of my own observations about my undergraduates may give you a sense of what students can tell you about themselves.

- They are ambitious but their work has been directed only toward meeting the technical requirements to get into a conservatory. Thus, they have little idea where their work might lead them or what options are out there in the world for an artist or musician. They are not in touch with the art world per se and have little sense of how wide is the professional sphere of concert music today. They have not experienced enough different styles or musical eras to have confidently chosen one as a "specialty."
- This is their first music history class. They have little experience thinking through music in a classroom setting or in lecture format, and have not considered what "music history" actually means. Their previous "classroom music" experience is via theory and aural skills courses and their first instinct will likely be to put themselves in the same frame of mind for my class.
- They have a remarkable ability to quickly immerse themselves in a topic that has caught their attention. This is partly a product of how much more media is available to them than was available to students even ten years ago.
- Finally, most of them are either performance majors or Music Education majors and as such their workload is heavy with skills classes and ensemble rehearsals. One result of this is that they have little time left in their schedule to take some of the standard liberal arts courses one might expect most any college student to experience. Thus, for better or worse, it is up to me to address some of this basic cultural, philosophical, and art history and I must find time to incorporate topics beyond musical style.

While not every student fits this profile, given a class of 30-100, it helps to have a template. Whatever the topic, for instance, I know that I must include something in almost every lecture to jolt them out of the "skills" practice mode that might carry over from their theory classes and into a more interpretive frame of mind. I frame my lectures in such a way as to remind them that history is less about "how music is put together" and more about "why it was put together that way." Likewise, I must relate the historical ideas and sounds of each class to today's concert life. My students need to be constantly reminded that you don't necessarily have to be interested in "music history" in order to be interested in the repertoire and ideas being discussed that day.

I am not in a department that generally produces future historians, and so my job is not to scout for future graduate students, or to prepare students for seminar studies in medieval or Renaissance music. Thus, when teaching the undergraduate "early music" survey, I now spend more time discussing twentieth-century recordings of Gregorian chant than I spend discussing the prayers and services that made up the medieval service or the generic differences between antiphonal and responsorial chants. When we discuss the organum of Notre Dame, I spend more time comparing the musical texture to 1970s minimalism than I spend on the historical details of the *Magnus Liber Organi*. I know that in order for my students to engage with the music, they need to see it as a viable, living avenue for expression in their own lives. Those who become interested in it as such will eventually get around to some of the historical details I've left out. But I know from the experience of my first year, that if I spend those lectures going over the names of Latin prayers and formal diagrams of mass texts, almost none of my students will be intrigued enough to look any further.

Fulfilling the mission I *do* have means taking more class time to deal with sound, with issues of recording and interpretation, and with comparisons between historical and contemporary expressive ideals. These are big topics that can lead to fun and useful discussion, but they also take time away from the "presentation of facts." Recently Melanie Lowe has addressed her ongoing anxiety over the need to make difficult cuts from the canon in order to make it through a four-semester undergraduate survey.[3] The cuts I've had to make are even more daunting, my department getting by for now with only a two-semester survey. As a TA, and even as a visiting post-doc., the consequences of curricular planning were no concern to me. So this new responsibility—for making drastic decisions about what will and will not be learned by hundreds of young musicians—caught me completely off guard and was a source of considerable angst.

Coming to terms with this in the aftermath of my first year meant a large-scale overhaul of my entire concept of the class. The lectures I delivered that first semester now seem ridiculous to me. They were miniature textbook chapters designed to impart as much historical information as possible. The class took on a more manageable shape once I accepted that, for *my* students in *my* department, my role is more complex and diffuse than simply teaching *The* (complete, ideal) History of Music. It is a job that requires appropriate compromises based on my students' career ambitions and the curricular structure of the department.

Stop Radiating All Your Brilliance

Coming out of graduate school, it can be hard to greet the necessity of such compromises with much enthusiasm. So much of what we do during our graduate school days is meant to demonstrate competence in the form of exhaustive knowledge. In our papers, during seminar discussions, even at "post-colloquium" dinner parties, we are under pressure to show off our brilliance. Even when you

---

    [3]   Melanie Lowe, "Teaching Music History Today: Making Tangible Connections to Here and Now," *Journal of Music History Pedagogy* 1 (2010): 45-59, accessed November 18, 2011, http://www.ams-net.org/ojs/index.php/jmhp/article/view/17.

teach as a graduate assistant you are aware of being under scrutiny from mentors and colleagues. Likewise, when you are on the market for a teaching job, you spend much of your time selling your mastery. It is a difficult habit to break as you begin your full-time teaching career, but you should set about shaking it off as soon as possible. Your students do not need to see you prove your credentials in front of them, and your class should not be a vehicle to demonstrate all your hard-won knowledge. The reality is that most of what you know is not useful to your students at this point in their studies. Their professional success or failure is unlikely to be affected by how much information you have offered them about the cyclic mass or the *formes fixes*. Much more useful are experiences that open their eyes to the value of historical criticism and give them the confidence to apply it in any situation they may encounter. But in order to create such experiences, you first need to allow them to project what they know and do not know, what they *think* they know, and what they are ready to take in. As you allow yourself to react to them, your view of which concepts and information are essential will then change greatly. This will take time, however, and it is again worth remembering our first axiom: Don't rush to judgment on your teaching. It's not as late as you think. It will be a number of years before you know *what* to teach, let alone how to teach it.

It will help to observe other teachers in your department. This is something I did not do enough my first year, but whenever I did, my understanding of the music majors in my school was suddenly enhanced. While the pedagogical sessions at AMS and other conferences are useful and inspiring, I have found that nothing has a more direct effect on your teaching than watching another teacher who has already adjusted to the same department and has already come to know the same students. This is not only useful for picking up new lecturing techniques, but also frees you up to observe how the students react in a class setting, something that is difficult to do while you yourself are lecturing. You will learn a lot from something as simple as your students' posture when listening, when they gain or lose interest, when they seem lost, and how they react to that feeling. It is also a chance to observe the physical demeanor of another professor as he or she commands the classroom. This may help to make you aware of your own physical and vocal habits, some of which may be detracting from the effectiveness of your presentation. I, for instance, learned a great deal about energizing a room by observing how some of my colleagues used their bodies within the class space, one by manically stalking the rows and another while never actually leaving the piano bench. Likewise, my own fear of any "dead air" during my lectures was alleviated when I observed how comfortable one of my colleagues was with long pauses, and how his students, too, were comfortable in taking time to think through their answers without the tension of a nervous professor expecting an immediate reply.

The most pleasantly surprising thing to come out of all this listening and watching was the effect it had on my students when I showed them, in turn, that I was paying attention to them. Midway through my first semester I handed out "mid-term student evaluations." They were not great. The most consistent complaint was about PowerPoint slides that were overly cluttered with information (as, I've already noted, were my lectures themselves). The next week I debuted a new PowerPoint system. From now on the slides themselves would only contain questions.[4] Those questions would serve as a basic frame for my lecture at that moment and would also likely end up on the following test. It would be up to the students to decide what bits of information from the lecture itself were most useful in answering questions on the slide. I also let them know that this change was due to their feedback. The response was overwhelmingly positive. The students felt a stronger sense of ownership over what went on in the classroom and my end-of-semester student evaluations reflected this as well. I now look for opportunities to credit student feedback with various changes in the course from semester to semester.

Getting to Know Yourself

As you become more accustomed to your new academic setting, you will begin to form a distinction between your relationship to knowledge as a researcher and as a teacher. This is an important step because the latter does not automatically flow from the former. One of the biggest impediments to my own development the first year was the residual effects of the "trickle down" myth of teaching, an unspoken axiom among my graduate school cohort that if you are a knowledgeable academic you will naturally be a good teacher. This came, in part, from observing our graduate-school mentors, all of whom were well-respected researchers and writers on music, and all of whom seemed to have effortless confidence and flair in the classroom. It did not occur to me at the time that there might be little connection between the two skill sets and that what I was seeing was not merely their native brilliance passively flaking off in dazzling sparkles, but was the end result of five, ten, in some cases twenty years or more of hard-won classroom experience, a process that remained hidden from us. It also did not occur to me then that their teaching style, tailored as it was to the students at that school, would be ineffective if transferred over to my new school.

This is a problem because much of what academics do is learned through emulation. We learn to write by reading good writing. We learn to research by following the steps of our predecessors as laid out in their published articles. We learn to read critically by observing how our graduate professors and our own graduate-student colleagues approach and discuss readings in seminar. Models of emulation are much more difficult to find for your teaching, and those mentors who guided you through your graduate work and dissertation writing may not end up being ideal as such. Their position, their school, and their teaching will likely be too different from what yours will become.

---

    [4]   It was looking for answers to the students' complaints that led me to this technique as mentioned in James M. Lang, *A Week By Week Guide to Your First Semester of College Teaching* (Cambridge, MA: Harvard University Press, 2008), 76.

This gets to the heart of the identity adjustment that defines that first year for, while you will arrive in your new position as a fully formed academic, you will not yet have as clearly defined an identity as a teacher. By the time you finish your dissertation, you will be well aware of your own strengths, weaknesses, and passions as a scholar. You will have a strongly identifiable scholarly voice, characterized by the methodologies and theoretical frameworks for writing history that appeal to you. You will have worked out these preferences carefully, through trial and error and countless debates with your graduate-school colleagues. As an academic, the path ahead is easy to visualize because your models for progress are clearly represented in all the best scholarly journals and are often discussed among your peers. Most importantly, you will be well aware of exactly what it is that you enjoy about research and writing.

None of this will be true of your teaching. Not only will you be unaware yet of your strengths and weaknesses, you will not yet even have a set of categories and methodologies by which you can begin to take stock of them. Worse, you will not yet know what you actually enjoy about teaching. The concept simply has not been theoretically defined for you in anything approaching the depth by which the term "scholar" has been. The solution to this sounds simple, but will require constant vigilance during your first semesters of teaching. In the midst of all of the crises and unexpected problems, you must find time to take stock of what you are actually enjoying, both when you are "in the moment" during class and during class preparation. You will hopefully be surprised at which parts of the teaching process become the most invigorating for you. Your teaching, for instance, may be the only time that you get to engage "academically" with the music of Beethoven if you are not a Beethoven scholar, or with Josquin if you are not a Renaissance specialist. I began my first year assuming that I would be comfortable lecturing from the podium and generally dread leading small seminar discussions. Up to that point my most successful experiences had been in large (400-student) lectures given behind an enormous podium. Thus, in my earliest seminars, I would often fall into the comfortable "lecture posture" automatically. I was also far more nervous before seminars than before survey classes. This, however, was deceptive. I was lecturing in undergraduate courses six to eight times a week and only led seminar discussions once a week, so of course I quickly became more comfortable doing the former. But as the semester wore on, I found that the seminar discussion provided a level of intensity that my lectures never approached. This was a first symptom that I did, in fact, quite enjoy the seminar setting. Now beginning my fourth year, I find that all of my teaching is influenced by the more casual tone and posture that I tend to assume during seminar discussions.

The Crisis of Authority

In talking with some of my former graduate-school colleagues about their first year, the most commonly cited anxiety had to do with the sudden assumption of "authority." The issue has been shadowing us the entire chapter, for instance in the anxiety, already mentioned above, that comes with taking responsibility for long-term curricular decisions. This is only one of many times in which you will be the final word on problems that might impact hundreds of people a year. During your dissertation research, the only potential casualty of your bad decisions was yourself. When you were teaching as a graduate assistant there was always an oracle to consult. Even as an adjunct you may often comfortably deflect many questions or problems toward the tenure-track faculty. Finding yourself without that higher power once you yourself are in charge of your own department can be dizzying. Of course, your new faculty colleagues will be helpful, but many problems are now yours alone to resolve and there is no orientation packet that can prepare you for every specific situation you will encounter in your first year. Take heart. In one form or another, the "crisis of authority" affects every new professor.

Again, past experience can be a psychological obstacle. A number of the people I spoke with noted how naturally and effortlessly our graduate-school mentors seemed to glow with authority. It can seem like an innate gift—you either have it naturally or not at all. It is not. It comes with practice, but graduate school affords few such opportunities. When you gained your first classroom experience as a teaching assistant, you were likely closer in age to your students than to your adviser, and in their eyes you were something of a buffer between them and the "real" professor. You may have found it convenient to foster that image because it made for easy, open discussion in your sections. But there was likely no point at which you were the final word on anything important. If a student had a concern, they may have come to you first because they felt you would be more sympathetic. But if a student was caught plagiarizing or cheating, you were not The Law. You referred the problem to the course professor and it was dealt with. It was not your responsibility to make sure that old test questions were not reused (it may catch you quite off guard your *second* year to find how well organized students are when it comes to archiving old tests and assignments for future generations). Nor were you setting deadlines, making final decisions on missed assignments or requests for makeup tests, or accepting/questioning claims of sudden mysterious illness or multiple expiring grandmothers.

As a newly minted full-time professor, you will feel the weight of your new authority every time you enter the classroom. I felt it, as did most of my graduate school colleagues. It is, however, the most illusory of first-year issues and a preoccupation with it can be unhealthy. Looking back now, I realize that the biggest problem my first year was not an inability to project authority from the beginning, but my constant worrying about it. This must have manifested itself to my students as a lack of confidence both in myself and in them. An early reader of this chapter suggested to me that such anxiety is symptomatic of an outmoded view of the classroom as a teacher-dominated lecture hall. Her antidote was simply this, humility: "My students have the sense that we're all in this knowledge-creating business together … building authority probably requires letting go of it.''[5] The notion that a lecture is like a performance is a common one.[6] We have all seen lecturers who can command a room with the power and panache of a Shakespearean actor or a Pentecostal preacher. But over the long term, for most of us, the performance element is best thought of as more Brechtian than Wagnerian. The more you open up to your students the work-in-progress of teaching—let them see your work, your thought process, even your struggles, rather than some final text delivered with the practiced air of omniscient mastery—the more constructive the classroom will become.

That said, there are a few everyday responsibilities in running a classroom that you should be aware of from the start. One of the first, hard lessons I learned was how quickly students make judgments about the nature of your classroom and how early patterns of behavior will set in. If you allow people to straggle in late the first few meetings, it will quickly become normal behavior for your class. The same thing goes for class participation. If you want your students to engage in regular discussion with you during class, you need to force them to talk in the first few meetings. They will decide within two weeks whether yours is a "listening class" or a "talking class" (or a "sleeping class"). You are no different. You will want to set up some habits for yourself in the opening weeks to insure that you are not caught off guard by your grading responsibilities. At the end of the term it is up to you and only you to have the numbers in order, and the sort of organizational prowess required for the accurate grading of two or three hundred students is not something that comes naturally to all humanities scholars. Force yourself right from the start to be more meticulous than you assume you'll need to be.

No matter how much effort you put in to your courses, a certain number of students each semester will simply be impossible to win over. Difficult situations will arise and it is foolish to assume that you should somehow naturally know how to diffuse them. The specter of discipline problems in the classroom is a major driver of first-year anxiety. While I cannot give any specific advice for how to handle specific problems, I strongly advise you to begin collecting anecdotes from your peers. Everyone will have stories about this and the more you hear about

---

[5] I would like to thank Jessie Fillerup for this observation. It is worth at this point remembering that the empowerment of students over the development of their own critical skills is a commonly encountered pedagogical goal (cf. L. Dee Fink, *Creating Significant Learning Experiences: An Integrated Approach to Designing College Courses* (San Francisco: Jossey-Bass, 2003), 19.) But ironically both "taking control" and "letting go" can be sources of first-year anxiety, depending on your own personality. Making this collaboration and being honest with your students about your own struggle to achieve the right balance may not only help foster such student empowerment, but also help lift some of the "authority anxiety" from the shoulders of the new professor.

[6] Just referencing sources already mentioned here, Conway and Hodgman, *Teaching Music in Higher Education*, 84, make the comparison as does Lang, *A Week By Week Guide*, 71-73. Likewise, many discussions I had as a graduate student about our own professors were something like reviews of a musical performance.

other people's problems (welcome to the sad fraternity!), the less the notion will rattle you. As you spend more time at the front of the class, you will naturally project a stronger presence. It is, on some level, just a matter of time. Near the end of my first year, I began counting up the hours I had spent teaching, as if I was logging training hours in an airplane. Now, as I begin my fourth year, I am approaching one thousand hours in front of a class. At this point, apart from the first few classes each term, I seldom feel the same sense of nervousness as I did throughout the first year and my own calmness gives my students a greater sense of freedom to carry the discussion where they would like.

You may be dismayed, or even devastated, if the first round of student evaluations you receive do not live up to your expectations (and worried that your personnel committee will only note the bad ones). Remember, however, the opening of this chapter. Your first classes *will* be among your worst and your first evaluations will reflect some genuine problems. However, you will also need to develop an eye for which student criticisms are genuine and thoughtful and which are not worth taking seriously. Scribbled screeds littered with exclamation points, pointless insults about how you dress or the tone of your voice, the words "worst … ever" or "ruined music for me"—these can all be safely discarded with the comforting thought that individual students will come and go quickly, but you will be around for a long time.

You will also (and this is less ideal news) age rapidly in the eyes of your students and this will quickly change how they view you. Yes, that first year, you will still have the whiff of the new and inexperienced and your students may react to that. Whether that means that they cut you a certain amount of slack or that they attack will depend on where you are teaching. Either way, it does not last. My own undergraduate survey, for instance, is mostly populated by sophomores. Thus, by my second year, even though I still felt new, none of my students had any memory of the department without me as a presence. As far as they knew, I had been at SUNY for thirty years. I had no less *gravitas* in their eyes than any other faculty member, even as I still felt like I was finding my feet in the department. You will be surprised how quickly you become just another ancient relic with an office. This is also worth bearing in mind when you make references to contemporary culture. Your jokes will age fast. A reference that made you seem relatable to your students five years ago is already outdated and needs to go. Your students' reactions to your jokes are the mirror that cannot lie. That is how you get old.

Outside Authority Transfers to the Classroom

Ironically, your own research and your university service, things that you might think of as a distraction from your teaching, can help to boost your confidence as much as anything that happens in the classroom. I made the mistake my first year of pushing both aside, assuming that the way to solve a crisis of teaching confidence was to work more on my teaching (logical, no?). The following summer, however, just a few weeks before the new semester began, I experienced some modest success presenting my first international conference paper. While it was nothing that shook the discipline, when I returned to begin preparing for my courses I had a swagger in my step that carried over into the next term. I had more energy and had the confidence to lead a much more relaxed classroom than if I had spent the summer working on my "issues." It is important, it turns out, to be reminded that your intellectual world extends beyond your own campus. Yes, it is difficult to find time to produce new work, particularly in your early years on the clock. But if you find the time to regularly present your work before your peers on the field of academic debate, suddenly a roomful of teenagers will seem less imposing.

Successes in service and committee work can have a similar effect. As a full-time tenure-track faculty member you will now be called upon to make decisions that impact your entire department and to act as an advocate for other professionals. In particular the adjunct lecturers and part-time faculty members will rely on your advocacy. These are people your own age or older with families and career goals, who will at some point need you to represent them within the college, whether it is an issue of salary, job security, or course load. The first time you find yourself successfully lobbying your department chair on behalf of one of your peers, you will "level-up" in your confidence in a way that almost no single classroom experience can match.

The classroom will undoubtedly be your biggest concern your first year. But as you take on responsibilities that expand your reach beyond it, into your department, your university, and the academic world, you will begin to see it as a different, freer space: a space for experimentation where you can have an idea and see its success or failure unfold before you in a matter of days rather than years, a space in which you are freed to comment on and compare works from vastly different cultural eras, a space in which you are allowed to engage in a discourse that is lofty but not constrained by the rules of academic publishing. A number of times over the last two years I have found myself at an academic paper session in my own field of specialty, the early Baroque, only to have my mind wander to Ives or Bartok or Verdi because I had a class on that topic coming up. Having travelled across the country (or the ocean) to "get away" from my teaching for a few days, I drifted back toward it, not because I had to, but because I was looking forward to it, to my classes, to my students.

Chapter 11
Professional Development

Jessie Fillerup

> I study and read. I bet I've read everything you read. Don't think I haven't. I consume libraries. I wear out spines and ROM-drives. I do things like get in a taxi and say, "The library, and step on it."
>
> David Foster Wallace, *Infinite Jest*

This was your life as a graduate student: reading books, haunting archives, tracking keywords in databases like a gumshoe detective. But once you secure a teaching position, you will be expected to perform many roles, and conducting research will be just one of them. Between preparing and teaching classes, attending to your scholarship, and providing service to the university and your profession, it may seem like there is little time or opportunity to work on improving your teaching—and indeed, negotiating this balance is a challenge even for experienced faculty. The skills you learned in graduate school may not transfer smoothly or easily to classroom teaching (see Chapter 10, on the first year of teaching). Even if your degree program included pedagogical training, you may feel that the workload in your first few years on the job prevents you from making the most of the practices you were taught. Reflecting on your teaching, experimenting with course design, and developing creative assignments are all worthy goals—but for the newly employed, are they practical? Once you have learned the ropes at your new position, you may find that responsibilities from which new faculty are exempt—advising students, or departmental administration, for example—start to interfere with your development as a teacher and scholar.

Academics and administrators often view professional development through a "deficit model" by seeking to add what is missing from a teacher's portfolio of skills.[1] Some institutions avoid using the phrase "professional development" because it implies that faculty have not fully formed as teacher-scholars.[2] Your own experience in transitioning from graduate student to faculty member may further contribute to the feeling that something was left out of your education. The extent to which you benefit from professional development activities is largely shaped by the value you place on them and the terms by which you define them.

---

[1]   The phrase "deficit model" derives from Gill Nicholls's research on professional development. See "New Lecturers' Constructions of Learning, Teaching, and Research in Higher Education," *Studies in Higher Education* 30 (October 2005): 613.

[2]   The University of Richmond, for example, eschews "professional development" for "faculty enrichment."

One researcher who examined faculty perceptions of teaching and learning found that certain beliefs about teaching placed constraints on professional growth: "The more limited an academic's conception of what growing and developing as a teacher can mean, the more limited their ways of approaching their own teaching development."[3] After interviewing faculty at various stages in their careers, she discovered five categories that they used to define their development as teachers:

1. Increasing content knowledge
2. Acquiring practical experience
3. Accumulating teaching strategies
4. Finding out what works, from a teacher's perspective
5. Finding out what works, from a student's perspective

Faculty who associated professional development chiefly with the first two categories seemed least likely to benefit from courses in pedagogy. The fifth category—finding out what works from a student's perspective—provided "the most complex and inclusive approach to developing as a teacher" by connecting teaching strategies to experience, reflection, and learning outcomes.[4] A comprehensive, student-centered perception of professional growth will help you focus on what may be gained from teaching development, not on what you lack as a teacher.

Working to improve your teaching early in your career can be practical, too, since it will save time outside the classroom and trouble inside of it. Learning to write syllabi that express course policies and goals clearly will help you avoid conflicts with students over assignments and grades; becoming more adept at connecting course goals to assessments should increase student learning and decrease complaints about busy work. Some techniques—like using technology to gauge student preparedness or to enhance the quality of class discussions—will help lessen problems with student engagement. Reading pedagogical sources, attending workshops, and writing grant proposals to support your teaching all pay dividends well beyond your investment. A study on the long-term effects of a five-day micro-teaching workshop showed that 89 percent of faculty who participated reported more confidence in their teaching, while 91 percent tried a new teaching strategy that they had learned there.[5] This chapter presents resources for professional development that should prove equally useful, helping you find the ideas, time, and funding necessary for you to identify and achieve your teaching goals.

[3]   Gerlese S. Åkerlind, "Constraints on Academics' Potential for Developing as a Teacher," *Studies in Higher Education* 32, no. 1 (February 2007): 33.

[4]   Åkerlind, "Constraints," 31.

[5]   Diane Persellin and Terry Goodrick, "Faculty Development in Higher Education: Long-Term Impact of a Summer Teaching and Learning Workshop," *Journal of the Scholarship of Teaching and Learning* 10 (January 2010): 5.

Teaching Centers and Research

An increasing number of institutions have opened teaching centers that assist both new and established faculty. The types of support available at these centers vary widely. Some offer financial incentives, like competitive grants for faculty to create new courses, stipends for innovative course design, and travel funds to attend pedagogical conferences and workshops. Others provide technology support, peer-to-peer teaching evaluations, and in-house workshops on specific teaching strategies. Some teaching centers have online resources that can be used by faculty at any institution. The website of the Center for Teaching at Vanderbilt University[6] features guides and short publications on many topics, including assessment, pedagogical theory, teaching activities, service learning, and educational technology.

One consequence stemming from the rise of university teaching centers is the implication that teaching development occurs independently from one's scholarly research. These centers, which help faculty with their day-to-day work as teachers, parallel the grants offices and library-based academic resources that assist faculty in their research. Resources for teaching and research are often housed separately for practical reasons: a scientist and a music historian may both benefit from a workshop at a teaching center, even if their research needs rarely overlap. But this separation, which is reflected in both the history and geography of an institution, may not be ideal for facilitating the free interaction of your research and teaching interests. Sometimes discipline-specific programs outside the university, such as grants and professional workshops (discussed below), more effectively bridge this divide.

Routinely evaluating the relationship between your teaching and scholarly activities is critically important to your progress in both fields, even if campus resources may project the notion that these activities are discrete. One researcher who interviewed faculty about their growth in academia found that many volunteered examples from both their teaching and research without being prompted to associate the two.[7] She also found parallels between teacher development—which progresses from the self (comfort and confidence in the classroom) to the other (student-focused learning)—and academic development, in which a scholar's focus on the self (one's own learning) expands to the other (one's contribution to the scholarly community).[8] A curious conclusion emerged from the study: when academics were asked to consider their growth as teachers independently from their development as academics, they exhibited a narrowed sense of awareness about their teaching. But when scholars thought about their

6   Vanderbilt University, 'Center for Teaching', accessed November 13, 2011, http://cft.vanderbilt.edu/.
7   Gerlese S. Åkerlind, "Separating the 'Teaching' from the 'Academic': Possible Unintended Consequences," *Teaching in Higher Education* 16, no. 2 (2011): 193-94.
8   Åkerlind, "Separating the 'Teaching' from the 'Academic'," 193.

careers holistically, encompassing teaching and research, they showed a more complex understanding of their development in both areas.

Professional Societies, Study Groups, and Symposia

You may already be familiar with professional music societies if you have applied for research fellowships or presented your work at regional, national, or international conferences. In addition to providing venues for scholars to share their work, these societies offer a variety of resources to help you improve your teaching, including workshops, conferences, symposia, and study groups. The descriptions below are by necessity selective, since they focus on professional development opportunities offered by four leading American music societies. There are many other organizations you may wish to investigate, including those with an international scope (like the International Musicological Society), national societies outside the United States (the Royal Musical Association or the Société française de musicologie, for example), or societies devoted to specific areas of research (like the Society for American Music).

College Music Society

The mission of the College Music Society (CMS) is to promote "music teaching and learning, musical creativity and expression, research and dialogue, and diversity and interdisciplinary interaction." CMS meetings typically feature many pedagogical presentations by faculty and graduate students in a variety of music disciplines, from applied instruction to music history and theory. Poster sessions may be more informal and experiential, inviting attendees to talk one-on-one with the presenter. Topic-specific symposia that the CMS offers each summer sometimes focus on musicology. Many attendees at CMS meetings find the environment friendly and supportive, particularly for graduate students.

   The diversity of music disciplines represented in the CMS means that you will be able to exchange ideas with musicians and scholars outside of your immediate teaching and research area. Sometimes teaching ideas translate with surprising ease from one discipline to another, and CMS members possess a broad base of knowledge and experience from which you may draw support. But the sweeping mission and musically diverse membership of the CMS requires a diffuse approach to its programming activities: music history teaching is just one of many pedagogical topics vying for attention.

   The CMS offers several conference events that are part of ongoing professional development initiatives. The pre-conference technology workshop, held the day before the national conference, serves both new faculty and experienced teachers seeking to improve their technological fluency.[9] Usually the workshop consists of several sessions organized by a theme, such as how to incorporate high-tech applications into the classroom, or how to use technology to integrate disciplines like music history and music theory. Other professional development opportunities at the CMS include mock interviews, career counseling, and mentoring sessions with experienced faculty. Meetings with mentors are confidential, and they give new faculty the chance to talk about sensitive topics that they may not feel comfortable discussing with their institutional colleagues—for example, maintaining collegial relationships, searching for a new teaching position, or issues surrounding academic freedom.

American Musicological Society

Founded in 1934, the American Musicological Society (AMS) claims its mission to be the "advancement of research in the various fields of music as a branch of learning and scholarship." Precisely what constitutes "learning and scholarship" has inspired debate among musicologists for decades, resulting in conference programs that gradually assimilate new technologies, disciplinary interests, and research methodologies. Attending regional and national meetings of research societies like the AMS will help you be informed about current disciplinary trends and provide opportunities to network with other scholars in your research area. Presenting your research for discussion and critique may improve your classroom presence, too: a sense of scholarly accomplishment can translate to confidence in teaching, and vice versa.

In recent years the AMS has started to consider teaching and pedagogical research to be pursuits that advance music scholarship. As a result, there are far more pedagogical resources available to musicology faculty today than there used to be. For several years the Committee on Career-Related Issues (CCRI) has featured the Master Teacher session, in which an esteemed, peer-nominated teacher-scholar talks candidly about life in the music history classroom. The CCRI also sponsors a mentoring program at the annual conference for graduate students and new faculty who seek an experienced hand to guide them through the maze of paper sessions, concerts, panels, social events, and networking opportunities. Often sessions organized by the CCRI are attuned to the current concerns of faculty and graduate students. Given the troubled global economy, recent CCRI sessions have focused on alternate career paths for musicologists, obtaining grant funding, and problems surrounding electronic access to research materials, which is particularly difficult for scholars unaffiliated with an institution.

Scholars with similar interests are allowed to form study groups, which provide plentiful opportunities to meet and exchange ideas with those who know a particular research area best. Study groups tend to give especially warm receptions

---

[9]   The event is convened with the annual meeting of the Association for Technology in Music Instruction (ATMI), whose interests often intersect with those of the CMS.

to graduate students and new faculty, whose participation helps ensure the robust health of the group's special research focus.[10] Each study group presents at least one session at the annual meeting, and many hold formal business meetings to elect officers and plan future events. The Pedagogy Study Group (PSG), which formed in 2006, often presents sessions with a practical focus on specific teaching strategies, themes, or problems confronting music historians in the classroom. PSG-sponsored events have included question-and-answer panels, poster sessions, position papers, and roundtable discussions. Recent session topics have considered the role of musicology in community engagement, reaching out to performance majors, and teaching music history in the digital age.

For several years the PSG has co-sponsored Teaching Music History Day, which originated in the AMS Midwest Chapter as a study day for local and regional teachers, including those who teach music history at the college level but do not consider themselves to be musicologists. The event offers a greater breadth of topics than a single PSG conference session, and the diversity of pedagogical backgrounds among attendees tends to generate lively discussion. Past study days have featured keynote addresses from accomplished teachers, as well as interactive events like the syllabus bazaar, in which attendees offer course syllabi for exchange and comment. Sometimes pedagogy sessions also appear on the programs of regional chapter meetings, providing a geographically accessible venue for those unable to attend pedagogy events at the AMS annual meeting or Teaching Music History Day.

Society for Ethnomusicology

Formally organized in 1955, the Society for Ethnomusicology (SEM) aims to "promote the research, study, and performance of music in all historical periods and cultural contexts." Ethnographic methods may be applied to a prodigious array of musical, artistic, social, and historical phenomena, and programs for the SEM's annual meeting reflect this diversity of approach. Papers at recent SEM conferences examined film scores, music and social justice, West African singing, the image of early blues musicians, Japanese hip-hop, and women's Andalusian musical ensembles. Documentary films, poster displays, and workshops (such as how to make videos without investing in elaborate recording equipment) round out the program. The proportion of pedagogical activities at the annual meeting is similar to that of the AMS, with one or two panels specifically devoted to teacher training or pedagogical practice. But the SEM strategic plan (2010-15) includes a goal to "strengthen K-12, undergraduate and graduate education in ethnomusicology" through two initiatives: to develop teacher-training programs on world music for elementary and secondary schools, and to support humanities

---

[10] Currently the AMS recognizes seven study groups: Cold War and Music, Ecocriticism, Ibero-American Music, Jewish Studies and Music, LGBTQ (Lesbian, Gay, Bisexual, Transgender, Queer), Pedagogy, and Philosophy.

education for undergraduates by sponsoring interdisciplinary summer institutes in ethnomusicology.

As with the AMS, members who share particular research interests may form special interest groups; these groups, in turn, may develop into sections once their membership has grown and they have established a stable presence in the society.[11] Both the applied ethnomusicology and education sections support pedagogical events at the annual meeting, often with a focus on K-12 education. The applied ethnomusicology section views education as one part of a multi-pronged mission that includes arts advocacy and social justice, and its program offerings—from service learning projects to museum education—express this approach.[12]

Society for Music Theory

If recent faculty job descriptions reflect new trends in the profession, then it is increasingly common for music historians and ethnomusicologists to teach in secondary areas like music theory, performance, or interdisciplinary studies. The Society for Music Theory (SMT), which incorporated in 1977, seeks to "promote music theory as both a scholarly and a pedagogical discipline." With pedagogy firmly embedded in its mission statement, the SMT supports a number of activities designed to improve music theory teaching and the education of music theorists. The annual meeting usually devotes a full three-hour session to pedagogy (sponsored by the Pedagogy Interest Group), which may involve open discussions, paper presentations, poster displays, hands-on demonstrations of technology, or some combination of these.

Additional learning and growth opportunities for faculty may be found through the SMT's many interest groups,[13] as well as the sessions sponsored by the Professional Development Committee. Among the latter are the one-on-one CV review sessions and the mentoring program, which consists of confidential meetings with established scholars for faculty at any career stage. The Professional Development Committee also presents a special session at the annual meeting exploring a topic of concern from various perspectives, such as steps to a successful

---

[11]   Special interest groups include Archiving, European Music, Historical Ethnomusicology, Indigenous Music, Improvisation, Irish Music, Medical Ethnomusicology, Music and Violence, Music of Iran and Central Asia, Sound Studies, Sacred and Religious Music, and the Society for Arab Music Research. There are SEM sections in African Music, Applied Ethnomusicology, Dance, Education, Gender and Sexuality, Latin American and Caribbean, Popular Music, Status of Women, and South Asian Performing Arts.

[12]   Thanks to Jeff Titon and Patricia Campbell for their insights about how the SEM is organized and the types of pedagogical activities it sponsors.

[13]   These groups include Improvisation, Jazz, Mathematics of Music, Music and Disability, Music and Philosophy, Music Cognition, Music Informatics, Music Theory Pedagogy, Performance and Analysis, Popular Music, and Queer Resource.

conference presentation, preparing an effective tenure dossier, or renewing one's career by discovering new pursuits in scholarship and teaching.

Other Professional Societies

If you have interdisciplinary interests, you may seek out professional societies whose focus intersects with your research. Meeting colleagues and hearing of scholarship outside your discipline may enliven your own work in unexpected ways. Some societies may also schedule events that deal specifically with teaching and pedagogy, similar to the sessions offered by study groups in music societies. The Modern Language Association, for example, holds one of the largest annual conventions in the humanities, but alongside thousands of research presentations, attendees who look carefully will find several sessions on teaching language and literature. (At a recent convention there were sessions on digital pedagogy, service learning, disability in the classroom, and teaching bibliography, among other topics.) Other musical societies, like the Music Teachers National Association and the National Association for Music Educators (previously the Music Educators National Conference, MENC) may prove useful if you perform, give applied lessons, or teach courses in the music education curriculum in addition to your other duties. To discover which professional societies might be relevant to your research, consult the list of constituent members of the American Council of Learned Societies (of which the AMS, the SEM, and the SMT are members).

Most societies have regional chapters that make meetings more accessible, particularly for those with limited access to travel funding. These smaller meetings are excellent venues for meeting new colleagues and trying out societies whose mission extends beyond your disciplinary reach. If you find that the regional or national meetings of a society do not offer pedagogy sessions, you might try contacting its officers to express your interest in seeing such topics on future conference programs. (Be aware that if you do this, you may be asked to help plan a pedagogy session, or even to organize one yourself.)

Grants and Fellowships

Faculty course loads might consist of two courses per semester or twice that number, and the total number of students that faculty teach could vary from 30 to 600. But despite differences in teaching responsibilities, we all have one thing in common: the need for more time. Faculty with smaller course loads tend to face a greater demand for research productivity, while those who are not expected to publish prodigiously may be asked to devote much of their time to university service. If teaching, scholarship, and service each occupy one side of a triangle, most faculty find that an equilateral shape is rarely, if ever, achieved.[14] Grants and fellowships can help you find that elusive balance. At institutions that emphasize teaching over research, pedagogy grants may satisfy requirements for scholarly productivity as well as teaching effectiveness.

Guidelines for grant proposals describe the various ways in which funding sources support research and teaching development. Some grants provide travel funds or material support (like equipment), but others simply offer a larger share of that most precious resource: time. Grants may fund an additional semester of sabbatical leave (which some institutions offer to pre-tenure as well as tenured scholars), or they may pay for your department to hire someone to teach one class for you giving you extra time to conduct research or develop a new course. Funding for scholarly activities and teacher development is still available from many sources even in times of scarcity. But before searching for grants, determine what is most valuable to you—time for research and writing, funds for travel, the purchase of materials, or the hiring of a research assistant, for example—and then pursue those that are most appropriate for your needs, since preparing grant proposals requires patience, thoughtfulness—and yes, time. The investment required in writing a proposal that may or may not be successful discourages some faculty from applying at all. But the grant-writing process requires applicants to clarify the purpose and scope of their projects, write persuasively about their work, and disentangle ambitious ideas from jargon, all of which will improve the quality of your forthcoming article or book.

The problem of time is notably acute when applying for grants, since the submission process can seem like one more prickly barnacle on your life raft. But this process merely illuminates a lurking problem for academics, and particularly for pre-tenure faculty: how to find time for research when teaching responsibilities encroach from every corner. Time management is a critical skill for faculty at every career stage, since much of our time is unstructured and, to the non-academic world, "free." Because most academics want to be better teachers—or, at the very least, feel more comfortable in the classroom and gain student approval—we can be tempted to devote all of our unstructured time to pedagogy. There is always something more that can be added to a lecture, some new article that might improve a seminar discussion. But if we lose sight of professional development as a holistic phenomenon, teaching activities can easily consume most of our working hours. Faculty handle this problem in different ways: some dedicate time for research in their daily agendas and refuse to do other activities during those hours; others accept the reality that little research will be accomplished during the academic year and schedule their research projects for the summer break instead.

---

[14]   And at many institutions, an equilateral shape may not be desirable. Faculty with high course loads, for example, may be expected to devote 50 percent of their time to teaching, with the remainder divided between service and research. But even in these situations, teaching often overwhelms other responsibilities to such a degree that the appropriate balance is difficult to achieve.

(If you pursue the former option, seek support from your department chair, who can help protect your research time from other responsibilities.) I find that I am most productive as a scholar when I write or research a little every day, knowing that articles and books, which can seem like insurmountable projects, come from smaller, humbler origins: words, sentences, paragraphs. The same is true for grant applications. As difficult as it is to find time for them, it may be helpful to treat them as emblematic of your research agenda: as the proposals go, so goes your research. This is not to say that unfunded grant proposals reflect unsuccessful research, but rather that making time to investigate and apply for grant opportunities should be an important, active dimension of your scholarship.

When applying for grants, first start with your own institution, which probably offers professional development funds for faculty at various career stages. Some institutions are more generous with pre-tenure than senior scholars, with special pools set aside to support conference travel or research in the first few years on the job. Policies for internal grants—those offered by an institution to its faculty—vary across institutions, so familiarize yourself with the types of grants available and the procedures for each. If departmental support for your project is limited, you may find that the dean, or another administrative office, provides supplementary funding for faculty on a competitive basis. Though conference attendance is valuable whether or not you are presenting research, it is usually easier to obtain travel grants if you are featured in some way on the program. If you did not have your work accepted by the conference program committee, you may still be able to present as part of a study group or panel, since these sessions are sometimes organized through informal channels. Other ways to get involved in the conference include volunteering for a committee, submitting your name as a session chair, or working on the editorial board of a publication that holds its board meeting at the conference.[15]

External grants come from funding sources outside your college or university. Many institutions have a grants office that requires faculty to follow certain procedures when applying for external grants, like having proposals reviewed internally before they can be submitted for competition. The grants office can also assist faculty with identifying funding sources, preparing effective applications, and creating project reports for grants you have received. Professional societies offer a range of grant programs, from travel and publication subvention to course development; the AMS Teaching Fund, established in 2010, offers a $1,500 award to support student-centered learning, which might be explored through pedagogical research or a practical, classroom-oriented project. Societies in disciplines outside of music may also have grants or fellowships that are relevant to your teaching and scholarship. (The American Society for Eighteenth-Century Studies, which sponsors an innovative course design competition, presented its

---

[15]   Societies often request nominations for session chairs (including self-nominations) several months in advance of the meeting. In the AMS, the call for session chairs typically appears in the August newsletter.

2009 award to musicologist Sarah Day-O'Connell.) If your project contributes to other disciplines, like cultural studies, literature, philosophy, or anthropology, you may be able to secure funding from their respective professional societies. The American Council of Learned Societies funds the Charles A. Ryskamp Research Fellowship, which supports the work of pre-tenure faculty with publication records, as well as fellowships in the humanities and social sciences that may replace a regular semester of teaching or extend a one-semester sabbatical to a full year.

Federal programs like the National Endowment for the Humanities (NEH) continue to provide funding for scholarly research and teaching development, but the shrinking pool of available funds makes their selection process highly competitive. Guidelines for NEH grants differ according to the grant program: NEH summer stipend applicants who teach at a college or university must be nominated by their institution before they can apply, but the same is not true for fellowships supporting six to twelve months of research. Several programs in the NEH education division provide course development opportunities, including the relatively new Enduring Questions grant, which supports faculty in creating and teaching a course that explores a pre-disciplinary humanistic question. But not all programs require teachers to invent new courses in order to win grants. The NEH Teacher Development Fellowship awards monthly stipends to reduce faculty teaching loads by half; faculty then use the extra time in their schedules to revise a course that they have taught previously in at least three different semesters.

The Fulbright Program, sponsored by the U.S. State Department's Bureau of Educational and Cultural Affairs, remains one of the best-known granting agencies for scholars in all disciplines. Applicants with U.S. citizenship may apply for support to conduct and share research abroad in participating countries; those originating from other countries may take part in the visiting scholars program. The level of financial support and the time frame for awards differ depending on the requirements of specific programs. (Some ask for an invitation letter from an institution abroad; others do not.) If your research requires only short-term support, you might apply for the Fulbright specialist program, which connects scholars with host institutions for two-to-six week collaborative research projects. Other governments around the world have programs similar to the Fulbright for which U.S. scholars may be eligible, provided they conduct research that will enrich knowledge and scholarship pertaining to the sponsoring country.

Publications and Online Resources

Music historians can be strange creatures. Some of our academic colleagues regard our field as a branch of the fine arts, which is reflected in campus geography: we are typically housed in music departments or performing arts centers. Yet often our research aligns us more closely with faculty in other departments or disciplines, like history, philosophy, or anthropology. From this perspective, musicology may be seen as belonging to the humanities or the social sciences. The curious disciplinary status of music history means that sometimes relevant pedagogical research comes from far afield—and sometimes the research far afield has little to do with music history teaching at all.

Journals that focus broadly on the scholarship of teaching and learning in higher education publish pedagogical strategies that may translate to the music history classroom, even if they do not specifically mention music or the arts. The peer-reviewed *Journal on Excellence in College Teaching* is one such publication, providing a forum for teachers to share successful techniques and inspirational classroom experiences. (Items in each issue often focus around a theme, like "Tools for Critical Thinking," or "Diversity and Inclusion on Campus.") The *International Journal of University Teaching and Faculty Development* has a similar focus while offering a global, multidisciplinary perspective on teaching. *The Chronicle of Higher Education*, which takes the form of a news magazine for academics, combines opinion pieces, blogs, and practical resources (like job postings) with research-driven articles on the politics and pedagogy of college teaching.

Often teaching music history presents special challenges to faculty and students alike, and pedagogy journals with a general focus may not meet the needs of musicologists. For example, teaching students how to listen to music is a perennial problem faced by music history faculty, and potential solutions to it are scarce: neither multidisciplinary education journals nor academic musicology journals (like the *Journal of the American Musicological Society*) provide much help. The *College Music Symposium* (the journal of the College Music Society) occasionally features articles on music history teaching, but it also publishes research—pedagogical and otherwise—from every music discipline. The *Journal of Music Theory Pedagogy*, a peer-reviewed journal published since 1987, includes articles on curricular design, classroom teaching, and applications of analytical and pedagogical research, but these may have limited use for faculty trying to teach twelve centuries of music history in one semester or designing a musicology seminar that will accommodate both Ph.D. and D.M.A. students.

Only recently has the field of musicology been served by a pedagogy journal dedicated to the challenges of music history teaching. The *Journal of Music History Pedagogy* (JMHP), an online, peer-reviewed journal, published its first issue in Fall 2010 with articles on class discussion in courses for music majors, the history of jazz through textbooks, and strategies to make music history relevant to today's students.[16] The issue that followed featured articles from three major textbook authors—Mark Evan Bonds, John Hill, and J. Peter Burkholder—as well as a review essay by José Bowen entitled "Six Books Every College Teacher Should Know." Every issue includes reviews of textbooks, multimedia materials,

16   The JMHP is supported by the Pedagogy Study Group of the American Musicological Society, and it is published on the AMS website at this address: http://www.ams-net.org/jmhp, accessed November 13, 2011.

and scholarly works relating to pedagogy. Reviews can be particularly valuable for new faculty, since they may save time when you are evaluating the strengths and weaknesses of a textbook or trying to choose which music writing guide might work best for your bibliography class. The JMHP also fills a void in musicological scholarship by providing a venue for scholars at all stages of their career to publish articles that bridge the gulf between their research and teaching.

A number of books examine best practices in teaching and provide helpful tips if you are seeking to improve a particular lecture or boost student engagement in your class.[17] Ken Bain's *What the Best College Teachers Do* reveals that great teaching is not necessarily the product of genetic programming or a charismatic personality.[18] Bain surveyed students to identify which teachers they remembered long after leaving school, then followed up with those teachers through interviews and classroom observations. He discovered that the most effective teachers are student-focused rather than teacher-centered, and their pedagogical approach is driven by scholarly models in which students formulate problems, questions, and debates. One technique that Bain suggests is to write "WGAD" ("Who gives a damn?") on the chalkboard for every class meeting, inviting students to interrupt at any time to question the relevance of the material they are studying.[19] Barbara Gross-Davis's *Tools for Teaching* presents ideas with immediate and specific applications, including how to personalize lectures for large classes, ask engaging questions, and set the stage for the first day of class. The book is replete with references to educational research, and it shows how small things—like a teacher's demeanor when fielding student questions—can have a significant effect on the learning environment.[20]

Textbooks have long been accompanied by instructor's manuals, which are coveted by students for their claims to having all the answers. Manuals contain these answer keys, of course, but the best guides also provide instruction for teachers about how to make use of textbooks and ancillary materials in a variety of classroom settings. Many texts now feature a suite of digital materials for teachers and students, including PowerPoint slides keyed to the reading, chapter outlines, practice quizzes, flash cards, and online listening labs that may be accessed through

---

[17]   Detailed descriptions and assessments of these books appear in José Antonio Bowen, "Six Books Every College Teacher Should Know," *Journal of Music History Pedagogy* 1 (Spring 2010): 175-82.

[18]   Ken Bain, *What the Best College Teachers Do* (Cambridge, MA: Harvard University Press, 2004).

[19]   Bain, *What the Best College Teachers Do*, 38-39. Bowen has adopted the technique to the music history classroom. He writes about the experience, "I allowed the question of musicology's relevance to be part of the course and was explicit with students that Schenker, Tovey, and Taruskin make radically different assumptions about what matters. I did not segregate the facts from the theories, or the compositions from the interpretations." See Bowen, "Six Books," 176.

[20]   Barbara Gross-Davis, *Tools for Teaching* (San Francisco: Jossey-Bass, 1993).

the publisher's website or course management software. For courses built out of the box—that is, designed around a specific textbook—these materials will save time when preparing your course and grading student assignments. If you teach a course without a textbook you may still be able to make use of certain readymade resources, allowing you to focus on creating activities for engaging students rather than developing content from scratch.

Informal Development

Informal mentorships may supplement the support provided by professional societies, institutions, and teaching centers. Though new faculty may feel the most vulnerable about their careers, and thus most in need of collegial guidance, mentoring may be useful at any career stage.[21] Within your department, you might ask colleagues to examine course materials you have created and to observe your classroom teaching. These same colleagues are likely to be reviewing your annual reports (which describe your productivity in teaching, research, and scholarship) as well as writing letters of support for your tenure file. Inviting them to actively participate in your development will improve your work as a teacher and scholar—and it will help your colleagues become personally invested in your professional success.[22] When asking colleagues to evaluate your work, be sure that you offer to reciprocate, too. Doing so will show that you value the time your colleague has volunteered, and it will help both of you to cultivate an understanding of professional development that extends through every stage of an academic career. Martha Fickett, a colleague of mine at the University of Mary Washington, showed me that no faculty is too experienced to benefit from the advice of a colleague. Though she had taught at the university for forty years, she often approached me—a first-year faculty member—about how I structured my courses or taught specific topics. I thought that she would have had all the answers, given her considerable experience. Instead, she showed me that teaching, creating knowledge, and growing professionally are endeavors that have no endpoint.

Digital means of communication make it possible to sustain professional friendships across broad geographical expanses. These relationships can be particularly helpful for faculty in small departments, or for those with disciplinary interests that fall outside the specializations of departmental colleagues. When

---

[21]   Professional societies that offer mentorships recognize this fact: both the College Music Society and the Society for Music Theory state that faculty may seek mentors through their programs regardless of their tenure status. Tenured faculty, having acquired that long-sought job stability following years of vigorous productivity, may feel that a mentor can help them discover new avenues to pursue in their research, or ways to re-orient themselves to the administrative responsibilities that loom post-tenure.

[22]   Thanks to Dean Kathleen Skerritt, who offered this advice at a luncheon she organized for pre-tenure faculty at the University of Richmond.

the time comes to apply for grants or new teaching positions, you will need the support of these friends, and you will be asked for their support in return. At times you will have needs that cannot be met by a teaching center, a pedagogy article, or a conference paper. In such situations, a trusted friend and colleague who can listen, empathize, and critique may be the most valuable resource you can have as a teacher. Collegial relationships like these, if nurtured from the beginning, can be a wellspring of mutual support and sympathy throughout your career.

Bibliography

Pedagogy Journals and Online Publications

Active Learning in Higher Education
Arts and Humanities in Higher Education
Assessment & Evaluation in Higher Education
Chronicle of Higher Education
College Music Symposium
College Teaching
Council for Research in Music Education
Educational Research Quarterly
Educational Technology
International Journal for the Scholarship of Teaching & Learning
International Journal on Teaching and Learning in Higher Education
International Journal of University Teaching and Faculty Development
Journal of Aesthetic Education
Journal of Educational Research
Journal of Effective Teaching
Journal on Excellence in College Teaching
Journal of Music History Pedagogy
Journal of Music Theory Pedagogy
Journal of Research in Music Education
Journal of Scholarship of Teaching and Learning
Journal of Student Centered Learning
Music Educators Journal
Philosophy of Music Education Review
Studies in Higher Education
Teaching in Higher Education

Works Cited

Åkerlind, Gerlese S. "Separating the 'Teaching' from the 'Academic': Possible Unintended Consequences." *Teaching in Higher Education* 16, no. 2 (2011): 193-94.
Åkerlind, Gerlese S. "Constraints on Academics' Potential for Developing as a Teacher." *Studies in Higher Education* 32, no. 1 (February 2007): 21-37.

Ashbee, Andrew. "Groomed for Service: Musicians in the Privy Chamber at the English Court, c. 1495-1558." *Early Music* 25 (1997): 185-97.

Auden, W. H. *Dyer's Hand*. New York: Random House, 1962.

Augsburg, Tanya. *Becoming Interdisciplinary: An Introduction to Interdisciplinary Studies*. Dubuque, IA: Kendall Hunt, 2005.

Bain, Ken. *What the Best College Teachers Do*. Cambridge, MA: Harvard University Press, 2004.

Barton, Jennifer, Paul Heilker, and David Rutkowski, "Fostering Effective Classroom Discussions." Accessed October 7, 2011. http://www.mhhe.com/socscience/english/tc/pt/discussion/discussion.htm.

Battista, David. "Making the Most of Multiple Choice Testing: Getting Beyond Remembering." *Collected Essays on Learning and Teaching* 1 (2008): 119-122,

Battista, David. "The Immediate Feedback Assessment Technique: A learner-centred multiple choice response form." *Canadian Journal of Higher Education* 35 (2005): 111-131.

Bellman, Jonathan. *A Short Guide to Writing about Music*. New York: Longman, 2000.

Benton, Thomas H. "A Perfect Storm in Undergraduate Education, Parts I and II." *Chronicle of Higher Education*, February 20, 2011 and April 3, 2011.

Berger, Arthur. "Problems of Pitch Organization in Stravinsky." *Perspectives of New Music* 2, no. 1 (Autumn-Winter 1963): 11-42.

Berrett, Dan. "Which Core Matters More?" *Chronicle of Higher Education*, September 25, 2011.

Biggs, John. *Teaching for Quality Learning at University*. 2nd edition. Maidenhead: Open University Press, 2003.

Bland, Mark, Gerald Saunders, and Jennifer Kreps Frisch. "Point of View: In Defense of the Lecture." *Journal of College Science Teaching* 37, no. 2 (2007): 10-13.

Bligh, Donald. *What's the Use of Lectures?* 5th edition. Exeter: Intellect, 1998.

Boethius, Anicius Manlius Severinus. *Fundamentals of Music*. Translated by Calvin M. Bower; edited by Claude V. Palisca. New Haven: Yale University Press, 1989.

Bonds, Mark Evan. *Listen to This*. 2nd edition. Upper Saddle River, NJ: Prentice Hall, 2011.

Bonwell, Charles C., and James A. Eisen. *Active Learning: Creating Excitement in the Classroom*. ASHE-ERIC Higher Education Report. Washington, D.C.: George Washington University, 1991.

Booth, Wayne C., Gregory G. Colomb, and Joseph M. Williams. *The Craft of Research*. 3rd edition. Chicago and London: University of Chicago Press, 2008.

Bowen, José Antonio. *Teaching Naked*. San Francisco: Jossey-Bass, 2012.

Bowen, José Antonio. "Rethinking Technology Outside the Classroom." *Journal of Music History Pedagogy* 2, no. 1 (Fall 2011): 43-59.

Bowen, José Antonio. "Six Books Every College Teacher Should Know." *Journal of Music History Pedagogy* 1 (Spring 2010): 175-82.

Bowen, José Antonio. "Teaching Naked: Why Removing Technology from Your Classroom Will Improve Student Learning." *National Teaching and Learning Forum* 16, no. 1 (2006): 1-14.

Briscoe, James R., ed. *Vitalizing Music History Teaching.* Hillsdale, NY: Pendragon Press, 2010.

Brooks, Kim. "Death to High School English." Salon.com. Accessed October 1, 2011. http://salon.com/mwt/feature/2011/05/10/death_to_high_school_english.

Burkholder, J. Peter, Donald Jay Grout, and Claude V. Palisca. *A History of Western Music.* 7th edition. New York: W. W. Norton, 2006.

Burkholder, J. Peter. "Peer Learning in Music History Courses." In *Teaching Music History*, edited by Mary Natvig, 205-23. Burlington, VT: Ashgate, 2002.

Burney, Charles. *A General History of Music, from the Earliest Ages to the Present (1789).* New York: Dover, 1957.

Conway, Colleen M., and Thomas M. Hodgman. *Teaching Music in Higher Education.* Oxford: Oxford University Press, 2008.

David, Hans T., and Arthur Mendel, eds. *The New Bach Reader: A Life of Johann Sebastian Bach in Letters and Documents.* Revised and enlarged by Christoph Wolff. New York: W. W. Norton, 1998.

Davis, James A. "Classroom Discussion and the Community of Music Majors." *Journal of Music History Pedagogy* 1 (2010): 5-17.

Dawes, James R. "Ten Strategies for Discussion Leading," *Derek Bok Center for Teaching and Learning, Harvard University.* Accessed October 7, 2011. http://isites.harvard.edu/fs/html/icb.topic58474/Dawes_DL.html.

deWinstanley, Patricia Ann, and Robert A. Bjork. "Successful Lecturing: Presenting Information in Ways That Engage Effective Processing." *New Directions for Teaching and Learning*, 89 (2002): 9-31.

Dubrow, Heather. "Teaching Essay-Writing in a Liberal Arts Curriculum." In *The Art and Craft of Teaching*, edited by Margaret Morganroth Gullette, 88-102. Cambridge, MA: Harvard University Press, 1984.

Dubrow, Heather, and James Wilkinson. "The Theory and Practice of Lectures." In *The Art and Craft of Teaching*, edited by Margaret Morganroth Gullette, 25-37. Cambridge, MA: Harvard University Press, 1984.

Duckles, Vincent H., and Ida Reed. *Music Reference and Research Materials: An Annotated Bibliography.* 5th edition. New York: Schirmer Books, 1997.

Eisler, Benita. *Chopin's Funeral.* New York: Knopf, 2003.

Facione, Peter. *THINK Critically.* Upper Saddle River, NJ: Pearson, 2011.

Fant, Jr., Gene C. "Class Size vs. Teaching Load." *Chronicle of Higher Education*, May 19, 2010.

Feather, N. T., ed. *Expectations and Actions.* Hillsdale, NJ: Erlbaum, 1982.

Fendrich, Laurie. "Ethics? Let's Outsource Them!" *Chronicle of Higher Education*, April 8, 2010.

Fiero, Gloria K. *Landmarks in the Humanities*. 2nd edition. New York: McGraw-Hill, 2009.

Fink, L. Dee. *Creating Significant Learning Experiences: An Integrated Approach to Designing College Courses*. San Francisco: Jossey-Bass, 2003.

Forney, Kristine, and Joseph Machlis. *The Enjoyment of Music*. 11th edition. New York: W. W. Norton, 2011.

Gee, James P. *What Video Games Have to Teach Us About Learning and Literacy*. New York: Palgrave Macmillan, 2003.

Gilles, Roger. "The Departmental Perspective." In *Strategies for Teaching First-Year Composition*, edited by Duane Roen, Lauren Yena, Veronica Pantoja, Eric Waggoner, and Susan K. Miller, 2-10. Urbana, IL: National Council of Teachers of English, 2002.

Gladwell, Malcolm. *Blink: The Power of Thinking Without Thinking*. New York: Back Bay Books, 2005.

Gross-Davis, Barbara. *Tools for Teaching*. San Francisco: Jossey-Bass, 1993; 2nd edition, 2009.

Grout, Donald Jay, and Claude V. Palisca. *A History of Western Music*. 4th edition. New York: W. W. Norton, 1988.

Hanning, Barbara Russano. "Teaching Music History through Art." In *Vitalizing Music History Teaching*, edited by James Briscoe, 139-60. Hillsdale, NY: Pendragon Press, 2010.

Hartley, James, and Ivor K. Davies. "Note-Taking: A Critical Review." *Programmed Learning and Educational Technology* 15, no. 3 (1978): 207-24.

Herbert, Trevor. *Music in Words: A Guide to Researching and Writing about Music*. Oxford: Oxford University Press, 2009.

Hess, Carol A. "Score and Word: Writing About Music". In *Teaching Music History*, edited by Mary Natvig, 193-204. Aldershot and Burlington, VT: Ashgate, 2002.

Hesse, Douglas D. "Writing and Learning to Write: A Modest Bit of History and Theory for Writing Students." In *Strategies for Teaching First-Year Composition*, edited by Duane Roen, Lauren Yena, Veronica Pantoja, Eric Waggoner, and Susan K. Miller, 38-43. Urbana, IL: National Council for Teachers of English, 2002.

Holoman, D. Kern. *Writing about Music: A Style Sheet*. 2nd edition. Berkeley: University of California Press, 2008.

Howard, Rebecca Moore. "The Ethics of Plagiarism." In *The Ethics of Writing Instruction: Issues in Theory and Practice*. Perspectives on Writing: Theory, Research, Practice 4, edited by Michael A. Pemberton, 79-89. Stamford, CT: Ablex, 2000.

Jenkins, Rob. "Accordions, Frogs and the 5-paragraph Theme." *Chronicle of Higher Education*, February 21, 2010.

June, Audrey Williams. "Some Papers are Uploaded to Bangalore to Be Graded." *Chronicle of Higher Education*, April 4, 2010.

Kamien, Roger. *Music: An Appreciation*. 10th edition. New York: McGraw-Hill, 2010.

Kerman, Joseph. *Contemplating Music*. Cambridge, MA: Harvard University Press, 1985.

Kerman, Joseph, and Gary Tomlinson. *Listen*. 6th edition. New York: Bedford/St. Martin's Press, 2008.

Keyworth, D. R. "The Group Exam." *Teaching Professor* 3, no. 8 (1989): 5.

Kivy, Peter. *The Corded Shell: Reflections on Musical Expression*. Princeton: Princeton University Press, 1980.

Kozma, Robert B., Lawrence W. Belle, and George W. Williams. *Instructional Techniques in Higher Education*. Englewood Cliffs, NJ: Educational Technology, 1978.

Lage, Maureen J., and Glenn Platt. "The Internet and the Inverted Classroom." *Journal of Economic Education* 31, no. 11 (Winter 2000): 11.

Lang, James M. *A Week By Week Guide to Your First Semester of College Teaching*. Cambridge, MA: Harvard University Press, 2008,

Leonard, Kendra. "Review Essay: Guides to Writing about Music." *Journal of Music History Pedagogy* 2, no. 1 (Fall 2011): 111-16.

Lockwood, Lewis. "*Beethoven* by Maynard Solomon." *19th-Century Music* 3, no. 1 (July 1979): 76-82.

Long, Holly E., and Jeffrey T. Coldren. "Interpersonal Influences in Large Lecture-Based Classes: A Socioinstructional Perspective." *College Teaching* 54 (2006): 237-43.

Lowe, Melanie. "Teaching Music History Today: Making Tangible Connections to Here and Now." *Journal of Music History Pedagogy* 1 (2010): 45-59.

Lowman, Joseph L. *Mastering the Techniques of Teaching*. San Francisco: Jossey-Bass, 1984.

Lyotard, Jean-François. *The Postmodern Condition: A Report on Knowledge*. Translated by Geoff Bennington and Brian Massumi. Minneapolis: University of Minnesota Press, 1984.

McKeachie, Wilbert J., *et al*. *McKeachie's Teaching Tips: Strategies, Research, and Theory for College and University Teachers*, 11th edition. Boston and New York: Houghton Mifflin, 2002.

Marshall, Robert L. "Bach's 'Choruses' Reconstituted." *High Fidelity* 32, no. 10 (October 1982): 64-66, 94.

Natvig, Mary. *Teaching Music History*. Aldershot and Burlington, VT: Ashgate, 2002.

Natvig, Mary, and Steven Cornelius. *Music: A Social Experience*. Upper Saddle River, NJ: Pearson, 2012.

Nicholls, Gill. "New Lecturers' Constructions of Learning, Teaching, and Research in Higher Education." *Studies in Higher Education* 30 (October 2005): 611-25.

Obendorf, Hartmut. *Minimalism: Designing Simplicity*. Dordrecht: Springer, 2009.

Parry, Marc. "Software Catches (and Also Helps) Young Plagiarists." *Chronicle of Higher Education*, November 6, 2011.

Partch, Harry. *Bitter Music: Collected Journals, Essays, Introductions and Librettos*. Edited by Thomas McGeary. Urbana: University of Illinois Press, 1991.

Persellin, Diane, and Terry Goodrick. "Faculty Development in Higher Education: Long-Term Impact of a Summer Teaching and Learning Workshop." *Journal of the Scholarship of Teaching and Learning* 10 (January 2010): 1-13.

Plato. *The Collected Dialogues of Plato Including the Letters*. Edited by Edith Hamilton and Huntington Cairns. New York: Pantheon, 1961.

Rifkin, Joshua. "Bach's 'Choruses': The Record Cleared." *High Fidelity* 32, no. 12 (December 1982): 58-59.

Rifkin, Joshua. "Bach's 'Choruses' – Less Than They Seem?" *High Fidelity* 32, no. 9 (September 1982): 42-44.

Rose, Adrian. "Angel Musicians in the Medieval Stained Glass of Norfolk Churches." *Early Music* 29 (2001): 186-217.

Roth, Marjorie. "The 'Why' of Music: Variations on a Cosmic Theme." In *Teaching Music History*, edited by Mary Natvig, 77-94. Aldershot and Burlington, VT: Ashgate, 2002.

Ruiz, Rebecca. "Twitter: The New Rules of Engagement." *New York Times*, January 9, 2011, Lifestyle, 4.

Russell, I. Jon, W. D. Hendrickson, and R. J. Hevert. "Effects of Lecture Information Density on Medical Student Achievement." *Journal of Medical Education* 59, no. 11 (1984): 881-89.

Samaras, Anastasia P., and Anne R. Freese. *Self-study of Teaching Practices Primer*. New York: Peter Lang, 2006.

Shaw, George Bernard. *Shaw on Music*. Edited by Eric Bentley. New York: Doubleday Anchor, 1955.

Sherr, Richard. "Competence and Incompetence in the Papal Choir in the Age of Palestrina." *Early Music* 22 (1994): 606-29.

Small, Christopher. *Musicking: The Meanings of Performing and Listening*. Middletown, CT: Wesleyan University Press, 1998.

Solomon, Maynard. *Beethoven: Revised Edition*. New York: Schirmer, 2001.

Steib, Murray, ed. *Reader's Guide to Music: History, Theory, and Criticism*. Chicago and London: Fitzroy Dearborn, 1999.

Struyven, Katrien, Filip Dochy, and Steven Janssons, "Students' Perceptions about Evaluation and Assessment in Higher Education: A Review." *Assessment & Evaluation in Higher Education* 30, no. 4 (2005): 331-47.

"Study: Most College Students Lack Skills." *USA Today*, posted January 19, 2006. Accessed September 20, 2011. http://www.usatoday.com/news/education/2006-01-19-college-tasks_x.htm.

"Suggestions for Leading Small-group Discussions." Prepared by Lee Haugen. *Center for Teaching Excellence, Iowa State University*. Accessed October 7, 2011, http://www.celt.iastate.edu/teaching/small_group.html.

Sundberg, Marshall D., Michael L. Dini, and Elizabeth Li. "Decreasing Course Content Improves Student Comprehension of Science and Attitudes towards Science in Freshman Biology." *Journal of Research in Science Teaching* 31, no. 6 (1994): 679-93.

Svinicki, Marilla, and Wilbert J. McKeachie, *McKeachie's Teaching Tips*, 13th edition. Belmont, CA: Wadsworth, Cengage Learning, 2011.

Taruskin, Richard. *The Oxford History of Western Music*. 6 vols. Oxford and New York: Oxford University Press, 2005.

Thomson, Virgil. *A Virgil Thomson Reader*. Boston: Houghton Mifflin, 1981.

Toppins, A. D. "Teaching by Testing: A Group Consensus Approach." *College Teaching* 37, no. 3 (1989): 96-99.

Tovey, Donald. *Chamber Music: Essays in Musical Analysis*. Oxford: Oxford University Press, 1989.

Walser, Robert. "Eruptions: Heavy Metal Appropriations of Classical Virtuosity." *Popular Music* 2 (1992): 263-308.

Walvoord, Barbara E. Fassler. *Helping Students Write Well: A Guide for Teachers in All Disciplines*. New York: Modern Language Association of America, 1982.

Walvoord, Barbara E., and Virginia Johnson Anderson. *Effective Grading: A Tool for Learning and Assessment in College*. 2nd edition. San Francisco: Jossey-Bass, 1998.

Weimer, Maryellen. *Learner-centered Teaching: Five Key Changes to Practice*. San Francisco: Jossey-Bass, 2002.

Weiss, Piero, and Richard Taruskin, eds. *Music in the Western World: A History in Documents*. 2nd edition. New York: Schirmer, 2007.

Wells, Elizabeth A. "Professionalism Marks vs. Participation Marks: Transforming the University Experience." *Collected Essays in Teaching and Learning* 1 (2008): 115-18.

Wiggins, Grant P., and Jay McTighe. *Understanding by Design*. 2nd edition. Alexandria, VA: Association for Supervision and Curriculum Development, 2005.

Willis, Judy. *Research-Based Strategies to Ignite Student Learning*. Alexandria, VA: Association for Supervision and Curriculum Development, 2006.

Wittrock, Merlin C., ed. *The Human Brain*. Englewood Cliffs, NJ: Prentice Hall, 1977.

Wright, Craig. *Listening to Music*, 6th edition. Stamford, CT: Schirmer Cengage Learning, 2011.

Wright, Craig, and Bryan Simms. *Music in Western Civilization*. Belmont, CA: Wadsworth, 2005.

Zull, James E. "The Art of Changing the Brain." *Educational Leadership* 62, no. 1 (September 2004): 68-72.

Index